Yankee Talk

A DICTIONARY OF NEW ENGLAND EXPRESSIONS

Robert Hendrickson

Volume III:
Facts On File Dictionary of American Regional Expressions

☑® Facts On File, Inc.

AN INFOBASE HOLDINGS COMPANY

Yankee Talk: A Dictionary of New England Expressions

Copyright © 1996 by Robert Hendrickson

Facts On File, Inc.
11 Penn Plaza
New York, NY 10001

Library of Congress Cataloging-in-Publication Data

Henrickson, Robert, 1933–
Yankee talk : a dictionary of New England expressions / Robert Hendrickson.
p.   cm. — (Facts On File dictionary of American regional expressions : v. 3)

ISBN 0-8160-2111-2 (hc)   ISBN 0-8160-3507-5 (pb)
1. English language—Regionalisms—New England—Dictionaries.
2. New England—Social life and customs—Dictionaries.   3. English language—New England—Terms and phrases.   4. Americanisms—New England—Dictionaries.   5. Figures of speech—Dictionaries.
I. Title. II. Series.
PE2906.H4   1996
427'.974—dc20   95-35938

Jacket design by Catherine Hyman

This book is printed on acid-free paper.

Printed in the United States of America

MP TT 10 9 8 7 6 5 4 3 2 1

For my granddaughter,
Brianna Ashlyn

"Everybody says words different," said Ivy. "Arkansas folks says 'em different, and Oklahomy folks says 'em different. And we seen a lady from Massachusetts, an' she said 'em different of all. Couldn't hardly make out what she was sayin'!"
—John Steinbeck, *The Grapes of Wrath*, 1939

Introduction _____

The New England, Yankee, Boston or Harvard accent, as it is variously called, has a formidable reputation. Back in 1920, for example, an Oxford professor of English, George Gordon, proclaimed that the King's English, or "standard" English, is spoken only in Boston, Richmond, Virginia and Edinburgh. In a study three decades later, the American Linguistic Institute polled "experts" to discover just where they thought the best English was spoken in the United States. The three winners were Boston, Nashville and Washington, D.C., with New York City coming in last! At about the same time, on March 10, 1948, the "Director of Speech Improvement" for the Boston public school system intoned that "Bostonians certainly speak the purest cultural English of any section of the country," a blessing she attributed to Boston's geographic location near the ocean, because "the salt in the air makes our Boston speech more forceful, gives it more strength."

It is probably safe to bet that the majority of Americans agree with the Director of Speech Improvement & Co. and still regard the New England accent as the "purest" English in the country—possibly because Harvard College has long been located there, or perhaps because so many of our earliest literary luminaries and statesmen were New Englanders, or maybe just because the Cabots, who spoke only to God, would be expected to do so in high style (though that would surely be a sin of pride). Then there is the "dominant WASPs" theory, explained by Bergen Evans: "It is more likely that God is conceived of as belonging to the dominant group. If He no longer speaks in Hebrew or Latin, He at least has a Boston accent."

All stuff and nonsense, certainly. What impresses most people about the Boston accent, for example, is its elegant or affected (depending on one's ear or psychology) pronunciations of such words as *ask, brass, class, grass, half, fast, dance, bath* or *can't* with the broad *ah* sound (*Bah-th, cah-nt, dahnce,* etc.). Granted, this is King's English too, but most people fail to realize that the broad *ah* sound in such words, the so-called Boston Brahmin *a,* is quite possibly an affectation introduced on the stage by the famed English actor David Garrick in the 18th century. Others say that the broad *a,* which a 1790 British pronouncing dictionary called "a characteristic of the elegant and learned world," is ironically of "vulgar" Cockney origin! In any case, it was unknown in polite circles during the Elizabethan era (when *a cahff came down the pahth to take a bahth* was simply pronounced *a calf came down the path to take a bath*) and is relatively a pompous upstart; the "flat" sound of *a* in words such as *dance* and *bath,* which is common to General American speech, preceded it by many, many years. It is interesting to note that the broad *a* is far from universal in England today. John Braine's lower-class heel of a hero in *Room at the Top* (1965), who is clawing his way up the social ladder, says before he gets to the top rung: "I was going to pronounce *Aunt* with a broad *a,* but decided not to attempt it yet."

While there is of course no "pure" or "proper" or "correct" or "best" pronunciation of American English, the New England accent is still decidedly *different* from other accents heard in America, even if television and the increased mobility of Americans has tended to blur many of its distinctions in recent times. Yankees proudly possess not only their own accent but a vocabulary peculiar to the region, as they have since the earliest days of the Republic. In searching for these words and expressions, some 3,500 or so recorded here in all, I have consulted all the standard etymological works, especially John Russell Bartlett's *Dictionary of Americanisms;* James Russell Lowell's *The Biglow Papers;* John Farmer's *Americanisms;* Mitford M. Mathews's *The American Dialect Dictionary* and *A Dictionary of Americanisms on Historical Principles;* Hans Kurath's *Linguistic Atlas of New England;* Sir William A. Craigie's and James Hulbert's *Dictionary of American English on Historic Principles;* H. L. Mencken's *The American Language; Webster's Third New International Dictionary; The Random House Dictionary of the English Language; The Oxford English Dictionary;* and the excellent *Dictionary of American Regional English* edited by Frederic Cassidy (two volumes of an estimated six published at this writing). Most valuable too were New England newspapers and specialized magazines such as *Dialect Notes, American Speech* and the *Journal of American Folklore.* New England friends and correspondents also have kindly supplied material, but the bulk of it comes from personal experience living or traveling in the region and hundreds of diaries, biographies, histories, essays, poems, songs, short stories and novels by New Englanders, many of which are cited in the text.

These New England authors (and authors who wrote about New England) range from Captain John Smith, who first recorded the term *New England* in 1616, to modern best-selling novelists such as Mainer Stephen King and George Higgins, who has been called "the man with the golden ear" for his command of the patois around Boston, home to some Irishmen with, in the happy phrase of Mark Helprin ("Palais De Justice," 1976), "a dialect strong enough to make the planet green." They include such renowned authors as Cotton Mather, Ralph Waldo Emerson, Henry Thoreau, Henry Wadsworth Longfellow, Nathaniel Hawthorne, James Russell Lowell, Herman Melville, Richard Henry Dana, Jr., John Greenleaf Whittier, Harriet Beecher Stowe, Louisa May Alcott, Emily Dickinson, Mark Twain, Amy Lowell, Edwin Arlington Robinson, William Dean Howells, Henry James, Edith Wharton, Thornton Wilder, Eugene O'Neill, Robert Frost, John P. Marquand, Kenneth Roberts, Robert P. Tristram Coffin and Robert Lowell, as well as comparatively little-known writers (often quite as good) such as Rowland Robinson, Sara Orne Jewett, Mary Wilkens Freeman, Thomas Bradley Aldrich, John Gould, Charles Haywood, Edith Holton, Joanna Colcord, Edward O'Connor, and André Dubus—to name a few.

All of these authors have provided interesting words and expressions peculiar to the region, whether they are au courant or obsolete and only of historical interest (although "obsolete" language often has an embarrassing way of turning up in current speech and writing). From James Russell Lowell on, they also have provided examples of New England pronunciation. Besides sometimes pronouncing *a*'s broad enough to launch a missile from, New Englanders often strengthen the *a* sound in such words as *far, park, dark* and *heart,* producing a sound somewhere between the one most Americans make in pronouncing *hat* and *father.* This characteristic is also found in the Southern Tidewater region, especially in eastern Virginia. A minority of dialectologists call it the Boston *a* and believe that it may have come over with the Irish in the 1830s—those same Irish whom Boston Mayor Theodore Lyman believed with Yankee certitude were "a race that will never be infused into our own, but on the contrary will always remain distinct and hostile!"

The lack of consonantal strength of the *r* in the New England accent is also a development that most likely began in southern England, proceeding until the end of the 18th century, when the *r* finally was heard no more in a Londoner's pronunciation of such words as *car*. In 1791 Walker's *Critical Pronouncing Dictionary* observed that "in England, and particularly in London, the *r* in *bar, bard, card, regard,* etc. is pronounced so much in the throat as to be little more than the middle or Italian *a,* lengthened into *baa, baad, caad, regaad.*" New England settlers brought this mannerism with them, and their slighted *r,* along with the broad *a* sound previously mentioned, eventually provided the color of the so-called Haavaad accent, which yields uranium such as *Pahk the cah in Hahvahd yahd* (Park the car in Harvard yard). It should be noted, however, that the *r* is *not* dropped before vowels, as in *carry,* or *Tory,* which are pronounced *carry* and *Tory.* Anyway, New Englanders were consistently dropping their *r*'s midway through the 18th century, which is why *liberty* is so often misspelled *libety* in early documents. The surest proof that *r* was not formerly sounded as *ah,* as it is in eastern New England and in parts of the South today, is the fact that it was once called "the dog letter." Since Roman times *r* had been thought of as the "dog's letter" or "the snarling letter," because its sound resembles the snarling of a dog—*r-r-r-r.* Said Ben Jonson, in his *English Grammar Made for the Benefit of all Strangers* (1636): "R is the dog's letter, and hurreth in the sound; the tongue striking the inner palate, with a trembling about the teeth." Shakespeare has Juliet's nurse in *Romeo and Juliet* call *r* the "dog name" when she tells Romeo that his name and rosemary, an herb associated with weddings, both begin with *r.* Today, however, *r* is pronounced as the dog letter only in parts of Scotland. In Anglophone North America, *r* has become "a vocalic glide or a retroflexed central vowel" (that is, sounded with the tip of the tongue curled back)—except, of course, in the coastal Southern states, New York City, and eastern New England, where the *ah* sound holds forth.

"*R*-dropping" America has inspired a humorous theorem called the Law of Conservation of R's (formulated by Edward Scher in 1985), which holds that an *r* missing from one word will turn up in excess in another: *fawth* (fourth), for example, is balanced by *idears* or the common second *r* in *sherbert.* "*R*-dropping" reached its zenith of popularity in the early 1960s, when John F. Kennedy was president. "Politicians all over the country began affecting his nasal *r*-dropping style of speech," columnist Mike Royko wrote in a recent nostalgic piece.

> I can remember a member of the Cook County (Chicago) Board, who had been born and reared on the West side, standing up at a political gathering, tucking his hand into his coat pocket, hunching his shoulders, and trying to talk like Kennedy. The effect on the audience was electrifying. Between his native West Side accent and his attempt to sound Boston Irish, nobody in the hall understood a word he said and thought he was drunk. The mayor was so alarmed at this kind of behavior that he ran the man for judge.

The vagrant *r* appears lucky when its fate is compared to that of *t* and *d* in regional speech, according to one New Englander. "Harsher is the fate of *t* and its soft sister, *d,* which often vanishes outright, albeit to a saving of time," William Howells of Kittery Point, Maine observed in a letter to *The*

New York Times. "In long words, it is usually every other *t* that goes, so I call the syndrome the all-knit *t*. Thus, in the television weather report: *Sal light pictures show inner mitten showers.* My favorite evening television newscaster manages to say nightly news with no *t* at all (he uses what cognoscenti call a glottal stop). By dispensing with many *t*'s and *d*'s he can save a *hun ridden twenny* seconds in half an hour, which translates into a lot of money.

While there is no such thing as the "correct" pronunciation of American, there is little doubt that New England, along with Virginia, still echoes accents of the *earliest* English immigrants to America, who came mainly from the eastern and southern counties near London, or that speech in the region is closer to "English English," the standard English spoken in England, than any other American dialect. It is the one region in the United States where the dialect clearly owes most to the migration of people from England, specifically Puritans from East Anglia, who constituted two-thirds of the 15,000 colonists who sailed to New England from 1620 to 1640. Even the nasalization, or "nasal twang," that the British twitted New Englanders (and Virginians) about had its origins in England, specifically in places where the Puritans held sway. English writers for many years associated this nasal twang (also called a *whine* and said to be affected to show piety) with the Puritans of East Anglia. Shelley described a rather nasty pious Puritan in this way:

> His eyes turned up, his mouth turned down;
> His accent caught a nasal twang.

Some New Englanders, their tongues arched up in the mouth, the pitch of their dialect somewhere higher than General American, still nasalize *cow* as *keow,* a pronunciation old Ben Franklin kidded them about and a habit that also results in the pronunciation of *k* and *q* as *ky* (*kyat,* cat) by many speakers. The *y* glide of the *u* sound after *d, n* and *t,* resulting in such pronunciations as *nyu* (now), *dyu* (due) and *tyune* (tune), is responsible for the "Yankee drawl" that Noah Webster tried to explain in terms of Yankee inferiority. Webster noted in his *Dissertations on the English Language* (1789) that Yankees were not used to commanding slaves and servants and didn't possess "that pride and consciousness of superiority which attend birth and fortune," all of which made them "give their opinions in an indecisive tone" and drag out their words uncertainly. Perhaps this is what Walt Whitman meant when in *An American Primer* he called "offensive" the Yankee flat, drawling nasal tone.

But there is generally a sharp, clipped quality to New England speech—"a dryness that almost crackles," as one writer put it. May Lamberton Becker, in *Golden Tales of New England* (1931), suggests that the frigid New England weather has something to do with "the habits of laconic speech" because of "what it does to your throat to do much talking in the open air." Anyway, a common characteristic is the glottal stop in the place of a final *t* or *nt,* so that *twant* (it was not) often becomes *twan.* New Englanders also commonly pronounce the *o* in such words as *not, box, pot* and *hot* as an open *o* sound, with the lips rounded, while the rest of America generally voices the *o* more like the broad *a* in *father*.

Another characteristic New England dialect feature is the vowel shift of *au* to *ah*, *Boston* thus becoming *Bahston* and *caught* transformed into something like *caht*. However, while this is common in the Boston area, the reverse is true in some New England areas, especially in Cape Cod, where *Cape Cod* is surrounded by *wotta*. Cape Codders, whose speech is less nasal than that of most New Englanders, also differ from Bostonians not only in dropping their *r*'s but in adding another syllable as well; a Cape Codder's *there* thus becomes *they-uh* (instead of the Bostonian's *theah*) and *air* becomes *ey-uh*.

Obviously, then, the Boston or New England accent is not the same in all parts of New England. Perhaps the designation *Boston accent* has stuck because the accent is so strong in the city, with specimens similar to the following commonly heard on streets around the Common:

back—bark	moa—more
bee-ad—bad	noo-klee-eh—nuclear
bey-eh—bear	outer—order
bee-eh—beer	owah—hour
cod—card	potty—party
cotton—carton	shop—sharp
dock—dark	shut—shirt
gahd—guard	such—search
gull—girl	sutton—certain
hot—heart	waw—war

More likely the term *Boston accent* is heard so often because Boston is the eastern New England dialect's "focal area"—that is, an area that strongly influences the speech of surrounding areas because of cultural, commercial, political and other factors. But the differences remain within the region. Another is the pronunciation of *home* and *stone* as *hum* and *stun*, once common in many New England areas but now largely confined to Maine, which has in many respects a dialect unto itself. While the *u* in words such as *up* is generally pronounced *aw* in New England, it is pronounced as a deep-back-of-the-throat *ah* in Maine: AHp. Mainers also pronounce the "pure" New England *ay* sound of *maybe* as *eh*, saying *meh-be*.

To give still another example of differences within the region, rural New Englanders often pronounce *far* not with the typical New England broad *a*, but as *fu-uh*. Rhode Islanders speak differently from Bostonians and New Havenites speak differently from both of them. There are, in short, many subtle pronunciation variations throughout the speech region, even among the "focal area" residents of Boston. In Maine many residents even speak a Canadian French dialect called *joual*. (See the text.)

Vocabulary also varies throughout New England. Nantucket, for instance, has the local expression *greasy luck* (good luck), a carryover from whaling days, when well-wishers hoped that a whaleman would fill his ship with oil on a voyage. The national expression *I wouldn't know him from Adam's off ox* (the ox in the yoke farthest away from the driver) also began life as a Nantucketism, originally having been *I wouldn't know him from God's off ox,* the *Adam* substituted as a euphemism. *Coof,* special Nantucket talk for a summer visitor and "off-islander," may derive from a Scottish word meaning a dull, spiritless person.

The expression *swatson* (to chat or chew the fat—probably from the German *schwatzen*) possibly originated in the Connecticut area, while *quzzle,* for a small channel between two sandbars of a stream through a marsh, comes from Cape Cod. *Schooner* supposedly came to life in Gloucester, where an onlooker is said to have exclaimed, "Oh, how she scoons!" when Captain Andrew Robinson launched the first vessel of this kind back in 1713 and she glided gracefully over the water. Captain Robinson, overhearing the remark, dubbed his ship a *scooner,* which came to be misspelled *schooner* over the years. (*Scoon* itself probably derives from the Scottish *scon,* to skip a flat stone over the water.)

One of the earliest New Englandisms was the amusing Vermont term *quyascutus* for a cow with shorter legs on one side so that it could better walk around the steep Vermont hills! The rutted roads winding over New England's hills in early times gave us the expression *kiss-me-quick,* for a ridge or depression in a roadway, one that caused a carriage to jolt and possibly throw a girl into her young man's arms. Similarly, *thank-ye-ma'am* (see text) is an American courtship term that dates back to 19th century New England.

Two seldom (if ever) recorded New England expressions that are very typical of the area are *mighty small potatoes and few in a hill* (something or somebody of little consequence) and *he has too many shingles to the weather* (he's trying to do too many things at one time). As would be expected, New England nautical life is responsible for many national and local expressions. *Switchel,* for example, is old Yankee sailor slang, origin unknown, for a very thirst-quenching drink of molasses and water seasoned with vinegar and ginger; and *quoddy boats,* the double-ended keelboats used in lobstering, take their name from the Passamaquoddy Bay between New Brunswick, Canada, and Maine, where they were first used.

Son of a sea cook, which can mean either a "good guy" or a "mean SOB," depending on the context, really has little to do with the sea, but it does concern New England. It seems that the earliest American settlers appropriated the word *s'quenk,* for *skunk,* from the Indians around the Massachusetts Bay Colony, pronouncing it *sea-konk.* Thus, a *son of a sea-konk* was first a stinking son of a skunk. But *sea-konk* sounded something like *sea-cook* and came to be pronounced that way long after the Indian word was forgotten. The fact that sea cooks were often cantankerous old men (but did dispense the food) probably reinforced the term's present ambiguous meaning.

The word *Yankee* itself was first applied, in America, to Yankee sailors. The most popular of dozens of theories holds that *Yankee* comes from *Jan Kee* (little John), a Dutch expression the English used to signify "John Cheese" and contemptuously applied to New England seamen. From a pejorative nickname for New England sailors, the term *Jan Kee,* corrupted to *Yankee,* was applied to all New Englanders and then to all Americans during the Revolution, the most notable example of this being found in the derisive song "Yankee Doodle." Nowadays, the British and others use *Yankee* for an American; Southerners here use it for Northerners; and Northerners use it for New Englanders, who are so proud of the designation that they gladly call themselves Yankees.

There are, of course, thousands more words and pronunciations characteristic of New England Yankee speech than those already mentioned. Among vowel changes, for example, the following stand out prominently:

■ The General American *aw* of *all* and similar words usually becomes *ah,* except when preceded by *w* or followed by *r,* when it becomes an *o* sound (wash = *wosh*).
■ The *aw* of *more* becomes *oh* (*mohuh*).
■ The *aw* of *cough* is often pronounced *o* (*kof*) by New Englanders.
■ The long *ee* of *he* changes to *i* (hi).
■ The *eh* of *there* becomes *aa* (*thaauh*).
■ The *er* of *curb* changes to *u* (*kub*), especially in rural areas.
■ In many but not all words, the long *oh* of *home* often resembles *uuh,* pronounced with a faint glide (*huuhm*).

Among the changes in New England consonant pronunciation from General American:

■ *D* at the end of a word is dropped after an *n* (*sand* becomes *san*).
■ *H* is frequently added to *ain't,* yielding *hain't.*
■ In *ing* endings the nasalized *ng* is usually dropped (especially north of Boston and on the East Coast) and replaced by a clear *n,* pudding thus becoming *pudin.*
■ Outside of Boston the initial *wh* sound generally is pronounced *w* — where, for example, becoming *waa.*

Like every dialect, the New England patois does have its share of typical grammatical "errors" or differences, mainly used by rural or uneducated people and all becoming less common in recent times. Among those historical examples not already noted, the following stand out conspicuously:

- *Be* used in place of *are*. (How *be* you today?)
- *Like* substituted for *almost*. (He *like* to drowned.)
- *Knowed* used for *knew*. (I *knowed* he was coming.)
- Verb and subject often don't agree, as in *Where's them boats?*
- The singular is used instead of the plural for quantitative words, as in *It's been eighty year now.*
- *Are* is omitted after *where*. (*Where you going?*)
- *Shouldn't wonder* takes the place of *think*. (*I shouldn't wonder but what it's true.*)
- *Should* is used in place of *to* after the word *want*. (*He wants you should stop it.*)

Most of western New England speaks what is often called Inland Northern, a branch of the General American dialect. What is probably the New England dialect, with numerous variations, is spoken from the Connecticut River north and eastward through the eastern strip of Connecticut and Rhode Island, the eastern half of Massachusetts and Vermont, all of New Hampshire except in the mountains and all of Maine. The dialect was the first to be recognized by visitors to the colonies. It is probably the earliest in the United States to be honored (or derided) with a name, *New England dialect,* first recorded in 1788, when the phrase was noted in the diary of a visitor to the region. A year before that the "Yankee type" made his debut on the stage in the first comedy written by an American, Royall Tyler's *The Contrast.* In the play Jonathan, the trusty Yankee retainer of the serious-minded American Revolutionary War officer Colonel Manley, is a servant full of homespun shrewdness, regional sayings and Down East dialect.

The Yankee type was elaborated upon by many humor writers, including Seba Smith. The shrewd political commentaries of Smith's Yankee peddler Major Jack Downing, under the guise of simplicity, made him the first in a long line of American political and social humorists, including James Russell Lowell and his Hosea Biglow, Finley Peter Dunne and his Mr. Dooley, Mark Twain, Will Rogers, and, in our day, Art Buchwald and Russell Baker, among others. Numerous cartoons of Major Downing appeared in the newspapers of the time, and the popular Yankee was widely considered a uniquely American character, his likeness becoming the prototype for Uncle Sam.

Another Yankee fictional character who greatly influenced American humor was the itinerant clockmaker Sam Slick, created by Canadian humorist Thomas C. Haliburton, who combined shrewd New England talk with the boastful tall talk of the frontier. Sam Slick consistently said "Yankee" things: "Now, Marm Pugwash is like the minister's apples, very temptin' to look at but desperate sour." Haliburton coined, or first recorded, a great many popular American words and expressions in the various adventures of Sam Slick. In *The Attaché, or Sam Slick in England* (1844), Haliburton may have coined the still-popular expression *fly off the handle* (to lose one's self-control or head, as an ax sometimes loses its head when wildly wielded). He was among the first to record *get one's dander up* (to become angry) and *cut a wide swath* (to swagger), his stories popularizing these and many other expressions. Our "Mark Twain of the early 19th century" also may have invented the Americanism *cry over spilt milk* in *The Clockmaker* (1863), and the just-as-popular *lock, stock, and barrel* (everything), which refers to the three main components of a rifle: the barrel, stock, and lock, or firing mechanism. These examples only reflect expressions I have chanced upon in my reading; a thorough study might well reveal a host of genuine New England American-isms that this premier humorist introduced—more, perhaps, than any other early writer.

The Yankee humorist tradition came to its apotheosis in James Russell Lowell's *The Biglow Papers* (1848 and 1867), two series of satirical verses written in Yankee dialect. New England farmer Hosea Biglow is the purported author of most of the "letters" in the work, and while Lowell's Yankee dialect has been criticized roundly on technical grounds, it is accepted by many scholars as "an effective literary presentation of rural New England speech of the early 19th century." There is no doubt that American humor had never before been put to more serious purposes, the first series of verses written in opposition to the Mexican War, which Lowell saw as an immoral one, and the second series supporting the North in the Civil War. In one stanza of the earlier series he writes:

> Ez for war, I call it murder—
>   There you hev it plan an' flat,
> I don't want to go no furder
>   Than my Tetymunt fer that!
> God hez sed so plump an' fairly,
>   It's ez long ez it is broad,
> An' you've gut to get up airly
>   Ef you want to take in God . . .
> Wut's the use o' meetin'-goin'
>   Every Sabbath, wet or dry,
> Ef it's right to go amowin'
>   Feller-men like oats an' rye? . . .

In a verse letter from Birdofredum Sawin to Hosea, Lowell has Birdof-redum add:

> Thet our nation's bigger'n theirn an so its rights air bigger,
> And thet it's all to make em free thet we air pullin' trigger,
> Thet Anglo Saxondam's idee's abrekin' 'em to pieces,
> An thet idee's thet every man doos jest wut he damn pleases . . .

Certainly no Hosea Biglow or Birdofredum today, the "typical" New Englander would be impossible to define, given the great variety of people in the region. But traditionally the native son or daughter has been depicted as a dry, conservative, unemotional, cautious, prudent person not much given to change or "newfangled" ideas or the latest fashions, a type that doubtless exists in great numbers everywhere. Albert Biglow Paine (the title of one of whose plays gave the familiar nickname *The Great White Way* to New York's theatrical district) described a typical New Englander like this in his turn-of-the-century dialect poem "Mrs. Smith":

All day she hurried to get through,
The same as lots of wimmen do;
Sometimes at night her husben' said,
"Ma, ain't you goin' to come to bed?"
And then she'd kinder give a hitch,
And pause half way between a stitch,
And sorter sigh, and say that she
   Was ready as she'd ever be,
     She reckoned.

And so the years went one by one,
An' somehow she was never done;
An' when the angel said as how
"Mis' Smith, it's time you rested now,"
She sorter raised her eyes to look
A second, as a stitch she took.
"All right, I'm comin' now," says she,
   "I'm ready as I'll ever be,
     I reckon."

A sampler of New England words and phrases follows, a number of them treated more fully in the text. Some of these characteristic expressions are heard only in certain areas of New England and others are used mainly by older people. Several of the terms are well along on the road to obsolescence, just as *to home* (for *at home*), *trading* (for *shopping*) and *clothes press* (for *closet*) are already probably obsolete in New England. As a further qualification, it should be added that many of these expressions, such as *conniption fit, scrimp, pesky* and *snicker* (four New England terms that come directly from England's Essex dialect), have national currency today, though they did originate in the region.

- The New England word for a pail is *bucket*.
- An earthworm is an *angleworm*.
- To swim is *to bathe*.
- A hero sandwich is a *grinder* (because you need a good set of grinders, or teeth, to chew one).
- *Cape Cod turkey* means baked cod.

- *'Lowed* or *allowed* is used for *thought*. (*She 'lowed it was true.*)
- *Ary* is used for *either*. (*Ary one or the other.*)
- *Master* is a synonym for *excellent*. (*He did a master job.*)
- *Aim* often takes the place of *intend*. (*I aim to go.*)
- *Look here* becomes *look-a-here,* especially in rural areas.
- *Flummydiddle* is *nonsense*.
- A *body* frequently means a *person*. (*What's a body got to do to get something to eat around here?*)
- *Spell* often replaces *while*. (*Let's set for a spell.*)
- *Fetched* is used instead of *gave*. (*He fetched the dog a kick.*)
- A cleaning woman or girl is more politely called a *cleaning lady*.
- *Nearly* often becomes *nigh*. (*It's nigh on five miles down the road.*)
- A cemetery is a *graveyard*.
- *The other* often becomes *t'other*. (*Give me t'other one.*)
- The verb *address* becomes *back*. (*Please back this letter for me.*)
- The movies is the *show*.
- *Tolerable* is used for *rather* and also for *pretty well* or *fair to middlin'*. (*He was a tolerable big man; I'm feelin' tolerable.*)
- Plain, thick unsalted crackers used with chowder are called *common crackers*.
- A basement is a *cellar*.
- *Nary* is used for *none*. (*I ain't got nary one.*)
- A sycamore tree is a *buttonwood*.
- Sneakers can be *tennis*. (*Put on your tennis.*)
- *That wasn't* sometimes becomes *twant* or *twan*. (*Twan no way to do it.*)
- One doesn't mow a lawn, but *cuts* it.
- *Dast* is sometimes used for *dare* and *dassn't* for *didn't dare*. (*He don't dast go; he dassn't come.*)
- A water cooler is a *bubbler*.
- Regular coffee, which is generally coffee with cream and sugar on the side, is in Boston and other New England areas coffee with cream added and sugar on the side.
- The zeroes in dates are sometimes pronounced *ought* (19 *ought* 3 = 1903), especially by old-time Mainers.
- *Please* is sometimes replaced by *thank you kindly*. (*I'll thank you kindly to leave.*)
- A milkshake is a *cabinet*.
- A refrigerator is often an *icebox*.
- A gardener is a *yardman*.
- To *play hooky* is sometimes to *slunk school*.
- *I can't be sure* is often *I can't rightly know for sure*.
- *Sitting* is often *setting*.
- *Let on* often takes the place of *pretended*. (*He let on he was ailing.*)
- Soured milk is *barney clapper*.

There are many, many others, including a *hummer* for any bad guy with some saving grace, such as a sense of humor, and the *banking* or *tree belt* for the stretch of grass between the curb and the sidewalk. (New York City has no name for this, while it is a *tree lawn* in Cleveland, a *boulevard* in Minneapolis and the *devil's strip* in Akron.) Common regional similes, at least ones I (not a native New Englander) have heard, include: *bright as a button; as blue as calm water; cool as a cucumber; leak like a sieve (or riddle); sharp as a meat ax; big as all outdoors; acts like folks; cross as Sam Patch; mad as a hopper; crazy as a loon; homely as a stone fence; like all get out; sleek as a whistle; tall as a beanpole; fast as a cat in a gale; slick as a whistle;* and *soft as mush.*

Tangy similes I haven't heard, and which probably aren't used much except by older people, include: *more airs than a country stud horse; puffing like a grampus* (whale); *easygoing as old Tilly; as mean as turkey bitters; deafern' a coot; as true as preaching; as bad as all possessed; sour as swill; tough as a boiled eel; right as bean water;* and *meaner than goose grease.*

New England cooking terms are among the most distinctive in the country. *Johnnycake* or *journey cakes* (they were used as food on long journeys) were invented in New England. The area is also historically noted for *bean porridge,* pronounced to rhyme with *Norwich,* as in *There was a young man from Noritch / Who burnt his mouth on bean porritch.* New England's butternuts are called *oil nuts.* In Maine, *huff-puffs* are small balls of raised bread dough fried in deep fat; they are called *holy pokes* in Connecticut and *Baptist bread* elsewhere. *Sap coffee* is a New England coffee in which maple sap has been added to the water. *Bean swagger* is stewed dried beans cooked with salt pork pieces, and *bloaters* are large cured herring. *Bean-hole beans* are beans cooked for 24 hours in a hole lined with coals and covered with soil; a *dido* is the slash made in a pie crust to let out steam; *garden sass* is rhubarb; and *slip gut* is an old-fashioned pudding. *Hasty pudding,* which of course has odes written to it, is a New England invention that has the honor of being the only food besides macaroni mentioned in "Yankee Doddle":

But father and I went down to camp,
Along with Captain Goodwin,
And there we saw the men and boys,
As thick as Hasty Pudding.

Our word *squash* comes from the vegetable's Narragansett Indian name, *asquatasquash* (eaten raw), which came to be pronounced *squash* by New Englanders, while the noted Hubbard squash takes its name from Mrs. Elizabeth Hubbard, the Massachusetts lady who first cultivated it. Similarly, the corn-and-bean mixture called *succotash* was early taken by New Englanders from the Algonquian *misickquatsh* (kernel of corn), and the name of the fish called the *menhaden* was adapted from the Algonquian *munnoquahatean* (that which enriches the soil).

In New England place-names reside many stories. To take just the Boston area, Milk Street is so named because country slickers used to water their milk at a stream there before selling it to city bumpkins; Beacon Hill recalls a beacon on a high pole there that guided ships into Boston Harbor; the Common was once used "in common" by all the people for grazing their cattle; and Damnation Alley was wide enough for only one oxcart, so that whenever two teamsters met going in opposite directions the air was blue with *damns* and much stronger curses. Pronunciation of New England place names is no easy matter, and there are no easy rules to follow. Groton, for example, is pronounced *Grah-ton;* Quincy is *Kwin-zi;* and Billerica is *Bill-rikker.*

Those interested in unusual and even outrageous New England family names should turn to the entry *Goddams* in the text. As for curses, these are plentiful there too—New Englanders aren't always the pious euphemizers they have often been depicted as. In the words of Burgess Johnson (*As Much As I Dare,* 1947): "Upon the farms of Vermont and New Hampshire, and along the coast and in the forests of Maine, there has been since the days of Ethan Allen an easy fluency in cursing that never sought the least disguise [because] . . . all of the northern territory was peopled by folk who had fled the Massachusetts and Connecticut clergy and their dour god."

New Englander exclamations often aren't euphemisms anymore and aren't heard as much today as in earlier times. In 1933 Hans Kurath listed no fewer than 42 New England euphemisms for the virile *bull,* the most widely used of these being, in order of popularity, *gentleman cow, male, toro, sire, animal, male critter, man-cow, cow-man, bullock, cow topper, doctor, bullit, paddy,* and *bungy.* The euphemistic exclamations most common associated with New England, at least in historical or literary use, would include the following, in no particular order:

Pshaw! landsakes alive! landsakes! sakes alive! gee whittakers! godfrey! dad blame it! my gracious! what in tarnation! what in tunket! don't that beat all get out! chowder! Jerusalem crickets! ginger! blow my shirt! gehosephatt! I swear! I'll be jiggered! I'll be dinged! I'll be danged! not by a jugful! and *gracious me!*

To which I finally should add the rather archaic but nice exclamation my dear old grandmother (a New Englander) used to exclaim:

My stars and body!

Which is as good a note to end on as any, except perhaps James Russell Lowell's good advice that "Life is short and prefaces [or introductions] should be."

—R.H.
Peconic, New York

A

A The capital letter adulterers were forced to wear as a badge when convicted of the crime of adultery under a law in force in New England from 1639 to 1785.

> There was likewise a young woman, with no mean share of beauty, whose doom it was to wear the letter A on the breast of her gown, in the eyes of all the world and her own children . . . Sporting with her infamy, the lost and desperate creature had embroidered the fatal token in scarlet cloth, with golden thread; so that the capital A might have been thought to mean Admirable, or anything rather than Adulteress. (Nathaniel Hawthorne, "Endicott and the Red Cross," 1838)

Hawthorne, of course, also wrote about the A of adultery in his novel *The Scarlet Letter* (1850). See also SCARLET LETTER, THE.

a (1) The broad *a* of New England (as in *cah* for *car, fah* for *far* etc.) is heard regularly in the Boston area (within an area of about 40 miles from the city) and again in Maine from about Portland eastward. Elsewhere in the region its occurrence is not as frequent and in western New England it is rare. (2) "The Yankee has retained something of the long sound of the *a* in such words as *ax* and *wax,* pronouncing them *ex, wex*

(shortened from *aix, waix*)." (James Russell Lowell, *The Biglow Papers,* 1866).

Aaron's rod A name used mainly in New England for the garden orpine (*Sedum telephium*). *Aaron's rod* comes from the sacred rod that the patriarch Aaron placed before the ark in Numbers 17:8, a rod that Jehovah caused to bend, blossom and bear ripe almonds. Many tall-stemmed, flowering plants that resemble rods, such as orpine, mullein and goldenrod, are called *Aaron's rod* in other regions.

A-B-Abs An old-fashioned term for the rudimentary ABCs of the schoolroom, or for basic knowledge of anything. "He don't know his A-B-Abs about it."

aback Stalled, at a standstill, behind. "I'm all aback in my chores."

abeam A nautical term sometimes used on land in New England to mean at a right angle to something. In nautical use it means at right angles to the fore-and-aft, or center line, of a vessel.

Abe Lincoln War See ABOLITION WAR.

able Strong. "He lifted it by himself. He's an able man, all right."

able to set up an' eat a few porridges In good health, or coming along fine after an illness. Cited as a common Maine and northern New Hampshire expression in George Allen England, "Rural Locutions of Maine and Northern New Hampshire," *Dialect Notes,* Vol. IV (1914).

Abolition War A historical name given to the Civil War in New England, the only region where names associating the war with slavery were commonly employed. The ABE LINCOLN WAR, The War for the Blacks, and *The War to Free the Slaves* were others.

about east A synonym for okay, all right, or the proper thing to do. "The late Mr. Horace Mann . . . commented at some length on the beauty and moral significance of the French phrase *s'orienter,* and called on his young friends to practice upon it in life. There was not a Yankee in his audience whose problem had not always been to find out what was *about east,* and to shape his course accordingly." (James Russell Lowell, *The Biglow Papers,* 1867)

Acadian owl Mainers and other New Englanders call the little sawwhet or barn owl (*Ulula acadica*) by this name.

accommodatin' as a hog on ice Very unobliging or disagreeable. Cited as a common Maine and New Hampshire expression in George Allen England, "Rural Locutions of Maine and Northern New Hampshire," *Dialect Notes,* Vol. IV (1914).

accommodation Short for *accommodation train.* A term for a train that stopped at every station, no matter how small, on a New England line, thus accommodating all the people in an area. Today *accommodation trains* are mixed passenger and freight trains.

acts like folks Said of a down-to-earth person, a regular guy, male or female.

Adam's ale Water. The humorous term is an old English one used in other regions as well. A variation is *Adam's wine.*

Adam's cup A folk name for the pitcher plant (*Sarracenia purpurea*) because of the cuplike shape of its leaves.

adder's tongue The origin of this New England name for the dogtooth violet (*Erythronium amercanum*) is unknown.

Admiration A vocabulary-testing word game very popular in 19th-century New England.

admire to To like to, be glad to. "I'd admire to go with you."

adrift A seafaring team used on land in Maine and other New England states, *adrift* can mean to be tied improperly, to become untied. "That package is all adrift; you don't know your knots."

advanced female This name was sarcastically bestowed upon any woman who fought for women's rights in the last half of the 19th century.

adz into   Used, primarily in Maine, to mean "bite," "dig into," "eat heartily." "He really adzed into that roast." The reference is to an adz or ax biting off chunks of wood.

afore   Before. "Afore we could say Jack Robinson." (Seba Smith, *Letters Written During The President's Tour, "Down East," by Myself, Major Jack Downing of Downingville,* 1833) Smith, a Mainer, was the first of the homespun Yankee political philosophers and had so many imitators that he said he knew himself only by the scar on his left arm. His character Major Downing inspired cartoons that were the prototype of Uncle Sam as a symbol of the United States.

afterclap   An old term for any unexpected or unpleasantly surprising happening. ". . . he shrinked and sheered away from whales, for fear of afterclaps." (Herman Melville, *Moby Dick,* 1851)

aftergrass   Heard in Maine for *aftermath*; that is, grass that grows after the hay has been harvested and is then cut itself. Also called *after cutting*.

agin   A pronunciation of "again" in Maine and other parts of New England.

ahp   The typical Maine pronunciation of *up*; pronounced with a deep back-of-the-throat *ah*: AHp.

aiglefin   A name French-speaking inhabitants of New England sometimes give to the cod-like fish more generally known as haddock (*Melanogrammus aeglefinus*).

aim   Intend. "I aim to go, Fred, whatever you do."

ain't all there   See HAS A SCREW LOOSE.

ain't got nothing?   Used in Maine to mean "Have you got a drink?" *Nothing* here is pronounced *nawthin'*.

ain't got sense enough to carry guts to a bear   Hasn't the most rudimentary common sense. Given as a common expression in George Allen England, "Rural Locutions of Maine and Northern New Hampshire," *Dialect Notes,* Vol. IV (1914).

ain't worth a fart in a gale of wind   Totally worthless.

ain't worth wrappin' your finger around   Is of little or no value.

alderman in chains   A Yankee recipe for turkey cooked with link sausages spread over it, resembling a potbellied alderman trussed in chains.

alewife   This member of the herring family returns in spring from the sea to spawn in fresh water. The Indians taught the early colonists how to trap the alewife both for food and for use as an excellent fertilizer. In *Cape Cod Yesterdays* (1935) Joseph C. Lincoln calls the fish the *Cape Cod herring*.

Writes Henry Beston in *The Outermost House* (1928):

> This "aloofe" of the colonists, better known as the "alewife," and often incorrectly called a "herring," is really not a herring at all but a related fish, *Pomolobus pseudoharengus*. It is distinguished from the true sea herring by its greater depth of body and by the serrations on the midline of its belly, which are stronger and sharper than those of the true herring—so sharp, indeed, that the fish is sometimes called a "saw belly." In April they leave the sea and run up our [New England] brooks to spawn in freshwater ponds.

In Maine, according to Robert P. Tristram Coffin's *Kennebec, Cradle of Americans* (1937), *alewife* "is pronounced *ell-y,* in case you don't know."

alewife in his air chamber Said of someone using a flimsy excuse to explain his poor performance on a job. The saying possibly originated when two fire engines were drawing water from a brook while attempting to put out a fire in a New England seacoast town. One engine company performed poorly; its crew claimed that its poor performance resulted from a big alewife caught in the engine's air chamber. See ALEWIFE.

all bones and sinner See ALL HIS (HER) BORN DAYS.

all chalk and water An old expression meaning worthless nonsense, balderdash. "That's all chalk and water."

all druv (drove) up Very busy, overworked; the *druv* (drove) derives from the droving of cattle in early times, a busy occupation. "I was all druv up trying to get things together."

all-fired An intensive meaning extremely that is heard in New England and other regions. "Don't be so all-fired sure of yourself."

all fluking Fast sailing; originally a nautical term suggesting the way a whale moves swiftly by strokes of its great flukes. "We arrived on the following day, having gone all fluking . . ." (Richard Henry Dana, Jr., *Two Years Before The Mast,* 1841)

all good Americans go to Paris when they die See FROZEN YANKEE DOODLE.

all hair by the nose Very angry. "He's all hair by the nose."

all hands and the cook! *All hands and the cook on deck!* was a cry probably first heard on New England whalers in the early 19th century when everyone aboard was called topside to cut into a whale, work that had to be done quickly. Fishermen also used the expression, and still do, and it had currency among American cowboys to indicate a dangerous situation—when, for example, even the cook was needed to keep the herd under control.

all her (his) born days All his or her life. "Ma herself was dreadful poor, never weighed ninety pounds in all her born days, but she was powerful strong, all bone and sinner to the last." (Annie Trumbull Slosson, "A Local Colorist," 1912)

all humped up like a hog going to war A Maine expression describing a determined person off on an unlikely mission that seems destined to fail despite his or her determination.

all in a pucker In a hurry. "He's all in a pucker to get home."

all nature Everybody or everything, "all creation." "All nature was at the fair."

all of a biver An old-fashioned expression meaning very excited. "She was all of a biver."

all of a high Heard in Maine for *very anxious, eager*. "They were all of a high to go."

all of a rush Suddenly, abruptly. "Everybody came at the last minute, all of a rush."

all of a scatter Widely scattered. "The papers were all of a scatter over the room." Also *all of a scatteration*.

all of a shiver An old expression meaning *shivering*. "The child was all of a shiver and we put her to bed."

all of a washing sweat Used in Maine to describe someone sweating profusely. Also *all of a lather*.

allot upon A synonym, rarely if ever heard anymore, for *intend*. "I allot upon going to Boston."

all over East Jesus Widely scattered, all over the place. ". . . Teddy's brushes with the law are scattered all over East Jesus. I have visited . . . Vermont . . . New Hampshire . . . Maine . . . Rhode Island . . . as counsel of record for Edmund M. Franklin." (George V. Higgins, *Kennedy for the Defense*, 1980)

all smiles and johnnycake Affable, happy. "Emily . . . was all smiles and johnnycake." (Susan Hale, *Letters*, 1989) See JOHNNYCAKE.

all standing A seafaring term meaning fully dressed that was once commonly heard on land. "He turned in 'all standing,' and was always on deck the moment he was called." (Richard Henry Dana, Jr., *Two Years Before the Mast*, 1840)

all stark alone Living without anyone else in the house or nearby. ". . . as nice an old man as you ever saw—all alone, all stark alone." (Dorothy Canfield, "Old Man Warner," in *Raw Material*, 1925)

all's well alow and aloft A Yankee nautical expression popular in 19th-century New England. It means everything is all right; *alow* means on deck or belowdeck and the *aloft* means in the rigging.

allus A pronunciation of "always." "It's the same as it allus was."

all used up Worn out, tired, very old. "He just worked a few hours and was all used up."

always astern of the lighter This Nantucket expression means always dead last, according to Marion Nicholl Rawson in *From Here to Yender* (1932).

always reefer down and standing on the inshore tack A Nantucket expression used to describe someone much too prudent or cautious; cited in William F. Macy, *The Nantucket Scrap Basket* (1916).

alst Common in Maine for *all* or *all that*. "That's alst I heard about it."

amalgamationist "Blending of the two races by amalgamation is just what is needed for the perfection of both," a white Boston clergyman wrote in 1845. Few American abolitionists were proponents of amalgamation (miscegenation), but many were call amalgamationists by slave holders in the two decades or so before the Civil War. This Americanism for one who favors a social and genetic mixture of whites and blacks is first recorded in 1838, when Harriet Martineau complained that people were calling her an *amalgamationist* when she didn't know what the word meant.

American The first person recorded to have used this term for a citizen of the United States or of the earlier British colonies was New England religious leader Cotton Mather in his *Magnolia Christie Americana* (1702).

Amherst Correctly pronounced AMM-urst in New England; the name of towns in Massachusetts and New Hampshire. Amherst, Mass. was the home of poet Emily Dickinson and is the site of Amherst College.

a mind to A rural expression meaning disposed to. "Don't matter what you say, she'll do as she's a mind to."

amongst Among. See FOLKSY.

amoosement In *Elsie Venner* (1861) Oliver Wendell Holmes gives this as a pronunciation of "amusement."

amost A common New England pronunciation of "almost."

ample Enough or more than enough; often used in reference to food. "I can't eat another morsel, had ample of everything."

anadama bread This Yankee cornmeal recipe offers one of the most humorous stories connected with any foodstuff. Tradition has it that a Yankee farmer or fisherman, whose wife Anna was too lazy to cook for him, concocted the recipe. On tasting the result of his efforts, a neighbor asked him what he called the bread. The crusty Yankee replied, "Anna, damn her!" Another version claims that the husband was a Yankee sea captain who endearingly referred to his wife as "Anna, damn'er." Anna's bread was much loved by his crew because it was delicious and would not spoil on long sea voyages. The captain is said to have written the following epitaph for his wife: "Anna was a lovely bride, / but Anna, damn'er, up and died.''

anesthesia After William Thomas Green Morton successfully employed ether at Boston's Massachusetts General Hospital in 1846, New England poet-physician Oliver Wendell Holmes wrote in a letter to him on November 21: "Every body wants to have a hand in a great discovery. All I will do is give you a hint or two as to names—or the name—to be applied to the state produced and the agent. The state should, I think, be called 'Anaethesia' (which derives from the Greek *anaisthesia*, "lack of sensation"). This signifies insensibility . . . The adjective will be 'Anaesthetic' . . .'' Thus, Holmes clearly coined the term *anaesthesia* so commonly used today, even though it had been recorded in a different sense over a century before in England. The word is usually spelled *anesthesia* today. See also BETTER A HASH AT HOME THAN A ROAST WITH STRANGERS.

angledog A name still occasionally heard for an earthworm that is used as bait in fishing.

animal An old-fashioned euphemism for *bull* used mainly in rural areas when it is used at all.

a'n't A pronunciation of *ain't*. "That a'n't my way." (Oliver Wendell Holmes, *The Professor at the Breakfast-Table*, 1860)

ant-bed An old-fashioned term for *ant hill*. Also *ant nest*.

ant heap Once a familiar term for *carbuncle;* so named for its shape.

antifogmatical An old humorous name used in Massachusetts for *rum*, which was said to be able to clear up any fog.

antimacassar A crocheted covering for the back or arms of a stuffed chair or sofa. It takes its name from the Macassar oil men used as hair tonic in the 19th century: men with the oily tonic on their hair or hands often soiled the chairs and sofas they sat on. Macassar oil was made from a bean Yankee ships brought back from Macassar in the East Indies.

antiques and horribles A historical term for men who used to march in small-town Fourth of July parades wearing masks and ragged clothing, parodying the veterans called "ancients and honorables" who marched in such parades.

any God's amint (amount) A large number of. "There's any God's amint of deer around here now." Given as a common expression in George Allen England, "Rural Locutions of Maine and Northern New Hampshire," *Dialect Notes,* Vol. IV (1914).

apple bee See APPLE CUT.

apple brown betty See APPLE PANDOWDY.

apple-cabbage A Maine term once commonly used for *rhubarb* or *pie-plant* (*Rheum rhubarbarum*).

apple cut An autumn social gathering at which apples were pared and strung to be dried for winter use. "A apple cut? A parin' bee? / You just try it an' see." (Rowland Evand Robinson, *Danvis Folks,* 1894)

apple duff The *duff* in this dessert's name simply means *dough,* which New England sailors often pronounced as if it rhymed with "rough."

apple John A kind of brandy made from apple cider.

apple Johnny Another Yankee name for APPLE PANDOWDY.

apple Jonathan See APPLE PANDOWDY.

apple knocker An outhouse; so called because outhouses are usually located back of the house, out in the trees where apples might fall and knock against the roof. This term is not related to the old slang term *apple knocker* meaning a rural person, hick.

apple pandowdy This is a Yankee dish, despite the popular song praising "Southern" treats such as "shoofly pie and apple pandowdy . . . I never get enough of that wonderful stuff." Imogene Wolcott's *New England Yankee Cookbook* (1939) gives several recipes for the deep-dish apple dessert, noting that the modern version is often called *apple brown Betty.* It is also called *apple pot-pie, apple Jonathan, apple Johnny* and *apple slump.*

apple-peru Another old-fashioned Maine term for *rhubarb* or *pieplant.* (*Rheum rhubarfarum*).

apple pie order An expression often heard in New England and elsewhere for *neat* and *orderly.* One old story holds that New England housewives were so meticulous and tidy when making their apple pies—carefully cutting their slices of apples, methodically arranging them in rows inside the pie, making sure that the pinches joining the top and bottom crusts were perfectly even, and so on—that the expression arose for prim and precise orderliness. While it is a nice story, the phrase *apple pie order* is probably British in origin, dating back at least to the early 17th century, and its derivation is unknown.

apple pot-pie See APPLE PANDOWDY.

applesauce turnover A turnover filled with applesauce rather than sliced apples. "Father helped himself to a handful of cookies and a fat applesauce turnover." (Hayden Pearson, *New England Flavor,* 1961)

apple shaker Any autumn storm short of a hurricane that shakes apples off the trees. "That was some apple shaker we had last night."

apple slump Apple slump, a popular New England dessert, takes on another meaning in Louisa May Alcott's story "Transcendental Wild Oats" (1876), an account of her father Bronson Alcott's failed utopian community Fruitlands 32 years earlier: " 'Poor Fruitlands! The name was as great a failure as the rest!' continued Abel [Bronson Alcott], with a sigh, as a frostbitten apple fell from a leafless bough at his feet. But the sigh changed to a smile as his wife added, in a half-tender, half-satirical tone—'Don't you think Apple Slump would be a better name for it, dear?' " The dessert is sometimes called *apple pandowdy* and *flummery*. So much did Harriet Beecher Stowe like the dish that she named her Concord, Massachusetts house Apple Slump.

apple snow A dessert made of apples, sugar and egg whites, according to Imogene Wolcott's *New England Yankee Cookbook* (1939), which gives the recipe for this frothy concoction elsewhere known as an *apple float*.

appletreer A ship that stays close to the coast, in sight of land or the apple trees; sailors have long used the word contemptuously. Also spelled *appletree-er*.

applicant An old term, possibly obsolete now, used for someone who applies him- or herself diligently to studies or work.

Arab Any wild, unruly child; said to derive from the savage Barbary pirates of old encountered by New England sailors. Often pronounced *Ay-rab* and used humorously.

Arlington Pronounced AAH-ling-tun by the natives; a suburb of Boston.

Aroostook County A county in Maine known throughout the state as *The County*.

around See HANGING AROUND.

around Cape Horn An expression once used in whaling communities to mean "being away on a whaling voyage." One old poem went:

"I'll tell your father, boys," I cried.
To lads at play upon my lawn.
They chorused back, "You'll have
    to go
Around Cape Horn!"

around time All over. "[He's] been fixing up all the roads around time but mine." (Hayden Pearson, *New England Flavor*, 1967)

arter (1) A pronunciation heard in Maine for *artery*. "He was so mad we thought he'd bust an arter." (2) A pronunciation of "after."

artistic purposes See MECHANICAL AND ARTISTIC PURPOSES.

ary An old-fashioned word meaning either. "Take ary one or the other."

asafetida bag Asafetida is a foul-smelling resinous material made from roots of several plants of the parsley family. Its odor was thought to ward off illness, and it was often placed in small bags that were worn under the clothing by children.

. . . we wore an asafetida bag beneath our long underwear [to fight off illness]. Unless you are personally acquainted with the aroma of this fetid Oriental gum, you can not comprehend the meaning of spring [in New Hampshire] a few decades ago. Day and night we wore that bag; the smell in the hot school room was something to lift the scalp. Mrs. Meigs, our beloved teacher, said more than once that the only thing she disliked about teaching was asafetida time. (Hayden Pearson, *New England Flavor,* 1961)

as bad as all possessed Used to describe someone who acts as if he or she is possessed by the devil.

as big as old Cuffey An old expression not often heard anymore describing someone or something of great size. After Captain Paul Cuffey, a black ship captain of New Bedford who in about 1787 recruited free African Americans to settle in Sierra Leone and transported them there on his ship.

as busy as a man on the town Indolent; a man on the town is someone on relief or welfare.

as chirk as a chitterdiddle on a pokeweed See CHIRK.

as close as the bark to a tree Cheap, stingy, tight.

ask no odds of anybody Ask no favors. ". . . as nice an old man as you ever saw . . . asking no odds of anybody . . ." (Dorothy Canfield, "Old Man Warner," in *Raw Material,* 1925)

as mad as a beaver An old simile meaning very angry that apparently originated in New England.

as Maine goes, so goes the nation A common political saying since the late 19th century; it means that the political party that wins the most votes in Maine in a national election will win nationally. This has often, but not always, been the case. The saying originally referred to New York, being first recorded in 1848 as "As goes Dutchess County, so goes the State, and as New York goes, so goes the Union."

as mean as turkey bitters A simile once common in New England.

as poor as Job's turkey An old saying possibly invented by Canadian humorist Thomas C. Haliburton, who combined shrewd New England talk with the boastful tall talk of the frontier. He apparently invented the common Americanism in one of his tales, explaining that the turkey was even poorer than the biblical Job, who had been stripped of all his worldly goods by God. Job's turkey so poor that it had but one feather to its tail, and so poorly fed that it had to lean up against the fence when it gobbled, lest the exertion make it fall down.

ass-up This small woodpecker of the family Sittidae, found in Connecticut and other New England states, runs up and down tree trunks with its head held lower than its tail. It is sometimes called a nuthatch.

astern the lighter Belated, far behind in doing something. The Nantucket expression is related in some unknown way to the barge called a lighter once used to transfer cargo between a ship and the shore. "You're astern the lighter a'ready with all your garden chores."

as the feller says As they say. "As the feller says, take things as they come."

as thick as huckleberries An expression common in the 19th century meaning very thick.

as tight (drunk) as a peep See quote. "[The] New England mind . . . has long since endorsed the locution 'as tight as a peep' to express an utter state of tipsification." (*Boston Daily Telegraph*, July 27, 1864)

ataunto A seafaring term meaning with all sails rigged that came to mean "all ready" among landlubbers, though it is rarely heard anymore. "[Some ships] were all a-taint-o . . ." (Herman Melville, *Redburn*, 1849) The word probably derives from the French *autant*, meaning the same. Pronounced *a-tanto*.

Atherton gag A historical term for a congressional resolution made in 1838 by Representative C.G. Atherton of New Hampshire, which provided that all bills relating to slavery should be tabled without debate. It remained in force until 1844. John Quincy Adams called Atherton "the man of the mongrel gag."

Atlantic Monthly A national magazine founded in Boston in 1857 by leading New England literary figures

and named by Oliver Wendell Holmes. The magazine, first edited by James Russell Lowell, has long been influential in literary and political affairs.

Augusty The way Mainers pronounce the name of their capital city, Augusta.

Aunt A large flavorful winter apple, considered to be one of the best eating apples in New England since at least the early 19th century. Also called the *Aunt Hannah*.

auntie Often used in the past as a respectful form of address for any unrelated old woman, as well as one's real aunt. *Aunt* was similarly used.

autymobile An old rural pronunciation of "automobile."

avast This was originally a nautical word meaning to stop hauling; it possibly derives from the Portuguese *abasta*, "enough." *Avast* came to be used figuratively in coastal New England areas to mean "stop doing anything," from talking to working.

away Down East A place far down in New England, usually meaning Maine; the term has been used since the early 19th century.

awful A synonym for ugly. "That's one awful face he's got."

awful old fart Someone, not necessarily old, who is compulsively neat and meticulous to the point of being prissy and unbearable.

awnt Aunt, commonly pronounced with a broad *a* in New England.

ayuh Yes, though the word has shades of meaning ranging from the affirmative to the sarcastic. Chiefly heard in Maine, *ayuh* is found throughout New England in variations such as *eyah, ayeh, eeyuh, ehyuh, aaay-yuh,* and even *ayup.* A touchstone of New England speech, it possibly derives from the nautical *aye* (yes), which in turn probably comes from the early English *yie* (yes). Another theory has *ayuh* coming from the old Scots-American *aye-yes* meaning the same. " 'Oh, ayuh, I guess I *did* hear that, but you know how people on the island talk.' " (Stephen King, *Dolores Claiborne,* 1993)

B

babbitt Congress deemed the invention of *babbitt metal* so important to the development of the industrial age that it awarded inventor Isaac Babbitt (1799–1862) a $20,000 grant. Babbitt is a soft, silver-white alloy of copper, tin and antimony used to reduce friction in machine bearings. It was discovered as a result of the inventor's experiments in turning out the first Britannia metal tableware ever produced in America. After the Taunton, Massachusetts goldsmith successfully manufactured Britannia in 1824, he experimented further with the same three metals and ultimately invented babbitt, which he used to line a patented journal box in 1839. The metal proved far better than any other substance used for reducing friction and is still widely used for machine bearings today. *Babbitt soap,* no longer marketed, also bore the inventor's name. Babbitt wasn't the prototype for Sinclair Lewis's ambitious, uncultured and smugly satisfied American businessman in his novel of the same name, but Lewis's early memories of advertisements for the soap probably suggested the character's name.

back An old term meaning to address. "Please back this letter for me."

back along In days past, in former times. "She said she was a good old-timer, dating back along."

back and fill Very little progress is made when you back and fill a sailing ship; that is, when you are tacking the craft while the tide is running with her and the wind is against her. In this sailing maneuver, the sails are alternately backed and filled and the ship seems to remain in roughly the same place, going backward and then forward. The term was a natural for landlubbers, especially New Englanders with their strong ties to the sea, to apply to any vacillating or irresolute action—to hemming and hawing.

Back Bay The Back Bay area, built on land reclaimed from the waterfront, has been a fashionable residential district in Boston, Massachusetts since the mid-19th century. So much so, in fact, that *Back Bay* has been synonymous for the culture of Boston for almost as long. " 'That's what they call in Boston being very 'thoughtful,' Mrs. Luna said, 'giving you the Back Bay (don't you hate the name?) to look at, and then taking credit for it.' " (Henry James, *The Bostonians,* 1886) "He had lodged himself in the grid of Back Bay a few blocks from where she had grown up." (John Updike, "Killing" in *Trust Me,* 1987)

backcheeks Heard in Maine for the posterior of a person.

backhouse An outhouse, so named because it was usually located in the rear of a dwelling. Most backhouses accommodated two people at a time (two-holers), but there were some one-holers and three-holers.

backhouse lily The day lily (of the genus *Hemerocallis*), which is a common "escape" from gardens and got this name because it often grew near backhouses or privies.

backlog The large log placed at the rear or back of a fire in a fireplace; the term is heard in other regions as well.

Back Side (1) The backyard of a house.

> "Back Side" and "Bay Side" . . . are terms to remember when you visit Cape Cod. A prim Wellfleet housewife who rents rooms to summer people once confessed to me that she had somehow shocked her guests by 'a perfectly civil answer' she had given them! They wanted to know the best place to take a sunbath and, of course, she told them the best place was on the Back Side." (Jeremiah Diggs, *Cape Cod Pilot,* 1937)

(2) See quote. ". . . Bath [Maine] was considerably more than a hundred miles from the backside (our word for the backshore) of Mount Desert [island] . . ." (Norman Mailer, *Harlot's Ghost,* 1991)

back states An old name for all the New England states. ". . . those folks from the back states are mighty green, they say." (James Hunter, *Western Border Life,* 1859)

backyard trots An old term for *diarrhea* or *the runs*.

bag plant The orpine (*Sedum telephium*), because the plant's leaves can be blown up like small bags or bladders until they pop.

bag yer head Be more modest, pull in your horns. "You better bag yer head!" Given as a common expression in George Allen England, "Rural Locutions of Maine and Northern New Hampshire," *Dialect Notes,* Vol. IV (1914).

bahstid A Maine pronunciation of "bastard." "He's a mean old bahstid."

Bahston A common pronunciation of *Boston* in Boston and environs. A recent ad employing two dialects heralded a coming "New York vs. Bahston" baseball game. Also *Bahstin*.

bake Short for *clambake,* where foods such as clams, lobsters and corn are not baked but steamed in the heat of a fire made of layers of wood, rock and seaweed.

baked beans A New England staple. "One ov the old blue laws ov Massachusetts wuz, *'thou shalt eat baked beans on Sunday.'* " (Josh Billings, *Old Probability, Perhaps Rain, Perhaps Not,* 1876)

baker's cart A small horsedrawn wagon bakers used a century ago to sell their bread, rolls, cakes and pies from door to door. Trucks later replaced it.

bakeshop meal An old-fashioned term for a meal cooked in a bakery oven, as baked beans and other dishes were in the past, or for a meal one doesn't take much time or effort to prepare. " 'He gets some sort of bakeshop meals together . . .' " (Robert Frost, "The Housekeeper," 1914)

baldheaded See quote. "Baldheaded: 'to go it bald-headed;' in great haste, as where one rushes out without his hat." (James Russell Lowell, *The Biglow Papers,* 1867)

bald-headed ship A colorful old term for a schooner without topmasts.

Baldwin In 1800 Colonel Loamine Baldwin (1740–1807) of Wilmington, Massachusetts found the seedling that was developed into the much-grown winter apple tree and the fruit that bear his name.

bale of hay An old name, its origin unknown, for a dish of peas, string-beans and pototoes mixed together.

balky A term for *wino* heard in Connecticut. "He's nothing but an old balky."

ballast for her (his) balloon A person who is a down-to-earth or steadying influence on another. "It was a little remarkable that only one woman ever joined this community [Bronson Alcott's utopian Fruitlands]. Mrs. Lamb [the fictional name for Alcott's wife] merely followed wheresoever her husband led—'as ballast for his balloon,' as she said, in her bright way." (Louisa May Alcott, "Transcendental Wild Oats," 1876)

balled up Dashing through the snow on a horsedrawn sled could be hazardous in old New England. One difficulty was the balls of snow or ice that formed in the curve of a horse's shoe and often made a horse slip and fall. When horses did fall, especially a team of them, the resulting confusion and entanglement gave rise to the expression *all balled up.*

Ballyhack A euphemism for *hell.* "You can go to Ballyhack."

balm o' Gilead Heard in New England and other regions for the balsam poplar (*Populus balsamifera*), the biblical name appropriate because the tree's resin was used for medicinal purposes.

balmy Used ironically by Mainers for *very cold weather.* "It's balmy out."

bange around To hang around; to impose on someone by staying where one isn't invited. "It'll interest him to go out there; and we can make him believe it's just to bange around for the winter." (William Dean Howells, *The Landlord at Lion's Head,* 1897) A *bandgeeing place* is a place, like a country store or courthouse, where people lounge around.

Bangor rule, the A rule devised by lumbermen in Bangor, Maine to determine the total of board feet in a log. Figuratively, the *Bangor rule* has become a measure of honesty and fairness in a person; one who goes by the *Bangor rule* is an honorable person.

banker Rudyard Kipling's *Captains Courageous* (1897) celebrates the rugged fishermen who worked the rich waters called the Grand Banks off Newfoundland. The two-masted Yankee schooners that worked these fishing grounds were called *bankers*.

banking (1) Dirt piled against a building's foundation as insulation for winter protection. (2) The stretch of grass between a curb and the sidewalk; however, the New England regional term for this is *tree belt*.

banned in Boston In its heyday during the 1920s, the phrase *banned in Boston* made a number of books best-sellers throughout the rest of the country. Books were frequently banned in Boston for foolish reasons because the local ultraconservative Watch and Ward Society wielded great power in the city. While this is no longer the case, the expression is still used jokingly.

bannock A bread made from (in one recipe) cornmeal, salt, boiling water and butter. It can be baked in an oven or cooked on a griddle. In Maine *bannock* sometimes has the connotation of poor food fit for the dogs, which were commonly fed bannock cakes before commercial dogfoods were available.

baptist cake The comparison is to Baptists baptized in water, for these sweet rolls, known also as *holy pokes,* are cooked by being dropped in hot fat.

barber A strong frigid northwestern wind bearing moisture that can cut the face and often clings to the hair and beard, forming ice crystals.

bare as a milkpan when the cat's been round Impoverished. " 'That Frome farm's always 'bout as bare's a milkpan when the cat's been round.' " (Edith Wharton, *Ethan Frome,* 1911)

bareassed Completely naked, an expression used mainly in New England and the Northeast.

barefoot See quote. " 'I take my tea barefoot,' said a backwoodsman when asked if he would have cream and sugar." (James Russell Lowell, *The Biglow Papers,* 1867)

bareneked A redundancy for *naked.* "They swam bareneked."

Bar Harbor The name of the famous resort in Maine is pronounced BAH-HAH-buh by the natives and most summer people too.

bark To scuff or skin a knee or elbow; usually said of children who fall and injure themselves this way. "He fell off the slide and barked himself."

bark nutmeg A false nutmeg made of tree bark reputedly sold by crooked Yankee peddlers. "We of the south are mistaken in the character of the people [New England Yankees], when we think of them only as peddlers in horn flints and bark nutmeg." (*Southern Literary Messenger*, III, 1837)

barm (1) A word used for *yeast* and *sourdough*, especially in Maine. *Barmbread* is made from it. *Barm* is an Old English word long preserved in New England. (2) A load, usually heard in coastal areas in expressions such as "They got a barm of fish"; origin unknown.

barmy A Maine word for *silly, foolish* that probably derives from *balmy*.

barney (1) Soured milk; also *barney clapper*. (2) A term used by Harvard students in the early 19th century for a poor recitation in class.

Barnstable Pronounced BARN-stuh-bul by locals; a town in Cape Cod, Massachusetts.

barnyard golf Horseshoes (the game), in the speech of old-timers.

Barre Properly pronounced BAA-ree; towns in Vermont and Massachusetts.

barred rock See quote. "[Connecticut poultrymen] crossed an American chicken, the Dominique, with a bright-eyed import from Asia, the Black Cochin. The new breed has become one of the most useful of all modern chickens, the familiar Barred Plymouth Rock." (*Science Illustrated*,

July 1947) Light and dark gray bars constitute the bird's distinctive plumage.

barrel Often pronounced *bar'l*. "He's a cracker bar'l philosopher."

Bartlett pear The yellow *Bartlett* grown commercially mostly in Oregon and Washington, where it is less susceptible to blight than in the East, represents 70% of the country's 713,000 ton pear crop and is certainly America's most commonly grown pear. It is a soft European-type fruit, in season from July to November, as opposed to earlier hard Asian varieties like the Seckel. The Bartlett was not, in fact, developed by Enoch Bartlett (1779–1860), a merchant in Dorchester, Massachusetts, as is generally believed. Bartlett only promoted the fruit after Captain Thomas Brewer imported the trees from England and grew them on his Roxbury farm. An enterprising Yankee, Bartlett eventually purchased Brewer's farm and distributed the pears under his own name in the early 1800s. They had been long known in Europe as Williams or William Bon Chretien pears.

Bartlett's For many years John Bartlett owned the University Book Store in Cambridge, Massachusetts, where Harvard teachers and students came for assistance in tracking down the source of a quotation. Bartlett's erudition soon made the saying "Ask John Bartlett" a customary one when anyone sought the origins of a phrase, a faith that was justified when *Bartlett's Familiar Quotations*, or *Bart-*

lett's, appeared in 1855. John Bartlett died in 1905 at age 85, and his book remains a standard reference today, unequaled by any similar English work except *The Oxford Dictionary of Quotations.*

barvel A leather or oilcloth fisherman's apron.

Bashaba A historical title once used for the chief of the Maine Abnaki Indians.

basket A leaky ship, the word used figuratively to mean "someone who can't keep a secret": "That old basket told everybody about it."

basket fish The brittle starfish (*Astronphyton agassizii*), which resembles a basket when the tentacles are not extended. Also called a *sandstar.*

bass-ackwards A euphemism for ass-backwards, head over heels. "He fell over bass-ackwards." Also *barse-ackward* in Maine.

basswood pumpkin seeds A humorous name for wooden pumpkin seeds carved from basswood and sold as real pumpkin seeds. Such seeds were said to be sold by YANKEE PEDDLERS.

Basting big An expression used mostly in Maine for *something very large of its kind.* "That's a bastin' big lobster." *Baster,* from which this expression derives, also means something very large, and was probably first a euphemism for bastard, as in

expressions such as "He's a big baster, ain't he?"

bate A pronunciation of *bet.* " 'I'll bate ye a quarter.' " (Oliver Wendell Holmes, *Elsie Venner,* 1861)

bathe Swim. "They went bathing."

baufat A probably obsolete term for a corner cupboard or a dresser that is a corruption of the French *buffet.*

bay A large, tall barn compartment for storing hay.

bayberry wax Wax made from berries of the common bayberry bush, which were sometimes called "light on a bush." "The vexed question of light was settled by buying a quantity of bayberry wax for candles . . ." (Louisa May Alcott, "Transcendental Wild Oats," 1876)

Bay Colony A 17th-century name for the colony of Massachusetts Bay.

bayman (1) An old name for a Yankee fishing vessel. (2) A name used in eastern Long Island, New York and Connecticut for fishermen who make their living from the local waters.

Bay Province, the Massachusetts. "The following story . . . awakened some degree of interest . . . in a principal seaport of the Bay Province." (Nathaniel Hawthorne, "The Wives of the Dead," 1832)

bay scallop The aristocrat of scallops, especially the unsurpassed Peconic Bay scallop of Long Island, New York, across Long Island Sound from New England. Bay scallops are found from the estuaries of Long Island Sound, up to the coast of Cape Cod, Nantucket and Martha's Vineyard.

Bay Psalm Book The popular name of the hymnal of the Massachusetts Bay Colony; published in 1640 and the first major work printed in the American colonies. Its proper name is *The Whole Booke of Psalmes Faithfully Translated into English Metre*.

bay shrimp A small, difficult-to-peel but delicious shrimp found off the Maine coast. Also called *Red shrimp*.

bay side See BACK SIDE.

Bay State Massachusetts, so called because its original name was the Massachusetts Bay Colony.

Bay State dialect See quote. " 'Tis but my Bay-State dialect—our fathers spoke the same!" (James Russell Lowell, "Look on Who Will," 1848)

Bay Stater A Massachusetts resident.

be (1) Sometimes used in place of "are." "How be you today?" (2) An old-fashioned way to say *is*. "Be there any other way to do it?"

beach out To wash ashore. "The boat beached out near the rocks there."

beach plum (1) A shrub (*Prunus maritime*) growing near the shore in New England and other areas; its fruit is used in making preserves. (2) An old name for the bunchberry (*Cornus canadensis*), a low-growing plant with scarlet berries.

Beacon Hill An area in Boston so named because a signal was placed there in 1635 to warn against Indian attacks, or because a beacon there guided ships into Boston Harbor at night. It is now the site of Beacon Street above the Boston Common. ". . . she had private pangs at committing herself to give the cold shoulder to Beacon Street for ever . . ." (Henry James, *The Bostonians*, 1886)

be all day with one Be in a hopeless situation. "It's all day with him now; and I must say it kinder sarves him right." (Thomas Haliburton, *The Clockmaker*, 1840)

Bean Eater A humorous nickname for a Bostonian since at least the late 19th century. "The second baseman of the Boston Beaneaters . . . never was noted for his long ball hitting." (*Chicago Tribune*, September 1, 1948)

bean hole A hole dug in the ground to hold a lidded pot filled with beans; the pot is set on top of hardwood coals and the hole is sealed with dirt until the beans cook, which can take as long as 24 hours.

bean swagger A New England dish made of stewed dried beans cooked with salt pork pieces.

Bean sweater, boots, etc. Clothing sold by the noted L.L. BEAN store in Maine. "He shrugged comfortably in his new Bean sweater; it was just the thing for this chill Sunday morning in October." (E.S. Goldman, "Way to the Dump," 1987)

Bean Town A nickname for *Boston*.

beat Superior, best. "What a fine party. I never saw the beat of it."

beat all nature To be extraordinary, almost unbelievable. "I hed to cross bayous an' criks, (wal, it did beat all natur',) / Upon a kin' o' corderoy, fust log, then alligator . . ." (James Russell Lowell, *The Biglow Papers*, 1867)

beat 'em all hollow Beat them decisively. ". . . she saw that he had given her two twenty-dollar bills. 'If it ain't enough there's more where that come from—I want you to beat 'em all hollow,' he repeated." (Edith Wharton, *Summer*, 1917)

beatenest Most unusual. "That's the beatenest thing as ever I seen."

beat out Tired. " 'I'm pretty nigh beat out a'ready,' said she, 'before any of the folks has come.' " (Oliver Wendell Holmes, *Elsie Venner*, 1861)

beat out all creation! An old exclamation meaning this surpasses everything. "If this don't beat out all creation!"

beau An old term meaning to escort or to date someone. "I'm going to beau her to the dance."

bee-ad A pronunciation commonly heard in Boston for *bad*.

beech seal A beech rod used in floggings in Vermont during the troubles of ca. 1775 over conflicting land grants. "The Vermonters . . . caught one of the [New York] officers, tied him to a tree, and laid upon him, what they called a 'beech-seal', which grows in the woods in the shape of what the boys call switches." (*Congressional Globe*, 1856)

bee-eh A pronunciation commonly heard in Boston for *beer*. "I cahn't believe they call this bee-eh."

beef To kill an animal for beef. "Well, I shant call it no disgrace / To beef that critter on the place." (Daniel Cady, *Rhymes of Vermont Rural Life*, 1919)

beef animal A cow raised for its meat. Also *beef cow, beef creature, beef ox*.

beef creature A mature bull or cow raised for beef.

beef critter A cow or bull.

beeline Any straight or direct path, like a bee's course to its hive, an expression that apparently originated in New England in the early 19th century. "He made a beeline for the food."

been known to Often used as a strong affirmative. "How about having a drink?" "I've been known to."

bee's honey A redundancy heard in Maine for *honey.*

begin with b! A venerable nautical saying regarding the naming of ships. Because ships whose names began with A had a history of misfortune, *Begin with B!* became almost a rule among sailors and shipowners when naming their vessels.

begrutch A pronunciation of *begrudge.* "If she'd ha' known that folks would begrutch craving a blessin' over sech a heap o' provisions, she'd rather ha' staid t'home." (Oliver Wendell Holmes, *Elsie Venner,* 1861) Also *begretch.*

being as Now that. "Being as I'm here, let's start."

being done for Having something done for one, having hospitality shown on. "Some don't think o' these things, but mother was very set about not being done fer when she couldn't make no return." (Sarah Orne Jewett, "The Guests of Mrs. Timms," 1895)

belay A nautical term used ashore in coastal towns to mean "stop," "wait," "stop talking." "Belay your jaw, I've got a headache."

bellows New England slang for the lungs, cited in James Russell Lowell's *The Biglow Papers* (1866). The plural of *bellows* was often *bellowses.*

belly-bump One of several New England terms meaning falling down on a sled for a ride over the snow. Also *belly-bunt, belly-bunk.*

belly bumping Running with a sled in the snow and falling down onto it to take a ride, usually down a hill.

belt of wampum A belt up to five inches wide used by New England Indians for ornamental and religious purposes. "These belts are made of shells found on the coasts of New England and Virginia, which are sawed out into beads of an oblong form, about a quarter inch long, and round like other beads. Being strung on leather strings, and several of them sewed neatly together with fine sinewy threads, they then compose what is termed a Belt of Wampum." (Jonathan Carver, *Travels Through the Interior Parts of North America,* 1778)

ben A common pronunciation of *been* heard in Maine and other places. "He's ben up to no good."

bendy bow ice Ice that is thin and flexible, barely bearing the weight of a person.

Berlin Properly pronounced not like the German city, but BURR-lin; towns in Connecticut and New Hampshire.

bespoke An old-fashioned term for *engaged to be married.* "She's bespoke to him."

best feller A term common a century ago in New England meaning a girl's favorite suitor. "He was her best feller and she secretly wished he'd propose.''

best parlor The living room in which guests are entertained. "In the 'best parlour,' with its black horsehair and mahogany weakly illuminated by a gurgling Carcel lamp, I listened every evening to another and more delicately shaded version of the Starkfield chronicle." (Edith Wharton, *Ethan Frome,* 1911)

be taken aback To be caught off guard, as in sailing when the wind is caught on the wrong side of the sails. Cited in William F. Macy, *The Nantucket Scrapbook* (1916).

be they Are they. "James Russell Lowell listened enchanted to the talk of two farm-boys watching a pair [of seals in Boston harbor]. 'Wal, neaow,' asked one, 'be them kind o' critters common up this way, do ye suppose? Be they—or be they?' and the other replied, 'Wal, dunno's they be and dunno ez they be.' '' (May Lamberton Becker, *Golden Tales of New England,* 1931)

better a hash at home than a roast with strangers A saying coined by New England poet-physician Oliver Wendell Holmes in a letter he wrote home while traveling far from Boston. See ANESTHESIA.

betterments A word coined in New England around 1785 meaning improvements made on undeveloped lands, including cultivation, erection of buildings, and so on.

bettermost An old-fashioned synonym for *the best.* "That's the bettermost of the two."

between grass and hay Between boyhood and manhood; an expression heard nationally that was originally a Nantucketism first recorded in 1848.

bey-h A pronunciation commonly heard in Boston for *bear.* "I cahnt bey-h it."

biddy A hen; usually in the call to chickens, "Here biddy, biddy, biddy."

big as a Dutch oven Very big. An old-fashioned simile not much heard anymore.

big as all outdoors Used to describe anything very big of its kind, from a house to a fat or imposing person.

big frog in a little puddle Someone important in a small place where he or she has little competition. Used by Daniel Webster in Stephen Vincent Benét's "The Devil and Daniel Webster" (1937).

big iron dollar A 19th-century term for the five-dollar bill customarily presented to a fisherman who had no share of the catch coming to him.

bigness The size of someone or something whether small or large. "He was about your bigness—a little feller."

big stick The ladder on a fire truck, such ladders in use since the late 19th century.

bile A common pronunciation of "boil." "She biled it about ten minutes."

biled cider apple sass A concoction of boiled thickened cider and apples often used as a relish. "In New England what the 'hired man' on the farm called 'biled cider apple sass' took the place of apple butter." (Alice Morse Earle, *Old Time Gardens,* 1901)

biled dinner A *boiled dinner.*

bill Short in New England for *bill of divorcement.* "He just got a bill from his wife."

billdad This little mythical woodland creature resides mostly in Maine, feeding mainly on fish; descriptions of it vary.

Billerica The name of the Massachusetts town is properly pronounced *Bill-rikker,* or *BILL-ri-kuh.*

birch Synonymous for a birchbark canoe. "The lake today was rougher than I found the ocean coming or returning, and Joe remarked that it would swamp his birch." (Henry David Thoreau, *Atlantic Monthly,* June 4, 1858)

birchen bark Birch tree bark.

bird See quote. "There are men in every college, of whom Yale has its full number, denominated in college slang as 'birds.' The 'birds' are firm believers in the old Epicurean theory

that everything in life is subservient to pleasure." (A. Jenks, *Lippincott's Magazine,* August 1887) The expression is now obsolete.

bird-foot violet A common pansy with large light blue or purple flowers.

bird of freedom The bald eagle; James Russell Lowell's character Birdofredom Sawin in *The Biglow Papers* (1846) preserves the old expression. In the same book Lowell also calls the bald eagle *the bird of our country*: "Ef the bird of our country ketch him, she'll skin him."

biscuit bread A redundant term for *biscuit*; the old pleonasm is still heard occasionally in New England.

bishop The word for a woman's bustle in late 18th-century New England.

bit Often used for *bitten.* " 'The mountain got bit away a few fractions of an inch.' " (Thorton Wilder, *Our Town,* 1938)

bitch hopper A derogatory term common in Massachusetts a century ago for a very provocative woman.

bitter as boneset Very bitter, like the plant boneset, once widely used in treating broken bones. "The preserves was bitter as boneset! I went hungry to bed, you'd better believe." (Rose Terry Cooks, "Town Mouse and Country Mouse," 1891)

bitters Any alcoholic drink; the expression is rarely used today.

black as the king of hell's riding boots Old-timers used this ornate expression to describe something as black or dark as could be.

black as zip Extremely black or dark. "It's black as zip out." Given as a common expression in George Allen England, "Rural Locutions of Maine and Northern New Hampshire," *Dialect Notes*, Vol. IV (1914).

Black Betts A historical term for any potent alcoholic liquor. "There I was loaded . . . with plenty of what some call 'Black Betts' or 'o be joyful' . . ." (L. Crawford, *History of the White Mountains*, 1845)

black cap An old-fashioned term for *black rasperries*, referring to their color and shape. Also called *thimbleberries*.

Black Daniel A nickname for Daniel Webster because of his black hair and eyes. Noted in Stephen Benét's "The Devil and Daniel Webster" (1937).

blacker'n a stack of black cats Heard in Vermont for a very dark night.

black growth See quote. "The fir has the darkest foliage, and together with the spruce, makes a very dense 'black growth.' " (Henry David Thoreau, *The Maine Woods*, 1858)

black ice A term used in New England and other areas meaning both smooth ice with a dark appearance that forms on ponds and lakes and the dangerous thin transparent layer of ice that forms on black road surfaces, making it appear as if the road is ice-free.

black jacks Old-fashioned candy sticks of many flavors originally made a century ago in Salem, Massachusetts.

black locust See quote. ". . . the golden yellow of our black locust grove [in autumn]. This tree isn't native to Cape Cod, but like so many of us who aren't, it thrives here. It was brought from the South in the 1800s, to grow in the nitrogen-poor soil, and Cape Cod would be a bleak place without it." (William Martin, *Cape Cod*, 1991)

black moose *Alcesa Americanus,* a color variety of the moose. "He had the horns of what they called "the black moose' that goes in the lowlands." (Henry David Thoreau, *The Maine Woods*, 1858)

Black Protestant A derogatory term not frequently heard anymore used by Catholics to describe Protestants.

black snap A folk name for the black huckleberry (*Gaylussacia baccata*) because its seeds snap when bitten into.

blackstrap An old term for a liquor made of rum and molasses. "It was afterwards observed . . . that instead of making SWITCHEL of the molasses, the Yankees had it converted into blackstrap." (J.M. Scott, *Blue Lights,* 1817)

blanket fever A lumberjack term for *laziness,* a liking for staying in bed under the blankets mornings. "The only thing wrong with him is blanket fever."

blare Used mostly in eastern New England for the sound made by a cow. "Listen to the cows blaring." Another New England word for this sound is *blart.*

blart See BLARE.

blind as a Burma bat Daniel Webster uses this expression meaning totally blind in Stephen Vincent Benét's "The Devil and Daniel Webster" (1937).

blinger Heard in Massachusetts for an uproarious joke, a thigh-slapper. "That's a real blinger!"

bloaters Large herring that are cured by salting, smoking and half drying them.

block (1) A large building in which space for stores and offices is rented. (2) A large building in which apartments are rented. (3) A pad or tablet of writing paper.

bloody back A contemptuous name New Englanders gave the red-coated British soldiers. "The Mob still increased, and were outrageous . . . calling out 'Come, you Rascals, you bloody Backs, you Lobster Scoun-

drels; fire if you dare.' " (*Massachusetts Gazette Extraordinary,* June 21, 1770)

bloomer car A streetcar once used in Providence, Rhode Island with a high side runningboard that forced women to hike their skirts, exposing their "bloomers," on boarding it.

blow (1) A single blossom or flower on a plant. "With us [New Englanders] a single blossom is a blow." (James Russell Lowell, *The Biglow Papers,* 1866) (2) An expression popular among Harvard students in the early 19th century for a drinking spree. "They were out on a blow." See BLOWTH.

blow-down A tree that has been uprooted and blown down by strong winds. "We've got three blow-downs on the place."

blowed An old-fashioned rural way to say "blew." "The wind blowed from the north."

blow in Someone who has recently moved into a town or area, though "recently" is subject to interpretation: "He's a blow in; just moved here ten years ago."

blowin' fit to make a rabbit cry Very cold and windy.

blowing A colorful old term meaning blossoming. "The apple trees are blowing."

blow leaf The orpine (*Sedum telephium*), so called because the leaves can be made into a small bladder that pops when blown up.

blow my shirt! An old-fashioned euphemistic exclamation. "Well, blow my shirt if it ain't Andy!"

blowth See quote.

> I thought as I see the apple trees with their spranglin', crooked, knotty branches showin' a'ready signs of the spring life, thinks I, "They'll be pink with blowth afore we know it." And then . . . I went and begun guessin' if there was any other word in any part of the world that stood for "blowth." Certain sure there couldn't be a word that described things so plain. Why, you can't only see the posies as you're sayin' it, but you can act'ually smell 'em. (Annie Trumbull Slosson, "A Local Colorist," 1912)

". . . *blowth,* which I heard again this summer after a long interval, means the blossoming in general. A farmer would say that there was a good blowth on his fruit trees." (James Russell Lowell, *The Biglow Papers,* 1866) See BLOW.

blue (1) Synonymous for a blueberry. "One day [she] came to her door with a bucket of fine ripe blues." (Edith A. Holton, *Yankees Were Like This,* 1944) (2) A term used at Yale and Dartmouth in the mid-19th century for a studious person or a grind.

blue as calm water An old-fashioned simile. "She had eyes as blue as calm water."

blue-bellied A contemptuous term Southerners used to describe a New Englander, or any Northerner, or any Northern soldier during the Civil War. ". . . the mackerel-eating, blue-bellied, psalm-singing Abolitionist . . ." (*Gold Hill Nevada News,* May 8, 1865)

blueberrying The gathering of blueberries. "The four of us went blueberrying this morning."

blue book The name for this booklet of blank pages used for college exams is first recorded in a 1893 book called *Harvard Stories.*

blue-bottles A fly with a metallic blue body of the genus *Calliphora.* "The garden was a poisonous tangle of nettles, burdocks and tall swampweeds over which big blue-bottles hummed." (Edith Wharton, *Summer,* 1917)

blue claw The blue crab (*Callinectes sapidus*); also called the *blue-clawed crab.*

blue laws *Blue laws* usually means excessive Never-on-Sunday moral laws. The expression may take its name from a nonexistent Connecticut "blue book" rumored to contain such fanatical laws. The vengeful rumor was spread by the Reverend Samuel Peters, an American Tory who returned to England after the Revolution. Peters claimed that the fictitious blue-bound book contained laws prohibiting such activities as kissing one's wife on Sunday.

Blue-law state A historical hame for Connecticut after the puritanical laws said to have been enforced there in the 17th and 18th centuries. See BLUE LAWS.

blue light *Blue light,* an early American term for a traitor, originated during the War of 1812 when pro-British Americans flashed blue lights to British ships off the coast as a signal that Commodore Stephen Decatur's two frigates would soon be sailing from their New London, Connecticut harbor. The British acted on this information and blockaded the port.

bluenose The term *bluenose* to describe a person of rigid puritanical habits was first applied to lumbermen and fishermen of northern New England and referred to the color of their noses, the blue induced by long exposure to cold weather. Only later was the word applied to the aristocratic inhabitants of Boston's Back Bay area in the sense that we know it today, possibly in alluding to their apparently "frigid" manner. *Bluenose* also is used as an opprobrious nickname for Nova Scotians, but there the word probably derives from the name of a popular Nova Scotian potato.

blue-skin Historically this now-obsolete term meant both an ardent patriot during the Revolutionary War and any person of grave deportment, especially a Presbyterian.

boat shell A designation heard in New England and nearby areas such as Long Island, New York for the slipper snail (*Crepidula fornicata*) be-cause it resembles a little rowboat with one bench. The boat shell is so named scientifically because it multiplies very rapidly.

boat steerers An old name, its origin unclear, for *clam fritters.*

bob house According to *Yankee Magazine* (January 1974), this is a little hut built on a frozen lake for fishing. The fishermen fish through holes cut through the wooden floor and through the ice. The term is mainly heard in New Hampshire.

bob-tail The New England word for *quail,* the game bird Southerners call partridge.

bodgo! Marblehead, Massachusetts sailors used to hail vessels passing in the fog or at night with the cry *Bodgo!* When the reply *Molly Waldo!* was heard from a vessel, it was known to be a Marblehead fishing schooner. The origins of both cries seem to be lost in history.

body, a Frequently means a person. "What's a body got to do to get something to eat around here."

body meeting An advertised public meeting held in Boston in the early 19th century that any citizen might attend in person.

body-pew A square church pew built to hold one person. "In one of the foremost body-pews sat John Arnold." (Mary Wilking Freeman, *The New England Nun and Other Stories,* 1891)

bogue in To pitch in, take part with. " 'I didnt get much done 'thout I bogue right in along'th my men.' " (James Russell Lowell, *The Biglow Papers,* 1866)

bog trotter A derogatory term heard mainly in New England for an Irishman, though it has a wider currency in print.

boiled dinner (1) A dinner of meat (usually corned beef) and vegetables boiled together. The term is recorded as early as 1805. (2) An old term for a heated argument.

bollicky Naked; probably derives from *ballock,* testicle. "We all went in bollicky at the old swimming hole."

boiling spring An expression used in Maine for a bubbling spring of fresh water.

bolt To split trees or timber into bolts.

bone dish A century ago, narrow curved dishes called *bone dishes* were set close to each dinner plate on a table for the disposal of bones and gristle from the meat that was served.

bones The popular name for Yale's Skull and Bones society, which is the university's oldest, founded in 1832.

bonnyclabber An old term for the sour curdled milk used in many New England recipes.

book larnin' Book learning, formal education; often used contemptuously. "He's got plenty of book larnin', but no common sense."

book-writer An old-fashioned term for *author.* "When I was a mite of a child, I was always sayin' that I'd be a book-writer when I growed up . . . just a plain author, no partic'lar sort." (Annie Trumbull Slosson, "A Local Colorist," 1912)

boots See quote. "Boston is the only city in America in which *boots* is a common equivalent for shoes . . ." (George Philip Krapp, *The English Language in America,* 1925) This is not common usage in Boston anymore.

boozefuddle Cheap liquor. Given as a common expression in George Allen England, "Rural Locutions of Maine and Northern New Hampshire," *Dialect Notes,* Vol. IV (1914).

born in the middle of the week and looking both ways for Sunday A colorful old expression describing someone extremely cross-eyed.

born with the gift of laughter and a sense that the world was mad These words became famous not because they are from Shakespeare, Milton or any of the great classical writers of antiquity, but because they were inscribed in a hoax over a door in the Hall of Graduate Studies at Yale University. The line is from contemporary novelist Rafael Sabatini's (1875–1950) rousing *Scaramouche,* beloved to generations of romantics, and the full quote, referring to the hero, is "Born with the gift of laughter and the sense that the world was mad, and that was his only patrimony." The words apparently were written on Yale's hallowed walls as the result of a hoax. At least the building's architect, John Donald Tuttle, confessed in a letter to the *New Yorker* (December 8, 1934) that collegiate Gothic repelled him. It is, he wrote, "a type of architecture that had been designed expressly . . . to enable yeomen to pour molten lead through slots on their enemies below. As a propitiatory gift to my gods . . . and to make them forget by appealing to their senses of humor, I carved the inscription over the door." Yale authorities apparently didn't enjoy the joke. After employing medievalists, classical scholars and Egyptologists to find the source of the quotation, only to learn it was from a mere adventure novelist, they planted the ivy that hides the words today.

borough A designation used in Connecticut for a municipal corporation roughly similar to an incorporated town or village.

Bosox A nickname for the Boston Red Sox baseball team. Also called the *Rouge Hose,* though not nearly so frequently. See BOSTON RED SOX.

boss This relatively recent nationwide slang for *excellent* seems to have first been used on Cape Cod in about 1850. "Those pancakes are boss."

Boston (1) The capital of Massachusetts, named for a borough in Lincolnshire, England. (2) A term once used by northwestern Indians for any white American, as opposed to the English or French. The Indians also called these people *Bostonians* and *Boston men* because so many settlers in the Northwest came on sailing vessels from the port of Boston or had connections with that great hub of commerce. (3) A name for the summer mackerel.

Boston accent Often used outside New England as a synonym for *New England accent,* perhaps because the accent is so strong in the city, although the New England accent is not the same in all parts of New England. In Boston one commonly hears such pronunciations as *gull* for *girl, shop* for *sharp, back* for *bark, hot* for *heart,* and *bee-ad* for *bad.* See the Introduction.

Boston bag An old name for a handbag with a handle on each side of the top opening.

Boston baked beans (1) Famous since at least the mid-19th century as the best of baked beans; made with navy beans flavored with molasses and slowly cooked with pork. Baked beans have been the traditional Saturday night supper in New England since early times, though recipes for them vary greatly. Leftover beans were traditionally Sunday breakfast fare. (2) See quote. "The choice of candies was extensive. There were all-day suckers, delicious sugar-coated peanuts in little pots (Boston Baked Beans) . . . Foxy Granpas, and Jackson balls. I had to look over everything before I made up my mind: the Chewy Bagdads, Half Hours, Gibraltars, Humbugs . . . Hokey Pokies . . . " (Hayden Pearson, *New England Flavor,* 1961) (4) A once-popular variety of the card game whist. (5) A modified form of the waltz.

Boston baseball A name once used in the Boston area for what is called stoop ball in other places. In the game a tennis ball is bounced (thrown) off the steps by the "batter" and the other players try to catch it to put him or her out.

Boston Bees The name given to the BOSTON BRAVES in 1936, after a contest was held to rename the team. The new name never caught on and the team became the Boston Braves again in 1941.

Boston bluefish Not really a bluefish but a pollack (*Pollachius virens*).

Boston boy See quote. "A 'Boston boy' is a melancholy picture of prematurity. It might be said that every man is born middle-aged in that and every other great city of the Union." (Thomas C. Grattan, *Civilized America,* 1859)

Boston Brahmin An aristocratic, upper-class, conservative Bostonian; named after the highest or priestly caste of the Hindus and first recorded in January 1861 by Oliver Wendell Holmes in his novel *Elsie Venner* as "the Brahmin caste of New England." Holmes found the Boston Brahmins a "harmless, inoffensive, untitled aristocracy . . . which has grown to be a caste by the repetition of the same influences generation after generation" so that it has acquired a distinct character and organization. In November 1947 the *Atlantic Monthly* noted: "The Brahmins do not think of themselves as Brahmins: the word is antique as the wooden cod hanging in the State House." Antique or not, the term is still used today. *Brahmin caste* is a synonym. (See BOSTON SCORN.)

Boston Braves A National League baseball team that was named after the New York City Tammany Hall political machine. Tammany politicians had invested in the club in 1912, and since members of the political club were called "braves," in honor of the Indian chief for whom Tammany was named, the name was applied to players on the baseball team. The Braves moved from Boston to Milwaukee in 1953 and later moved on to Atlanta. See BOSTON BEES.

Boston brown bread A steamed brown bread flavored with molasses that is often served with Boston baked beans.

Boston chips An old term for *house shingles*.

Boston coffee (1) A name common in other regions for a cup of coffee that is half coffee and half cream, perhaps because coffeeshops in Boston often serve coffee with cream already added. (2) A humorous term used in the early 19th century for whiskey.

Boston Common See BOSTON GARDEN; COMMON.

Boston cooler Currently heard in Pennsylvania for a half cantaloupe with a scoop of ice cream in it. Apparently the term isn't used in Boston for this or for a tall glass of root beer with vanilla ice cream—a Cleveland specialty.

Boston cracker A thick round cracker often served with New England clam chowder. Also called the COMMON CRACKER.

Boston cream pie A two-layer cake with a custard filling between layers and covered with chocolate icing.

Boston culture Once a widely used term denoting a culture superior to most others in the United States.

Boston dip An old, rather stiff and ungraceful form of the waltz. Also called the *Boston.*

Boston dollar A humorous historical term used in the West for a penny, so called by cowboys who regarded New Englanders as tight-fisted.

Bostonese (1) See quote. "Bostonese . . . is a method of speech or manners supposed to be specially affected by the residents of that city." (John Farmer, *Americanisms,* 1889) (2) An obsolete term for *learned talk.* (See also BOSTONITE.)

Boston fern *Nephrolepis exalta,* var. *Bostoniensis,* a very popular variety of the sword fern, which originated with a sport or mutation in a shipment of these ferns from Boston.

Boston folks are full of notions Once a common rural New England saying referring to the "newfangled" ways of Bostonians.

Boston Garden The now-closed Boston sports arena, former home of the Boston Celtics and Boston Bruins. " 'Boston Garden,' I said, 'Singular, as in the Public Garden. Hayshakers from New York and Los Angeles are always looking ignorant by saying Boston Gardens and Boston Commons, and generally disgracing themselves in front of us Beantown sophisticates." (Robert P. Parker, *Spenser's Boston,* 1994)

Bostonian See BOSTONITE.

Boston is a state of mind An old saying dating back to the 19th century.

Bostonism A typical Boston expression; also *Bostonianism.*

Bostonite A native of Boston, the term recorded as early as 1775. Also *Bostoner,* first recorded in 1671, *Bostoners* and, most commonly today, *Bostonian.*

Boston ivy An attractive climbing vine (*Parthenocissus tricuspida*) native to eastern Asia that first became popular in the United States in Boston.

Boston mackerel Another name for the Atlantic or summer mackerel (*Scomber scombus*).

Boston massacre (1) March 5, 1770, when British troops fired into a Boston crowd and killed three people, inflaming the colonists. (2) A nickname for the 1978 fall of the Boston Red Sox baseball team when they were in first place, which they had held by 14½ games.

Boston notions Small items, such as beads or pottery, used as trade articles by Yankee traders.

Boston philosophy See quote. "What is the Boston philosophy? Why, it is not to care about anything you do care about." (*Harper's Magazine*, November 1886)

Boston pine A popuar midseason strawberry variety of the 19th century.

Boston Pops A nickname for the Boston Symphony orchestra, founded in 1881 and one of America's oldest symphony orchestras.

Boston Red Sox The name of Boston's American League baseball team since 1904. The team had previously been called the *Boston Americans, Boston Somersets, Boston Puritans, Boston Plymouth Rocks* and *Boston Speed Boys.* See BOSOX.

Boston resolves Laws originating in Boston in 1767, with the intention of seeking a return to puritanical simplicity by not importing any luxuries from abroad.

Boston rocker A modified form of the Windsor wooden rocking chair with a spindle back and curved seat.

Boston scorn A look supposed to be a typical expression of what Boston Brahmins thought was their superiority. "Graven on his face was what is called the 'Boston scorn.' " (Winston Churchill, *The Crisis,* 1901) See BOSTON BRAHMIN.

Boston screwdriver A humorous disparaging term used in the Boston area for a hammer, which some workers use to drive in screws, thus saving time.

Boston strawberries A humorous slang term for Boston baked beans. " 'Give me a plate of beans,' he said to the waiter. 'One plate of Boston strawberries,' yelled that functionary." (*American Speech,* February 1945, citing a usage of the term made in 1884)

Boston strong boy A nickname of John L. Sullivan, late 19th-century bareknuckle boxing heavyweight champion. He was also called *The Boston Hercules, Boston's Pet, Boston's Pride and Joy, The Boston Miracle, Young Boston Giant, Boston's Goliath* and *Boston's Philanthropic Prizefighter,* among many more nicknames.

Boston style See quote. "To do a thing in 'Boston style' is proverbial throughout the county, as signifying a thing done with superior promptness and execution." (*Monthly Magazine,* January 1834)

Boston Tea Party The first act of violence in the disputes leading to the Revolutionary War, occurring on

December 16, 1773 when members of the Sons of Liberty, incensed by the tax on tea, boarded British ships and dumped 342 chests of tea in Boston Harbor.

Boston terrier A dog bred from the English bulldog and white English terrier.

Boston type An embossed type for the blind that a Boston doctor, S.G. Howe, invented in about 1830.

Boston Whaler A trademarked small boat noted for its seaworthiness. "Geoff leaned on the throttle of Rake Hilyard's Boston Whaler and pointed toward Eastham." (William Martin, *Cape Cod,* 1991)

botheration! An exclamation indicating impatience. "Botheration! Ain't you finished yet?"

bouchots See MOULES.

boughten An old-fashioned word meaning something store-bought as opposed to being homemade.

boughten beans A disparaging term for *canned baked beans* used instead of beans prepared and baked at home (or baked in a baker's oven).

bound Often pronounced with the *d* dropped. "When a Yankee skipper says that he is *boun' for Gloster* (not Gloucester, with the leave of the Universal Schoolmaster), he but speaks like Chaucer or an old ballad singer, though they would have pro-

nounced it *boon.*" (James Russell Lowell, *The Biglow Papers,* 1867)

bouquets A name for shrimp in parts of New England, Louisiana and Canada where there is a French influence. Also *crevettes.*

box tortoise A New England land turtle of the genus *Terrapine* that can close itself up completely in its shell.

boxwood An old name once widely used in Connecticut for the dogwood tree (*Cornus florida*).

braces Suspenders. "He's so cautious he wears braces and a belt."

Brahmin See BOSTON BRAHMIN.

Brahmin caste See BOSTON BRAHMIN.

brash (1) Coarse, unrefined. "This meal is too brash." (2) An old term, rarely used anymore, for wood that is brittle.

brass-eyed whistler A New England name for the American golden-eye duck (of the *Bucephala* genus).

Brave An often derogatory designation heard in Massachusetts for someone of Portuguese descent. " 'I haven't got time to do that, sit here entertaining a bunch of stupid Braves . . . having them yell at me in Portuguese.' " (George V. Higgins, *Imposters,* 1985)

breachy Said of a cow that often breaks out of or breaches enclosures.

breakers ahead! Watch out, your action or conduct is leading you into trouble. Originally a nautical phrase warning of the breakers or white water that usually form over submerged rocks or other dangerous objects.

break the Pope's neck An indoor children's game once played in New England, its name reflecting anti-Catholic prejudice a century and a half ago.

breedin' up a storm Said when the sky turns from clear to cloudy.

brewis A kind of pudding made of brown bread, salt, water, butter and cream, according to Imogene Wolcott's *Yankee Cookbook* (1939). Also called New England Hard-Scrabble. See HARDSCRABBLE.

breezing up Said of increasing winds. "It's really breezin' up out there."

Brewster chair A spindle chair named after William Brewster (1566–1644), elder of the Pilgrim Church.

bridesman An old-fashioned term for an usher at a wedding.

bright as a button A common New England simile.

Brimstone Corner A nickname for Park Street Church in Boston because it served as a munitions store during the War of 1812 and because fiery sermons were preached in the landmark church.

brindle In the past, *brindle* was not always used by New Englanders in the sense of its dictionary definition. It often meant any dark color, usually a cow of no known breed. *Shit brindle* meant a dark unattractive color.

Bristol This Connecticut city takes its name from its sister city in England. Bristol, England, in turn, got its name from the habit its residents had of tacking an *l* onto words ending in a vowel. This local dialectical eccentricity, which persists there today, changed the seaport's name from Bristowe to Bristol.

British soldier An old name heard in Nantucket for the star moss, a lichen whose light red color suggests a British soldier's uniform.

broke of one's rest To be deprived of one's rest. " 'I ain't goin' to be broke of my rest this way.' " (Mary Wikens Freeman, *A New England Nun and Other Stories,* 1891)

brook See CRICK.

Brook Farm A famous socialistic and literary collective that was established in Massachusetts in 1841 and failed five years later.

brook-southerntine An old name for the snapdragon (*Antirrhinum majus*).

broom clean Said of a room swept up with a broom but not mopped or scrubbed. "Within, the cluttered kitchen floor, unwashed (broom-clean I think they called it) . . ." (James Greenleaf Whittier, *Among the Hills*, 1869)

Brother Jonathan See JONNY-CAKE.

Brothertown Indians According to records of the Massachusetts Historical Society dated 1795, these were "the scanty remnant[s] of the Moheakaunuck Indians, called formerly *the seven tribes on the sea coast.* They lived in Farmington, Stonington, Mohigan, and some other towns in the state of Connecticut, and Narragansett, in the state of Rhode Island."

brown bread A dark steamed bread traditionally served with baked beans. Made from various recipes, but usually including molasses. Also called *Boston brown bread*.

brown bread brewis See HARDSCRABBLE.

brunonian Any student or alumnus of Brown University in Providence, Rhode Island. Also called *Brownies*.

brush See U.

brustle Bristle. "He got all brustled up about it."

bub A term of address. " 'Why, yes, bub,' said the old man, beaming down a kindly glance through his round glasses . . . 'it's turrible nice . . .'" (Rowland Robinson, "The Paring Bee," 1900)

bubblegum machine Used in New England and elsewhere for a police car with a flashing light on the roof.

bubbler The water cooler common in business offices.

bubble-work Insubstantial work, work that comes to nothing. ". . . I am wearing half my life away / For bubble-work that only fools pursue . . ." (Edward Arlington Robinson, "Dear Friends," *The Children of the Night*, 1897)

bucket The preferred New England term for *pail*.

buckle A cake filled with cooked fruit that often "buckles" in the middle as it cooks in a hot oven.

bucky (1) An old name for the alewife (*Alosa pseudoharengus*), which is also called the *buckboard herring*. (2) A whelk found in southern New England waters. See ALEWIFE.

buddy Maple sap dark in color and strong in flavor. Maple syrup is buddy when made from sap running at the time the maple buds begin to open.

budge Friendly with, familiar with. "She's very budge with Mary."

buffle-brain A stupid person. "He's the buffle-brain of the buffle-brained." Given as a common expression in George Allen England, "Rural Locutions of Maine and Northern New Hampshire," *Dialect Notes*, Vol. IV (1914). The word derives from the English dialect word *buffle* meaning fool.

bug Lobsterman lingo for *lobster*. "He already had eighteen 'bugs' in the box, he'd likely have thirty or more by the time he was through . . ." (Peter Benchley, *White Shark*, 1994)

bug-bite and moonshine Unbelievable nonsense. "That's bug-bite and moonshine!" Given as a common expression in George Allen England, "Rural Locutions of Maine and Northern New Hampshire," *Dialect Notes*, Vol. IV (1914).

build a better mousetrap Ralph Waldo Emerson is often credited with "If you build a better mousetrap the world will beat a path to your door," mainly because a book entitled *Borrowings* by Sarah S.B. Yule and Mary Keene, published in 1889, reported that he had said it in a speech. But many scholars believe that Emerson was too wise to believe that the world would always seek out the best, and nothing concerning a mousetrap can be found in any of Emerson's published writings.

bulkhead A term heard in eastern Massachusetts and elsewhere for an outside cellar entrance with sloping doors, one opening to the left, the other to the right. "The bulkhead double-doors were double-locked / and swollen tight and buried under snow." (Robert Frost, "The Witch of Coos," 1923) "An old woman came out and fastened the door of her bulkhead." (Henry David

Thoreau, *Cape Cod,* posthumously published 1865)

bull To labor long and hard. "The old-timers bulled from sunup to sundown."

bullheads A name New England colonists gave to the freshwater catfish, which they also called *bullhead cats.*

bull pad Once commonly heard in Massachusetts for *frog*. Also *bull-paddock, bull-paddy.*

bull's-eye A small, thick, silver watch. "With some trouble he dragged up an ancient-looking, thick, silver bull's-eye watch . . . then opened the watch and handed me the loose outside case without a word." (Oliver Wendell Holmes, *The Autocrat of the Breakfast Table,* 1858)

bully boy A historical term for the class leader at Yale; an enforcer of order and discipline, he was usually the strongest of his class and carried a thick oak stick called a bully club as an emblem of his office. "The bully club is said to have been taken from a sailor by a powerful student in 1801, and, until 1841, was handed down from class to class as an emblem of supremacy." (*Bachelor Arts Monthly,* May 1895)

bully club See BULLY BOY.

bundling A historical term for a custom that was practiced mainly in New England and other parts of the

Northeast. In the late 1700s many tracts pro and con were written about the custom of *bundling,* which was all the rage in America at the time. When *bundling,* courting couples would lie in the same bed partly or fully clothed, sometimes with a special bundling board between them. Often the bundling board was breached or hurdled and the couples groped in the dark for additional ways to keep warm, and that is where the controversy came in. In his *Classical Dictionary of the Vulgar Tongue,* Grose defined *bundling* as "A man and woman lying on the same bed with their clothes on; an expedient practiced in America on a scarcity of beds, where, on such occasions, husbands and parents frequently permitted travelers to 'bundle' with their wives and daughters." But there was more to the practice than the scarcity of beds or the lack of heat, as Washington Irving noted in his *History of New York.* Irving cited those "cunning and ingenious" Yankees who permitted young couples to bundle due to their "strict adherence to the good old pithy maxim about 'buying a pig in a poke.'" On the other hand, one old gentleman, explaining the custom to his grandson late in the last century, emphasized the practicality of *bundling* and denied any wrongdoing on the part of the participants. "What is the use of sitting up all night and burning out fire and lights, when you could just as well get under cover and keep warm?" he said. "Why, damn it, there wasn't half as many bastards then as there are now!"

bung up and bilge-free (1) An old Nantucket way to describe good health, in reference to the way casks are correctly stowed in a ship's hold. Cited in William F. Macy, *The Nantucket Scrap Basket* (1916). (2) In proper order, stowed neatly. Originally a nautical term, referring to casks of whale oil stowed neatly on whalers. " 'Bung up, and bilge free!' he cried, in an ecstasy." (Herman Melville, *White-Jacket,* 1850)

Burbank potato Plant breeder Luther Burbank (1849–1926) was born in Lancaster, Massachusetts and there developed the *Burbank potato,* his most important achievement, while just a boy experimenting with seeds in his mother's garden. At 26 he moved to Santa Rosa, California, using the $150 he made from the sale of his potato to pay for the journey. It was in Santa Rosa, his "chosen spot of all the earth," that he bred almost all the other varieties of fruit, vegetables and ornamentals for which he became famous.

burden An old term for *crop.* "We had a good burden of corn."

burn off Said of fog that lifts or clears up; a term heard on Long Island, New York and in other areas, but mainly in New England. "The fog burned off before noon."

burnt blacker than a crow Said in Maine of anything burnt so that its inedible, especially toast burnt to a crisp.

buryin' A Maine expression for *funeral.* "We had his buryin' yesterday."

burying ground A graveyard. "Poor little widow's boy, riding tonight in the mad wind, back to the village burying ground where he never dreamed of sleeping! Ah! the dreamless sleep!" (Emily Dickinson [of a widowed neighbor's son killed in the Civil War], *Letters*, ed. by Thomas H. Johnson, 1958)

bury the hachet

> Buried was the bloody hatchet;
> Buried was the dreadful
>   war-club . . .
> There was peace among the nations.

Longfellow wrote this in *Hiawatha* (1855), but the expression *bury the hatchet*, "to settle all differences, to let bygones be bygones," goes back much further. Recorded as early as 1794, it stems from an old Indian custom. Crude stone axes, or hatchets, were long the most important weapon of northeastern American Indians. Such ceremony was attached to these tomahawks that when peace was made between two tribes, it was customary to take the tomahawks of both chiefs and bury them. If hostilities broke out again, the hatchets were dug up as a declaration of war. The earliest record of this practice is found in a 1680 letter of New England author Samuel Sewall: "Meeting with the Sachem they came to an agreement and buried two axes in the ground . . . which ceremony to them is more significant and binding than all the Articles of Peace, the hatchet being a principal weapon."

bust your haslet out See HASLET.

butcher An old term for *copyeditor,* because copyeditors typically cut short reporters' stories. "These are the manuscript poems we receive, and the one sitting at the table is commonly spoken of among us as The Butcher." (Oliver Wendell Holmes, *The Guardian Angel,* 1867)

butcher cart The horse-drawn wagon butchers used in selling meat door to door. See BAKER'S CART.

butter and sugar corn Yellow and white kerneled ears of corn; sometimes called *bicolor corn* in southern New England and Long Island, New York. The scientific name is *Zea mays* var. *rugosa.*

butternut *Juglans cinera,* a common New England tree sometimes tapped for syrup and whose fruits were used by pioneers to make a yellow dye.

buttery An old word for *pantry* not often heard anymore.

butt fiend A compulsive cigarette smoker.

butt floss Slang heard in New England for a skimpy bikini bathing suit, or string. "She was wearing one of those bikini bathing suits . . . what did they call them. Butt floss . . ." (Peter Benchley, *White Shark,* 1994)

buttonball A name for the sycamore tree (*Platanus occidentalis*), which has fruits resembling ball-like buttons. Also called the *button tree* and *buttonwood*.

button box A box in which odd buttons are kept. "Hand me my button box—it must be there." (Robert Frost, "The Witch of Coos," 1923)

button up for the winter To get ready for winter, making sure storm doors and windows are in place, that the woodpile is full, and so on.

buttonwood See BUTTONBALL.

buy your luck An old nautical expression describing the practice of throwing a lucky charm or coin overboard before departing on a voyage to bring good luck.

by fire! A common exclamation in days past.

by Godfrey A euphemism for *by God* heard mainly in New England.

by guess and by God At random, without planning. "I did it by guess and by God." Also *by guess and by gosh; by guess and by gorry;* and *by guess and by golly.*

by the great horn spoon An early euphemism for *By God!* "Sez Mister Foote, / I should like to shoot / The hull gang, by the gret horn spoon!' sez he." (James Russell Lowell, *The Biglow Papers,* 1848)

by the livin' law! Cited as a common exclamation by George Allen England, "Rural Locutions of Maine and Northern New Hampshire," *Dialect Notes,* Vol. IV (1914).

by the Old Lord Harry! A common exclamation heard in Maine and elsewhere.

by the prophet's nippers! A colorful nautical exclamation noted by Shebnah Rich in *Truro-Cape Cod,* 1883.

by the snakes of Babylon! An old exclamation rarely, if ever, heard anymore. Other old-fashioned New England exclamations include: By chowder! By crackie! By crimus! By dad! By fire! By gary! By ginger! By gorry! By the great deludian! By gull! By gum! By gravy! By hen! By the holy smut! By hokey! By Joe Beeswax! By King! By the livin' laws! By mighty! By scissors! By smutt! By swan! and By zounds!

C

cabbage night A name in times past for the night before Halloween when young pranksters (usually in rural areas) dumped cabbage roots, rotten cabbages, and other field refuse on people's porches.

cabinet A term heard in Massachusetts and Rhode Island for what is commonly called a milkshake in other areas; it was possibly so named because the drugstore that first concocted it in Fall River, Massachusetts kept the ice cream in a cabinet attached to the soda fountain. But perhaps the name has something to do with the earlier CABINET PUDDING, which is also a sweet dessert.

cabinet pudding A dessert made of layered ladyfingers, macaroons and custard; the origin of its name is apparently unknown.

caboose A word once commonly used by New England sailors for the galley of a ship.

cade Used in Massachusetts and Rhode Island to describe an orphan lamb raised by bottle-feeding as a pet.

caht A common pronunciation of "caught."

Calais Pronounced CAL-is by the natives; a town in Maine.

calculate To reckon, guess, figure, expect, suppose, intend. Often used in place of *know,* as in "I calculate he's comin'." "She calculated to have one piece of work join on to another." (Sara Orne Jewett, "A Lost Lover," 1878) Frequently pronounced *cal'late.*

calibogus An alcoholic drink usually made with rum, spruce-beer, and molasses, though the term is sometimes applied to any drink. The word is of unknown origin.

called aft Died. Originally a nautical term referring to a seaman being called to the captain's quarters at the rear (aft) of the ship for "final judgment" about his conduct.

calling hours, the A funeral wake. "When are the calling hours?"

call it up Recall, recollect. " 'You see, I can look back and call it up in his mother's day, before their troubles." (Edith Wharton, *Ethan Frome,* 1911)

calm as a clock Said of someone very calm, unexcited no matter what the situation, going like a clock at the same pace.

cambric tea A tealess children's drink served at play tea parties made of cream and sugar added to hot water. Also called *Cambridge tea*.

Cambridge A city across the Charles River from Boston in which Harvard University, Radcliffe College and the Massachusetts Institute of Technology are located. " 'Cambridge is not,' Rachel Wallace said, 'technically part of Boston . . .' 'That's right,' I said. 'There are those who say that, technically, Cambridge is not part of this world.' " (Robert P. Parker, *Spenser's Boston*, 1994)

Cambridge flag A popular name for the first flag of the American Continental Army at the start of the Revolutionary War. Its official name was the Grand Union flag (because it had been patterned on the British Grand Union flag with its red and white stripes and crosses) but was popularly called the *Cambridge flag* because it was first flown near Boston and Cambridge, Massachusetts.

camphor chest A chest containing camphor, which protects against moths that might ruin clothes and fabric stored in it.

candleberry bush Another name for the bayberry bush, whose berries often were used to make candles in days past. Also called the *bayberry tallow, candleberry tree* and *light on a bush*.

Candlemas Day, Half Your Wood, and Half Your Hay This old farmer's saying indicated how one's supply of hay and wood should stand by Candlemas Day, February 2.

candle wood A resinous wood like pitch pine, whose splinters were burned for lighting.

canker rash An old term for *scarlet fever* accompanied by throat ulcerations.

cannikin A covered wooden bucket generally used to store flour or sugar.

can't rightly know for sure I can't be sure; I'm not positive.

can't spin a thread Is powerless to act. Given as a common expression in George Allen England, "Rural Locutions of Maine and Northern New Hampshire," *Dialect Notes*, Vol. IV (1914).

canoodle To caress, fondle, pet, "fool around," usually in secret, out of sight. "There they were canoodlin' in the parlor while Mother made the tea."

can't for the life of me Utterly unable to. "I can't for the life of me understand."

Canuck *Canuck* as a derogatory name for a French Canadian has been around since about 1865, with both Canadians and Americans using it. It derives from *Can*ada + the Algonquin Indian ending *uck*. " 'Polish town's across the tracks, and some Canuck families.' " (Thornton Wilder, *Our Town*, 1938)

Cape, the The name most New Englanders use for *Cape Cod* in Massachusetts. "It is true they had a place on the Cape and trips to Europe in the years they didn't go to Florida, but then so did everybody else, more or less." (John Updike, "The Afterlife," 1986) See CAPE CAUD.

Cape Ann turkey Same as CAPE COD TURKEY; named after Cape Ann, Massachusetts.

cape catboat A fishing and pleasure boat developed in Cape Cod and once common there.

Cape Caud Commonly heard on Cape Cod as a pronunciation of the place-name. Thoreau called Cape Cod "the bare and bended arm of Massachusetts" in his *Cape Cod* (1865). The place was named by English navigator and colonizer Captain Bartholomew Gosnold on his voyage to the New World in 1602 when "Neere this Cape . . . we tooke great store of Codfish . . . and called it Cape Cod." See also the LANGUID CAPE.

Cape Cod cat The name of a popular pleasure boat, said to have been designed by one Andrew Crosby and finished by his sons in 1850 after he had died and they consulted him about several construction problems in a seance held by his wife. The boat takes its name from an old sea captain's remark that "She comes about as quick as a cat." All this from Donald G. Trayser's *Barnstable: Three Centuries of a Cape Cod Town* (1939).

Cape Cod clam chowder A milk-based clam chowder.

Cape Cod clergyman An old humorous name for the large, flat-headed sculpin fish (of the genus *Cottus*). "They might have been permitted . . . to take some few sculpins . . . known in the rude dialect of our mariners as Cape Cod Clergymen." (James Russell Lowell, *The Biglow Papers*, 1846)

Cape Cod cottage A type of cottage common on Cape Cod. It is usually one or one-and-a-half stories high and has a gabled roof and a central chimney.

Cape Codder (1) A native or long-time resident of Cape Cod. (2) A drink of cranberry juice and vodka. " 'For a nice change of pace, grapefruit juice and vodka makes a salty dog. Cranberry? A Cape Codder.' " (George V. Higgins, *Imposters*, 1985)

Cape Cod fence A white picket fence, like those often seen on Cape Cod.

Cape Cod Girls A sea chanty once very popular on Cape Cod and in other parts of New England. It has many verses, including: Cape Cod girls they have no combs . . . / They comb their hair with codfish bones . . . and Cape Cod doctors have no pills, / They give their patients codfish gills."

Cape Cod measure See quote. "We call it four miles, more or less. That's Cape Cod measure—means most anythin' lineal measure." (John McLean, *Cape Cod Folks*, 1881)

Cape Cod turkey New Englanders have called baked codfish *Cape Cod turkey* for many years, at least since the mid-19th century, but Imogene Wolcott in the *New England Yankee Cookbook* (1939) points out that it has come to mean any cooked fish, "what kind doesn't matter unless you are literal." If one is literal, she says, it is "stuffed codfish well-larded with salt pork." In times past *Cape Cod turkey* was a large cod nailed on the wall of the barn, a piece regularly cut off for supper. People of Irish descent in the Boston area use the term to refer to the Friday night meal of fish.

Cape Flyaway A nautical expression used in the New England and Long Island, New York areas for a cloud bank that appears like a cape of land from a distance.

Cape of Eternal Peace See the LANGUID CAPE.

capful of wind A gentle, pleasant breeze for sailing.

Cap'n *Cap'n* is the title of almost anyone along the New England coast who captains anything bigger than a rowboat.

Captain's walk Another name for the WIDOW'S WALK, so named, in this case, for the retired sea captains who liked to walk these small fenced platforms on the roofs of houses and look out at the ships coming in and going out of the harbor. "When he sighted it, he would come down from his Cap'n's walk . . . and cart an empty keg over to the packet landing." (Joseph Lincoln, *Cape Cod Yesterdays,* 1935)

cardboard carton Pronounced *kahdbooud kaht'n,* which is as good a test of Yankee speech as *pahk y'r cah in Hahvud yahd* or *Hahdah than a hoah's haht.* See the Introduction.

cards beat all the players, the Fate or luck is all. It is not certain that this saying originated in New England, but Ralph Waldo Emerson was familiar with it, meditating on the words in his essay "Nominalist and Realist" (1844): "For though gamesters say that the cards beat all the players, though they were never so skillful, yet in the contest we are now considering, the players are also the game, and share the power of the cards."

Careboo The Maine pronunciation of Caribou, as in Careboo County.

careful Very conservative in spending money. " 'I would not have been able to run this house and keep my head above water, if I had not been 'careful.' There's another word for you, Mr. North.' " (Thornton Wilder, *Theophilus North,* 1973)

carrelet Used in parts of New England for the saltwater fluke (*Paralichthys dentatus*).

Carver chair A type of chair with three vertical and three horizontal spindles named for John Carver, first governor of the Plymouth Colony, who first owned one so designed.

case Used in Maine to describe a practical joker. "He's a case, ain't he?" Cited in E.K. Maxwell, "Maine Dialect," *American Speech* (November 1926).

Castine Pronounced cas-TEEN; a Maine town.

cast-iron sweat Once a common term for a highly nervous state but rarely heard anymore.

cat and bull story An old expression not much heard anymore that is euphemistic for a *cock and bull story*.

catch a crab When an oarman *catches a crab*, he of course doesn't catch one on his oar. The expression, dating back to the 19th century, means that the oarsman has slowed down the speed of the boat either by missing the water on a stroke or, more commonly, by making a poor, awkward stroke that doesn't clear the water when completed. The phrase is heard most frequently in Maine.

catch a weasel asleep To catch an aware, shrewd person off guard. "Trying to trick him is like trying to catch a weasel asleep."

catch a Yankee, to To catch a Tartar, that is, to deal with someone or something that proves unexpectedly troublesome or powerful.

catching weather Getting caught in a storm. "He said just what anybody anywheres would say, that it was goin' to be catchin' weather like the day afore, when he got soppin' wet over to the medder lot, and he cal'l-ated 'twould keep on thataway till the moon fulled." (Annie Trumbull Slosson, "A Local Colorist," 1912)

catering Not plumb, askew; from *cater-cornered*. "He built it all catering."

caterpillar An old-fashioned term meaning body hair standing on end, gooseflesh. "I was so scared it made me caterpillars."

cat-ice See quote. " 'Cat-ice' is a good old New England word and thing; it is the thin layer of brittle ice formed over puddles, from under which the water has afterward receded . . ." (Alice Morse Earle, *Old Time Gardens*, 1901)

catouse A commotion, a big fuss. "What a big catouse he made about it." See MAKE A TOUSE.

cat-road A poor narrow dirt road. "I shall never forget . . . in Dublin, New Hampshire, driving through what our delightful Yankee character and guide called 'only a cat-road.' " (Alice Morse Earle, *Old Time Gardens*, 1901)

cat's hind foot! An exclamation of contempt, disgust or disbelief for another's foolish remark or action. "Cat's hind foot! There he goes again with those opinions of his." Also *cat's foot!* Possibly a euphemism for *Christ's foot!*

catslide roof house A term used on Nantucket for a saltbox house.

cat spruce The white spruce (*Picea canadensis*), because of its strong smell.

catstick (1) A historical term for a bat used in a ball game. (2) A small piece of kindling wood. (3) Spindly sticks of cut wood or growing wood, wood of poor quality. "Don't bring me a load of catsticks next time."

cattle show An old term for a county fair, where cattle usually were exhibited and judged for prizes.

caught Froze. "We ran out of oil and the pipes caught, bust in a few places."

caught milk A phrase used in Portsmouth, New Hampshire for slightly burned milk, according to Frederic D. Allen, "Contributions to the New England Vocabulary," *Dialect Notes*, Vol. I (1890). *Caught* is used in this sense of other foods too.

cellar bang A colorful term for a sloping cellar door, which makes a loud noise when dropped closed instead of gently closed.

cellar case An outside cellar entrance with sloping doors.

cellar way Same as CELLAR CASE.

cemetery pink Pink flowers of the *Dianthus* species that were often planted near grave markers in cemeteries.

cent shop A historical term describing a small shop in which all or many cheap articles were sold for only a cent each. "Reduced now, in that very house, to be the huckstress of a cent-shop!" (Nathaniel Hawthorne, *The House of Seven Gables*, 1851)

certain See quote. ". . . Chapman and Ben Jonson use *certain*, as the Yankee always does, for certainly." (James Russell Lowell, *The Biglow Papers*, 1867) Lowell was referring, of course, to people of his time.

chair bottomer The occupation Yankee humor gives to a lazy man. Cited in E.K. Maxwell, "Maine Dialect," *American Speech* (November 1926).

chalk above, a Superior to. "They [foreigners] reckon themselves . . . a chalk above us Yankees." (Thomas Haliburton, *The Clockmaker*, 1836)

chamber A bedroom on the upper floors of a house.

chocorua plague A plague of cattle also called *cripple all,* which occurred in New Hampshire near the foot of the White Mountains, apparently due to the lack of phosphate in the area. According to Frederick Hodge in *Handbook of American Indians* (1907), Chocorua was the name of an Indian, "the legendary last survivor of a tribe . . . who, previous to 1766, inhabited the region about the town of Burton, New Hampshire. He was pursued by a white hunter to the mountain which bears his name and driven over the cliffs or shot to death. Before dying he is reported to have cursed the settlers and their cattle."

chamber mug A historical term heard mostly in New England for *chamber pot.*

Champ A fabled water creature said to reside in Vermont's Lake Champlain, the American counterpart of the Loch Ness Monster. Samuel Champlain first sighted the creature in 1609, describing it as a "barrell thick monster . . . [with a] horse-shaped head." Descriptions have varied since.

chance blow A euphemism for an illegitimate child. "Some chance-blow of a splendid worthless rake, doomed to inherit both parts of her infecting portion—vileness and beauty." (Herman Melville, *Pierre,* 1852)

chaney An ancient Cornish word for *China* commonly used in 19th-century Cape Cod, according to Shebnah Rich's *Truro-Cape Cod* (1884).

chankings A corruption of "chewings," the peels, cores and other remains of apples pared for a pie or the like, or discarded when eaten out of hand. "Put those chankings in the compost pile."

Chappy A local nickname for *Chappaquiddick,* a small island off Martha's Vineyard, Massachusetts. *Chappaquiddick* means separated island in Algonquian.

charge Amount, quantity. "He ate some charge of them."

charge all outdoors To charge an exorbitant price. "[He] fixes up your teeth and don't charge all outdoors for it." (Joseph C. Lincoln, *Cape Cod Yesterdays,* 1935)

Charlie Noble Commander, captain or ship's cook Charles Noble (ca. 1840) demanded that the cowl of the copper funnel of his galley stove always be kept brightly polished. So obsessed was he with the idea that galley funnels were dubbed *Charlie Nobles* in his honor. The Charlie Noble in question may have been a Mainer, though others have claimed the honor.

charter oak A tree that stood until 1856 near Hartford, Connecticut; said to be the hiding place of the colonial charter of New England.

chat See quote. "Nor is there any government, however despotic, that ventures to deny the least of its subjects the privilege of a sociable chat . . . For chat man must and by our immortal Bill of Rights, that guarantees to us liberty of speech, chat we Yankees will . . ." (Herman Melville, *White Jacket,* 1850)

Chatham Properly pronounced CHAT-um; towns in Massachusetts and New Hampshire.

cheap John For well over a century *cheap John* has meant inferior goods, a person who deals in them and, by extension, any cheap person. There is even a chain of stores called Cheap John's today in New England. "None of your cheap-John turnouts for me. I'm here to have a good time, and money ain't any object." (Mark Twain, *Roughing It,* 1872)

chebacco See quote. "Certain fishing-boats, used in the Newfoundland trade, were called, from Chebacco, the name of a place near Ipswich, Mass., where they were fitted out, 'chebacco-boats.' Through corruption, or by jesting alteration of the name, they were also known as 'tobacco boats.' " (*American Folklore,* April 1902) The boats were the progenitors of the popular pinky schooners.

checker bee A gathering of people who play checkers until one person emerges as the winner. "The jiff the prison guards was free / They'd start a guardroom checkerbee." (Daniel Cady, *Rhymes of Vermont Rural Life,* 1919)

cheeky as a man on the town Nervy, overbearing, conceited. Given as a common expression in George Allen England, "Rural Locutions of Maine and Northern New Hampshire," *Dialect Notes,* Vol. IV (1914).

cheese and crackers! A euphemistic Maine oath.

cherrystone The name for a small quahog clam (*Venus mercenaria*).

chestnutting The gathering of chestnuts in the fall, at a time before the great chestnut blight killed all the native American chestnut trees. "There are still many of us living who remember with delight those joyous occasions when we went 'chestnutting' in the crisp October days." (*Yankee Magazine,* September 20, 1946)

chew over Think about carefully. "James would take time, of course, to chew it over / Before he acted . . ." (Robert Frost, "The Code," 1914)

chewy bagdads See BOSTON BAKED BEANS.

chickadee The state bird of Maine; of the genus *Parus.*

chicken bird Another name for the chicken plover (*Arenaria interpres morinella*), because of the clucking sounds it makes.

chicken lobster A small lobster of about one to one and a quarter pounds in weight; the term is also heard on Long Island, New York, where it once also meant a lobster weighing under the legal size limit.

chimbley An ancient Cornish word for *chimney* said to be commonly used in 19th-century Cape Cod in Shebnah Rich's *Truro-Cape Cod,* 1884.

chimney shelf The mantel over a fireplace.

chirk Cheerful, full of good spirit. The old-fashioned term was once heard in the expression *as chirk as a chitterdiddle on a pokeweed. Chitterdiddle* is an old word for *katydid.*

chism Heard in Maine for *gravy* or *cream sauce.*

chist A common pronunciation of "chest," as in *chist of drawers,* a bureau.

chit The shoot or sprout that germinates from a seed or plant, like the sprouts on old potatoes.

chivey A name used in Maine for *whitefish* (of the genus *Coregonus*), which is called *poisson blanc* in French-speaking parts of New England.

chockablock Originally a nautical term meaning no more slack can be taken on rope, *chockablock* came to mean "completely full" ashore. *Chukfull,* which has more currency countrywide, comes from the same source.

chock full Very full. "It was chock full of gold dollars." (Mary Wilkins Freeman, *A New England Nun and Other Stories,* 1891)

chocolate root A plant (*Geum revale*) whose boiled roots are said to taste like chocolate. Also called *Indian chocolate* and *water avens.*

choice of Appreciative of. "Because he was very choice of it, they were to have only one drink apiece." (Imogene Wolcott, *The New England Yankee Cookbook,* 1939)

chopping An area of forest where the trees have been felled or are being felled. ". . . the state of Maine had paid for a 'chopping' of five acres on each of the hundred acre lots . . ." (John Wilson, *Aroostook,* 1937)

chore To work. "He chores down at the post office."

choring round Doing general chores that need to be done. "Moses White [the name used for Joseph Palmer in Louisa May Alcott's fictional recreation of her father Bronson Alcott's Fruitlands community] placidly plodded about, 'chorin' raound', as he called it, looking like an old-time patriarch, with his silver hair and flowing beard, and saving the community from many a mishap by his thrift and Yankee shrewdness." (Louisa May Alcott, "Transcendental Wild Oats," 1876) See also MEN WITH BEARDS.

chowder (1) Breton fishermen who settled the Maritime Provinces of Canada contributed the word *chowder* to the language. The soup called a *chowder* or *clam chowder* is made with milk in Maine and Massachusetts, this being the famous *New England clam chowder.* But in Rhode Island and farther south, it often is made with water and tomatoes. The two schools are not at all tolerant of each other. One Maine state legislator, in fact, introduced a bill making it *illegal* to add tomatoes to chowder within the state of Maine, the penalty being that the offender must dig a barrel of clams at high tide. (2) In New England *chowder* also can mean "wobbling" or "vibrating": "The drill chowdered back and forth." (3) An old-fashioned euphemistic exclamation equivalent of *damn!* (4) A party or social gathering where chowder is made for all. "Nearly 10,000 persons assembled [at a political meeting] in Rhode Island, for whom a clambake and chowder were prepared." (John

Bartlett, *Dictionary of Americanisms,* 1848) See also CLAM CHOWDER

chowderhead A term that has currency nationwide but is associated with New England. According to one theory, neither clam chowder nor any other chowder has anything to do with the expression *chowderhead,* used to mean "a dolt, a stupid clumsy person." *Chowderhead,* this theory holds, is a mispronunciation of *cholterhead,* which dates back to the 16th century and derived from the older term *jolthead.* Unfortunately, we're all a bunch of chowderheads when it comes to the origin of *jolthead.* On the other hand, *chowderhead,* defined as "a muddle-brain" in James Russell Lowell's *The Biglow Papers* (1867), does suggest a mixed-up mind, in pieces, like the ingredients of a chowder. "We resumed business; and while plying our spoons in the bowl [of chowder], thinks I to myself, I wonder how if this here has any effect on the head. What's that stultifying saying about chowder-headed people?" (Herman Melville, *Moby Dick,* 1851)

christened in salt water Said of old salts. ". . . but as uncle Parker used to say, they have all been christened in salt water, and know more than men ever learn in the bushes." (Nathaniel Hawthorne, "The Village Uncle," 1835)

christer (1) A wild hell-raising person. "He's a real christer." (2) Said of anything unrestrained, excessive. "What a christer of a winter we

had." Variations are *christly* and *christless.*

Christopher Columbus! A once-common exclamation. " 'Christopher Columbus! what's the matter?' " (Louisa May Alcott, *Little Women,* 1868)

chrysocracy Coined by Oliver Wendell Holmes in his novel *Elsie Venner* (1861). Holmes later wrote in a letter: "In 'Elsie Venner' I made the word *chrysocracy,* thinking it would take its place; but it didn't; *plutocracy,* meaning the same thing, was adopted instead." See also ANESTHESIA.

chum Sometimes used as a hostile form of address. "Watch your mouth, chum."

chunked Chunky, thick and short. "She was a chunked baby."

chunkwood Large, knotted pieces of firewood so big that they burn all the night in a stove and a roaring fire can be made from their coals in the morning.

church stick A staff with a foxtail or rabbit's foot attached to th end. Ushers monitoring church aisles used this stick to tickle the face of and awaken anyone who fell asleep during Sunday services.

church supper A supper held in a church kitchen to which parishioners bring various dishes. Also called a *grange supper.*

cider beggar See quote. "In olden times there was a distinct class of itinerants in New England called 'cider beggars.' " (*Knickerbocker Magazine*, no. 37, 1851)

cider frolic An old term for a party at which hard cider was drunk in great quantities.

cider toast Toast with cider poured over it.

citified Said of someone having the ways of city people. "It's all citified . . . They're all getting citified." (Thorton Wilder, *Our Town*, 1938)

City of Elms A nickname for *New Haven, Connecticut*.

City of Nations An old nickname for *Boston, Massachusetts*.

City of Spindles A nickname for *Lowell, Massachusetts*, when it was one of the world's greatest textile centers.

clabbered milk See LOPPERED MILK.

clam boil Not a clambake but often prepared on the beach, a *clam boil* consists of potatoes, carrots, onions, clams, frankfurters, sausage and corn boiled or steamed in a pot together.

clam cakes An old name for *clam fritters*.

clam chowder Soup made with clams. "Oh sweet friends! hearken to me. It was made of small juicy clams, scarcely bigger than hazel nuts, mixed with pounded ship biscuit, and salted pork cut up into little flakes; the whole enriched with butter, and plentifully seasoned with pepper and salt." (Herman Melville, *Moby Dick*, 1851) See also CHOWDER.

clam pie A pie of one or two crusts filled with a clam mixture.

clamshell hoe A hoe made of a long stick with a clamshell tied to the end that was used by Indians in early New England.

claw out A term, probably nautical in origin, used in Portsmouth, New Hampshire and elsewhere in New England meaning to make excuses or extricate oneself from a difficult situation. "He sure clawed out of that one." Cited by Frederic D. Allen in "Contributions to the New England Vocabulary," *Dialect Notes*, Vol. I (1890). *Claw off* also is used.

cleaning lady A common term in New England for a cleaning woman.

cleanser Heard in Boston and vicinity for a dry cleaner. "My clothes are in the cleansers."

clear A historical term for someone whose ancestry is regarded as "unmixed, full-blooded." Said of both Indians and settlers. "I am as clear a Yankee . . . as the Major himself." (Charles Davis, *Letters of J. Downing*, 1834)

clear thing An old expression meaning the real thing, the genuine article. "That's the clear thing, that chowder."

clearing See CORNER.

clever (1) Said of animals that are docile, managed easily. (2) An old expression meaning good-natured but not especially smart.

cleverly A term, little used now, that means in good health, well. "She is cleverly now, although she had a severe turn for a week." (Abigail Adams, *Letters,* 1784)

click A perhaps obsolete word meaning to walk in a sprightly manner. "He clicked across the green."

clim Heard in Maine for *climbed.* "The little one clim a tree and fell out of it."

cling john An old term for a kind of soft cake. "I subjoin a few phrases not in Mr. Bartlett's book [the *Dictionary of Americanisms*] which I have heard . . . *Cling-John*; a soft cake of rye." (James Russell Lowell, *The Biglow Papers, 1866)*

clip in Make a hasty call upon someone. "I'll just clip in on Mary." Cited in William F. Macy, *The Nantucket Scrap Basket* (1916).

clitchy An old term that used to be common for *clammy* or *sticky.*

close Cheap, stingy, closefisted. "Mr. Cranston laughed. 'In Rhode Island say close [instead of 'near' used in most of New England]. I'm not ashamed to say that I am fairly close in my dealings.' " (Thornton Wilder, *Theophilus North,* 1973)

closed the door A Mainism describing someone who falls in the water and goes under (not necessarily to drown). "She fell off the boat and closed the door."

close upon Nearly. "So began the worst winter on the Cape for close upon fifty years." (Henry Beston, *The Outermost House,* 1928)

clothes press An old, perhaps obsolete, term for a closet.

clove apple "Do you remember the clove-apple on grandmother's parlor whatnot long ago?" Imogene Wolcott writes in *The New England Yankee Cookbook* (1939). "Call it a 'pomander' today, but it still remains an apple solidly embedded with cloves and guaranteed to last half a century."

cloy Full, satisfied. "He was cloyed, couldn't eat another morsel." Sometimes pronounced "cly."

coasting A venerable term for riding down hills on a sled. "We used to go coasting every winter."

cobbler This may originally have been a tropical fruit drink New England sailors encountered in the West Indies, but it came to mean a fruity filling covered with pastry. Others say its name derives from its "cobbled" look when the fruit filling is topped with dollops of dough.

cock the hay To arrange hay cut in the fields in conical piles called cocks. " 'To cock the hay?—because its going to shower? / I said that more than an hour ago.' " (Robert Frost, "The Code," 1914)

cod A pronunciation commonly heard in Boston for *card*. "He's a real cod."

codfish aristocracy The term *codfish aristocracy,* for a pretentious, newly rich person, apparently comes from the Boston area. It's hard to think of any group haughtier than the Lowells and Cabots (who spoke only to God in the land of the bean and the cod), but the Boston nouveau riche who made their money from the codfishing industry in the late 18th century apparently gave a grandiose imitation of those haughty Yankees in Back Bay Boston. As Wallace Irwin's old poem goes:

> Of all the fish that swim or swish
>   In ocean's deep autocracy,
> There's none possess such haughtiness
> As the codfish aristocracy.

codfish ball A codfish cake or patty made of codfish and mashed potatoes and generally fried.

codfish chowder A chowder featuring codfish. See CHOWDER.

codfish gentility A synonym for the CODFISH ARISTOCRACY.

Codfish State A nickname for Massachusetts.

codge up Heard on the Maine coast for *botch up*. "He codged it up again."

codhead boots Knee-high leather boots once common on Cape Cod.

coffin A humorous term once used for a large shoe.

coffin canoe An unsturdy canoe. "Like a whaleboat these coffin canoes were without a keel." (Herman Melville, *Moby Dick,* 1851)

cohoes An area overgrown with pine trees; from a Native American word of the same meaning. Often used as a place-name.

cohog A northeastern New England term for a quahog (*Venus mercenaria*) clam.

cohosh A medicinal plant (*Actaea spicata*) of New England popularly named from the Algonquian *koshki* meaning it is rough.

Cold Arse One of the most uniquely named places in New England: an island near Port Clyde, Maine, said to be so called after a fisherman who was marooned there one freezing night.

cold as a clam digger's hands in January Very cold indeed.

cold as a dog and the wind northeast A colorful expression that means extremely cold and suggests a dog huddling out in the middle of nowhere while a brutal northeast wind blows.

cold as Christmas A Mainism for a very cold night.

cold as the north side of a January gravestone by starlight Quoted as a contemporary saying in James Russell Lowell's *The Biglow Papers* (1867).

cold cellar A walled-off cellar room where foods including fruits, vegetables, and meats were stored for later use. It was the refrigerator of its day.

cold enough to freeze the tail off a brass monkey Brutally cold. The origin of the expression, possibly a nautical one, is unknown. The unexpurgated version substitutes *balls* for *tail*.

cold enough to freeze the tail (etc.) off an iron dog The "iron dog" here refers to the iron ornament often seen on the lawns of the well-to-do in days past.

cold enough to freeze two dry rags together A Maine expression recorded in John Wallace, *Village Down East* (1943).

cold-water man A term once used commonly to mean "a man who didn't drink" or "a temperance worker."

college ice Once a common synonym in Massachusetts and Maine for an ice-cream sundae.

collywobbles, the An old-fashioned term for *stomachache*. "He had an attack of the collywobbles."

combat zone The name of a well-known red-light district in Boston featuring prostitutes, porno shops, topless bars, and the like. See ZONE.

combed with a hatchel See quote.

> Hatchel-combs consisted of sets of iron teeth inserted in strong boards . . . Flax was moistened and pulled between the teeth, in such a way that the short pieces were combed out and only the long, even fibers were left . . . Hatcheling brought a pithy saying into New England conversation, for many a mother, reprimanding her tousled-haired boy, reminded him that his hair "looked as if it had been combed with a hatchel!" (Ella Shannon Bowles, *Homespun Handicrafts*, 1931)

come day, go day, God send Sunday Said of a worker who doesn't do more than he or she has to do, if that; a clockwatcher or loafer; the expression is probably nautical in origin.

come it over Once common in Massachusetts for *trick, deceive*. "Don't try to come it over me."

come on the town Go into the town old-age home or the like. "And then he was ninety-one, and then ninety-two; and we were surer he would 'come on the town' before the fiscal year was over." (Dorothy Canfield, "Old Man Warner," in *Raw Material*, 1925)

come-outer See quote.

> A name originally applied to certain religious dissenters . . . Such

a group flourished in New England about 1840, including that group of non-resistance Abolitionists who advocated "coming-out" from the church and state because of the attitude of both toward the slavery question. Also applied to ultraradical reformers, particularly in political and religious matters. (*The Cyclopedia of American Government*, 1917)

come out of here, you damned old rat See IN THE NAME OF THE GREAT JEHOVAH AND THE CONTINENTAL CONGRESS.

come out the little end of the horn To end in failure, in allusion to the pointed end of the cornucopia or horn of plenty. "Can you wonder that people who keep such an unprofitable stock, come out of the small end of the horn in the long run?" (Thomas Haliburton, *The Clockmaker*, 1838)

come up amongst the missing To die, or to be lost. Given as a common expression in George Allen England, "Rural Locutions of Maine and Northern New Hampshire," *Dialect Notes*, Vol. IV (1914)

come up with To even the score with. "He cheated me, but I got come up with him."

come Yankee over To cheat, the expression inspired by Yankee peddlers of old. "He come Yankee over him."

comfort powders See quote. "These were tiny bits of folded white paper filled with medicinal powders (and often peddled door to door). Opened, each revealed a verse of Scripture of a distinctly comforting nature." (Mary Ellen Chase, *A Goodly Heritage*, 1932)

common (1) A piece of land in a central spot belonging to or used by the community as a whole. The word is first recorded in this sense in New England in 1634 in a law stating "No man shall fell or cut down any timber trees upon the Common." (2) Short for the Boston Common, a public park in Boston once used in common by all the people for grazing their cattle. " 'Common's full of elms,' he said." (John Cheever, "The President of the Argentine," 1976) (3) Can be used to describe someone unaffected, one of the guys, a nice guy. "He's a real common, doesn't put on airs."

common crackers (1) A famous light crisp cracker originally baked in Vermont and known as *Montpelier biscuits* because they were made with water from hill springs around the Vermont capital. (2) Hard round unsalted crackers often served with clam chowder; these are also called *Boston crackers*.

common pin Used mostly in New England for a straight pin.

common talk Common knowledge. "It's common talk that he's going out of business."

Commonwealth Officially, Massachusetts is not a U.S. state, but a commonwealth, as are Virginia, Pennsylvania and Kentucky. Technically, Rhode Island is not exactly a state either; its official title is the State of Rhode Island and Providence Plantations.

complications Serious medical problems.

> Ethan knew the word for one of exceptional import. Almost everybody in the neighborhood had "troubles," frankly localized and specified; but only the chosen had "complications." To have them was in itself a distinction, though it was also, in most cases, a death-warrant. People struggled on for years with "troubles," but they almost always succumbed to "complications." (Edith Wharton, *Ethan Frome,* 1911)

Concord (1) Properly pronounced *Con*-cord; cities in Massachusetts and New Hampshire. (2) A coach made in Concord, New Hampshire in the 19th century; weighing about 2,500 pounds, it could carry nine passengers inside.

Concord grape A large blue-black grape developed by Ephraim Wales Bull, who lived in Concord, Massachusetts next to Nathaniel Hawthorne's "Wayside." Bull found a wild vine of good flavor on his property and cultivated seedlings from it for six years until he developed the Concord grape, which brought him fame but little money. His grave-stone in Concord states "He sowed—others reaped."

conducts like To conduct or behave oneself like. "The preacher was glad to see she conducts like a Christian."

Connecticut See quote. "Connecticut derives its name from the river by which it is intersected, called by the natives Quonectacut. This word, according to some, signifies *the long river*; it has, however, been stated that the meaning of the word is River of Pines, in allusion to the forests of pines that formerly stood on its banks." (Maximillian Schele De Vere, *Americanisms,* 1871) Other authorities say the Connecticut River takes its name from the Mahican *quinnitukqut*, "at the long tidal river."

Connecticut Jonathan The name for a country bumpkin a century ago.

Connecticut peddler Same as YANKEE PEDDLER.

Connecticut River pork A common name for shad (*Alossa sapidissima*) when the fish were abundant in the Connecticut River.

Connecticut stone A coarse garnet-colored stone found in Connecticut.

Connecticut warbler This bird (*Oporornis agilis*) is not seen much in Connecticut and New England. It is so named because the first specimen was collected while migrating through Connecticut. It is mainly found in south-central Canada and northern Minnesota, Wisconsin and Washington.

Connecticut Yankee An old term for a very sharp and cunning person; Mark Twain used it in his *A Connecticut Yankee in King Arthur's Court* (1889), in which an ingenious Yankee mechanic, knocked out in a fight, awakens to find himself in Camelot.

conniption fit Though this term, meaning a fit of violent emotion, is national in use, it originated in New England, possibly introduced there directly from England's Essex dialect.

conquedle Another name for *bobolink*, the name imitative of the bird's cry.

consarn A euphemism for *damn*. Jabez Stone's mother frequently admonishes him for using it in Stephen Vincent Benét's "The Devil and Daniel Webster" (1937).

considerable Considerably. " 'Joe . . . got smoothed down considerable." (Sarah Orne Jewett, *"Miss Debby,"* 1883)

consult your feelings Reconsider. "[He] brought home a lovely turn of phrase from a lonely farmhouse where he had stopped for dinner . . . and where he had regretfully declined a second portion of mince. 'Consult your feelings, sir, about the meat pie,' said his host." (May Lamberton Becker, *Golden Tales of New England,* 1931)

coof Heard on Nantucket island for a Cape Codder, any off-islander or anyone not a Nantucket native. Originally it meant a lout or coward, but it has lost most of its contemptuous bite. Cited in William F. Macy, *The Nantucket Scrap Basket* (1916), the word may derive from a similar Scottish word meaning a dull spiritless person.

coon cat A long-haired cat with a ringed tail once believed to be a cross between a raccoon and a cat. The breed is actually the descendant of Angora cats that were probably brought to New England from Turkey.

coot stew Apparently a few generations ago some New Englanders enjoyed this dish. Wrote one feisty Yankee world traveler in the late 19th century: "Frederick's pressed duck at the Tour d'Argent isn't bad, but it can't hold a candle to coot stew." There is a real recipe for coot stew, but the anonymous old Maine recipe for it is more famous:

> Place the bird in a kettle of water with a red building brick free of mortar and blemishes. Parboil that coot and brick together for three hours. Pour off the water, fill the kettle, and again parboil three hours. Once more throw off the water, refill the kettle, and this time let the coot and brick simmer together overnight. In the morning throw away the coot and eat the brick.

corker Something or someone extraordinary in some way. "Crandall regarded him . . . and said, 'Ayuh, corker, ain't she?' '' (Stephen King, *Pet Sematary,* 1983)

corky Said of tough, stringy vegetables. "These turnips are so corky I can't eat them."

corn chowder A thick soup made with milk or cream and corn niblets.

corner (1) In the early 19th century, the west end of all New England villages. (2) A name for small New England villages, which are also called *notches, hollows* and *clearings.* A famous example is Grover's Corners in Thornton Wilder's *Our Town* (1938).

corn husk mattress A mattress made of corn husks that was commonly used up until the early 1900s. These mattresses rustled every time one moved and often contained corncobs to add to one's discomfort.

corn lightning A name for heat lightning heard in Maine.

corn money A historical term for corn used as currency in 17th-century New England.

cornstealers Humorous old slang for *hands.* "Give us a shake of your cornstealer."

corn weather Hot weather in July and August that is excellent for the corn crop, a time when one can almost hear the corn growing.

corpse candle A nautical term for St. Elmo's fire, which was considered an omen of bad luck among Maine sailors, though it is generally considered a good luck sign by mariners elsewhere.

cosset (1) A pet lamb brought up without a mother. (2) Any favorite or spoiled child in a family.

cottage cheese This nationwide term is widely used throughout New England except in cities. Regional terms for it include *pot cheese* in southwestern Connecticut and along the upper Housatonic to the Berkshires; *sour milk cheese* in eastern New England and Narragansett Bay to the Penobscot; and *Dutch cheese* in western Massachusetts and Vermont as well as farther east, where it competes with *sour-milk cheese.*

cotton A pronunciation commonly heard in Boston for *carton.*

couldn't hit a bull's arse with a barn shovel Said of a poor marksman, someone who couldn't hit the broad side of a barn, a barn shovel being a wide shovel.

counter A Maine lobster that is big enough to be kept under the state's legal limits law; called a *keeper* in other places.

country-fair job, a An extensive job. " 'Now I already said I'm going to do a country-fair job of talking before we're done in here . . .'' (Stephen King, *Dolores Claiborne,* 1993)

County, the See AROOSTOOK COUNTY.

courting stick A slender wooden tube about six feet long, round at one end and octagonal at the other, and fitted at either end for ear- and mouthpieces. It is said by some historians to have been used by New England courting couples to speak to each other privately while in the presence of others. Some regard the story as folklore.

cousining Visiting distant relatives. "I went cousining in California."

coverlid A coverlet. "Our rustic coverlid is nearer its French original than the diminutive *coverlet*, into which it has been ignorantly corrupted in politer speech." (James Russell Lowell, *The Biglow Papers*, 1866)

cow See quote. "It is said that one of Calvin Coolidge's remarkable achievements was the pronunciation of 'cow' in four syllables." (Charles Edward Crane, *Let Me Show You Vermont*, 1937) The U.S. president, a Vermonter, was noted more often for his laconic speech.

cow, the A humorous term for *can of condensed milk*.

cowberry A popular name for the mountain cranberry (*Vaccinium Vitis-idaea*).

cow corn Field corn.

cow dressing Cow manure.

cow puncher A term used in Maine for a veterinarian a century or so before it was used in the West for a cowboy. Said to derive from the practice of veterinarians' punching a

cow's stomach with a sharp instrument to let excess gas escape.

cowslop A humorous name for the cowslip or marsh marigold (*Caltha palustris*).

cow tight See quote. "A lady summoned a jack-of-all-trades to repair her fence. After contemplation he enquired, 'Well, marm, will you hev it hen-tight or cow-tight?' She replied: 'As we haven't any hens, I think cow-tight will do.'" (Katharine M. Abbott, *Old Paths and Legends of the New England Border*, 1907)

cow yard tar A farmer who also works at lobstering.

coydog A cross between a coyote and a dog; coyotes came east through Canada and into Maine.

cracked See HAS A SCREW LOOSE.

cracker Unlike its use in Southern speech for a poor, ignorant white person, *cracker* for many years in Maine speech meant a fine-looking, stylish lively person, as in "She's a real cracker!" The expression is old-fashioned today, if used at all.

crackling A name New Englanders give to the crisp tasty skin of turkey, chicken and other fowl, as well as crisp bits of fried pork.

Cradle of American Liberty (1) A nickname for Massachusetts, where the Revolutionary War began. (2) A nickname for Faneuil Hall in Boston.

Also *Cradle of Liberty*. See GRASSHOP-
PER.

Cradle of New England A nickname
for *Plymouth, Massachusetts,* where
the Pilgrims landed.

Cradle of the Revolution A nickname for *Boston* since at least the early
19th century.

Cranberry Capital of the World A
nickname for *Carver, Massachusetts.*

crawm Garbage, rubbish. "Clean
up that crawm over there." Also
crom, krom.

crazier than a backhouse rat Utterly
stupid, to the point of being unbal-
anced; an expression heard chiefly in
Maine.

crazier than Gideon's geese A biblical expression meaning very crazy,
disoriented.

crazy Using *crazy* as a synonym for a
crazy person didn't originate in
modern slang, as this 19th-century
quotation shows. " 'There ain't no
use bringin' that kind of crazy on the
town." (Mary Wilkins Freeman, *A
New England Nun and Other Stories,*
1891)

crazy as a loon Someone very crazy.
This old simile is heard in New England and other regions. The loon has
a laughlike cry that sounds crazy or
deranged to many people.

crazy bone A name once common
for the funny bone, technically the
medial condyle of the humerus.

cream toast Toast served covered
with a cream sauce made of milk,
flour and butter.

creatures A Maine term for *women*;
said to be a borrowing from the
Canadian French *les creatures* meaning
the same. "The creatures are out in
the parlor."

creeter Creature. "Some poor
creeter came a-beggin', and your ma
went straight to see what was needed." (Louisa May Alcott, *Little
Women,* 1868)

crevettes French-speaking New Englanders use this name for *shrimp.* See
BOUQUETS.

crick Commonly used in colonial
times for what is generally called a
brook in New England today; a pronunciation of creek.

crimmy An old term used in Marblehead, Massachusetts for chilly, or
"under the weather."

cronch To chew noisily, "crunch."
"I heard the cronching of the
snow." (Henry David Thoreau,
Walden, 1854) Also *craunch.*

croping Stingy, mean. "He's a
croping person all right."

cross as Sam Patch Very angry. "He
was cross as Sam Patch." The iden-
tity of the original Sam Patch is a
mystery.

crossing See JUNCTION.

crotchical A 19th-century synonym for *crotchety*. "He's a crotchical old cuss."

crowbait Originally an exclusively New England term for a broken-down horse or mule, this term spread to other regions as well.

crowner, the The final, crowning act. " 'Wal if that a'n't the crowner!" (Oliver Wendell Holmes, *Elsie Venner*, 1861)

cruelize To treat a person or an animal cruelly. "He cruelized his wife." (Joseph Lincoln, *Cry Whittaker's Place*, 1908)

cruller A term for *doughnut* throughout New England.

cruncher A synonym for a large male deer.

crust coffee An old-fashioned beverage made from hard crusts of brown bread and hot water, sometimes sweetened with molasses, that was used as a coffee substitute.

crusting A method of hunting once widely practiced in New England and other areas. "Crusting is the term applied to taking large game amid the deep snows of winter, when the crust of ice which forms upon the surface after a slight rain, is strong enough to support the weight of a man, but gives way at once to the hoofs of a moose or deer; while the animal, thus embarrassed, is easily caught and despatched with clubs." (*The Mirror*, October 28, 1837)

cry one's wife down To disown all the debts of one's wife in a newspaper ad, such as "As of 1/1/95 I will no longer be responsible for the debts incurred by anyone but myself . . ."

cry over spilt milk Canadian humorist Thomas C. Haliburton, whose Down East humor strongly influenced American literature, had a friend say this to his famous character Sam Slick, a shrewd Yankee peddler, in *The Clockmaker; or the Sayings and Doings of Samuel Slick of Slickville* (1836). The exact words were "What's done, Sam, can't be helped, there is no use cryin' over spilt milk." This is the first use of the expression in print, though to *cry over spilt milk* seems homely enough to be of much older origin. It expresses, of course, the folly of vain regret, meaning to grieve over something beyond saving, something you can't do anything about. Haliburton, a Canadian jurist, later returned to England and became a member of Parliament.

culch See quote:

Culch is the New England word for that clutter of partly worn-out or obsolete objects that always gathers . . . There's everything there—old bolts, old wrought-iron cut nails, bits of unrelated metal, old wool, wiping rags, coffee cans, broken hacksaw blades, a divorced work glove or two, parts of a dog team harness . . . It's a mess, but it's better to have this one big mess in the corner of the kitchen than a patina of messiness spread all over the house. (Louise Dickinson Rich, *We Took to the Woods,* 1942)

cup plate An old-fashioned plate in which a teacup was set after the tea in the cup was poured into its saucer for cooling, and then poured back into the teacup.

curfew Up until the end of the 19th century, church bells in many New England towns rang at nine at night to warn children that they must be off the streets. This curfew became less strict with time and finally vanished completely.

cusk *Brosmius brosme,* a large fish that looks like the cod and is common in New England waters.

cut along To run along; heard along the New England coast and probably originally a nautical term.

cut a pie, to To meddle in something. "You had better not cut that pie, mind to your own affairs."

cut behind To hitch a ride on a wagon or sleigh. ". . . a boy that loves to 'cut behind' anything on wheels or runners." (Oliver Wendell Holmes, *The Professor at the Breakfast Table,* 1860)

cut dingdoes An old-fashioned term meaning to put on airs, show off.

cut dirt To depart quickly, run away. "Why two-thirds of the Rebbels would cut dirt." (James Russell Lowell, *The Biglow Papers,* 1862)

cute An obsolete synonym for *acute, sharp, keen.*

cute as a shithouse rat Clever, in a devious, often criminal way. "Teddy is cute as a shithouse rat. He is an expert." (George V. Higgins, *Kennedy for the Defense,* 1980)

cut it To run off, skip out. " 'You thought I meant to cut it?' " (Edith Wharton, *Ethan Frome,* 1911)

cutter A large sled. " 'But look a here, ain't it lucky I got the old man's cutter down there waiting for us?' " (Edith Wharton, *Ethan Frome,* 1911)

cutting A clearing in the woods where logging has been done.

cuttyhunk An especially strong fishing line made of linen that is named for Cuttyhunk Island, Massachusetts, where it was developed early in the century.

cutty pipe A pipe with a short stem used for smoking.

cut your foot To step in cow flop. Used in rural Maine, though it seems to have first been recorded in the Appalachians in 1899.

cultch This word describing objects placed in the water for oyster spawn to grow on has come to be a synonym for *rubbish* in New England, especially Maine, and also can mean a worthless person. Anything *cultch* is worthless or inferior. See CULCH.

cunner A common name for saltwater perch (*Tautogalabrus adspersus*) in New England.

curious A New England term, historical now, for *something fine or interesting*. "These are curious apples."

cuss The use of "cuss" for "curse" in New England is recorded as early as 1759. ". . . man the cus o' man." (James Russell Lowell, *The Biglow Papers*, 1846)

cut one's eyeteeth To come to maturity; heard since early times in New England, though the expression is British in origin. "The expression is somewhat literal, for the implication is that by the time a person has got his permanent set of canine teeth, has reached the age of twelve or fourteen, he has passed out of babyhood and has reached years of discretion." (Charles Funk, *A Hog on Ice and Other Expressions*, 1948)

cutting cross-lots Taking a shortcut. "We cut cross-lots to get there."

cymbal See quote. "The genteel form of doughnut called in the native dialect *cymbal* . . . which graced the board . . ." (Oliver Wendell Holmes, *The Guardian Angel*, 1867) Also called *simball*.

czar This Russian title is given to any powerful person today, but the first American to be called a czar was the Maine congressman Thomas B. Reed (1839–1902), who was Speaker of the House of Representatives and so nicknamed for his strict application of parliamentary rules and great power.

D

D A historical term that was used in colonial New England as an abbreviation for *Drunkard* and required to be worn as a red badge for a year by anyone convicted of drunkenness. See A.

d The final *d* in many words often is dropped in New England, resulting in pronunciations like *san* for sand and *han* for hand. For more about the syndrome of the vanishing *d* and *t* in New England speech, see the Introduction.

dander Anger, temper. " 'Whut'll git your dander riz?' " (James Russell Lowell, *The Biglow Papers,* 1866)

dad blame it! An old-fashioned euphemistic exclamation.

daddock Once a common term for an old log rotting in the woods.

daisy ham A boned and rolled pork shoulder butt; the term is heard mainly in the Boston area.

Dalton plan An educational plan in which students work at their own speed to learn; named for Dalton (Mass.) High School, where the plan was first used in 1922.

Damnation Alley An alley in Boston so named because it was wide enough for only one oxcart, so that whenever two teamsters met going in opposite directions, the air was blue with *damns* and much stronger curses.

damn yankees See YANKEE PEDDLER.

damn-you-straight-to-hell See SUICIDE SIX.

danburite A yellow or white silicate of lime; the mineral was found first in Danbury, Connecticut.

dandle A name for a children's seesaw in the Narragansett Bay area of Rhode Island. Also *dandle board.*

dandy funk See quote. "This appears to have been a dish of class . . . made of powdered hard-tack, molasses and water and baked in the oven—evidently a sort of pudding." (William F. Macy, *The Nantucket Scrap Basket,* 1916)

dangleberry Another name for the common huckleberry (*Gaylussacia frondosa*).

daow! An authentic Maine expression meaning an emphatic *No!*

daown A common pronunciation of "down."

dark as a pocket Heard in Vermont for a very dark night. "It's dark as a pocket out."

dark as Egypt Very dark. " '. . . it's as dark as Egypt outdoors. We might go tomorrow if there's a moon.' " (Edith Wharton, *Ethan Frome*, 1911)

dark-hole An unlighted closet under the stairs or in another dark place.

darnation An old-fashioned term that can be a euphemism for *damnation*, or mean very ("I had a darnation good time").

darning needle See DEVIL'S DARNING NEEDLE.

darsn't Dare not. "Used indiscriminately, either in singular or plural." (James Russell Lowell, *The Biglow Papers*, 1866). " 'You darsn't!' he shouted out with sudden passion." (Edith Wharton, *Summer*, 1917)

darst Dared. See quote. "When he [the Yankee] says *darst*, he uses a form as old as Chaucer." (James Russell Lowell, *The Biglow Papers*, 1867)

Dartmouth College Named for British Lord Dartmouth because he financed it in large part after it was founded as a free school for Indians by the Reverend Eleazar Wheelock in 1769.

dast An old-fashioned word meaning dare; *dasn't* is sometimes used for *didn't dare*. "He dasn't come."

Daughters of Liberty A woman's society formed in Boston in 1769 to boycott British products and shopkeepers.

daur A term once used in Maine for *small village*.

day-lazy An old euphemism for *damned lazy*. ". . . that day-lazy rascal's been fixing up all the roads around time but mine." (Hayden Pearson, *New England Flavor*, 1961)

deacon To make something seem better than it is, as in arranging strawberries in a box with the biggest berries on top. ". . . the strawberries [were] not as ripe as they looked, having been skillfully 'deaconed.' " (Louisa May Alcott, *Little Women*, 1870)

deacon off To give a cue to. "An important part of the office of deacon was to deacon off, to read aloud the hymns *given out* by the minister, one line at a time, the congregation singing each line as soon as read." (James Russell Lowell, *The Biglow Papers*, 1866)

Deacon Porter's hat A tasty sweet pudding named after Andrew W. Porter, a trustee of Mount Holyoke College in South Hadley, Massachusetts, whose stovepipe hat was similar in shape to the pudding mold. Holyoke students gave the pudding its name in 1837, and it became traditional to serve it every February 28 to honor the birthday of Mary Lyon, the college's founder.

deader than a pelcher (pilchard) Indisputably dead. Variations are *deader than a mackerel* and *deader than a duck*.

dead horse See quote. "A dead horse was something you got paid for before you finished it. Say you had half a case [of shoes] put on the books as done, and you'd get your money for it. But then on the next Monday morning you'd have that empty case to do, and no pay for it. A dead horse sure looked dead on Monday morning." (John Healy, "The Lynn Shoe Worker," *Living Lore of New England*, Federal Writers' Project, 1938)

dead whale or a stove boat, a An old motto of Yankee whalemen, which meant either they would kill the whale they were pursuing or it would wreck the boat.

deafer n' a coot A venerable simile describing someone completely deaf.

deal, a A lot, a good deal. "Tonight she had on a deal of wide cotton lace." (Mary Wilkins Freeman, *A New England Nun and Other Stories*, 1891)

dear Besides being used as an exclamation of surprise ("Oh, dear me!") *dear*, pronounced *de-ah*, is an old-fashioned term of address to anyone, regardless of sex, even from one grizzled old lobsterman to another.

dear dear, bread and beer / If I were rich I wouldn't be here An old rhyme that possibly originated in Massachusetts.

dear me suz An exclamation. "Oh, dear me suz, I dunno what I am goin' to do." (Mary Wilkens Freeman, *A New England Nun and Other Stories*, 1891) *Suz* is said to be a corruption of *sire*, or the phrase may be a corruption of the French *Dieu mon suzerain*. The expression also has been recorded as *La suz; Suz; Dear suz; Suz a day;* and *Law suz*.

dear only knows, the Perhaps a euphemism for "God only knows." "The dear only knows / What will next prove a rose." (Robert Frost, "The Rose Family," 1928)

dear suz See DEAR ME SUZ.

death baby A name for a toadstool of the genus *Ithyphallus* that is fabled to foretell death.

deep cake See quote. "A deep cake is a Yankee dish not unlike a fritter." (Imogene Wolcott, *The New England Yankee Cookbook*, 1939)

deep cold Heard for *bitter cold* in Maine. " 'Hangin sheets in deep cold is a kind of torture.' " (Stephen King, *Dolores Claiborne*, 1993)

deep-dish pie An old name, now heard in other regions as well, for a fruit pie made in a deep pie pan or casserole dish.

deermeat A synonym for *venison*.

democrat A versatile wagon much used in New England in olden times. ". . . farm families drove to the village in sturdy democrats in summer and pungs in winter." (Hayden Pearson, *New England Flavor,* 1961)

derail Heard in Maine for a cheap, toxic alcoholic drink. " '. . . not Jim Beam, not Old Duke, not even derail, which is antifreeze strained through cotton battin'.' " (Stephen King, *Dolores Claiborne,* 1993)

Derne Street A street near the State House in Boston named in honor of the battle of Derne during the war with Tripoli. In this famous battle General William Eaton of Massachusetts led eight U.S. Marines and a company of Greek soldiers to victory.

Derryfield beef An old name for eels, Derryfield being the original name of Manchester, New Hampshire. Wrote an anonymous New Hampshire poet in explanation:

> From the eels they formed their
> food in chief,
> And eels were called the Derryfield
> beef;
> It was often said that their only
> care,
> And their only wish, and their only
> prayer,
> For the present world and the world
> to come,
> Was a string of eels and a jug of
> rum.

despizable A despizable person, in Maine, is someone a notch below *despicable.*

devil and Tom Walker!, the Once a common exclamation, apparently it derived from an old folktale about

the devil and a greedy New Englander named Tom Walker. The folktale may have inspired Stephen Vincent Benét's story "The Devil and Daniel Webster" (1937).

devil's apron A long kelp of the genus *Laminaria* that often washes up on New England beaches.

devil's dancing rock A name given to wide flat rocks the size of tabletops often found in New England fields. It was once believed that the devil did wild solo dances on such rocks in the light of the full moon.

devil's darning needle Thoreau and other New Englanders called the dragonfly the *devil's darning needle* and *devil's needle* because of its big eerie eyes, which are far out of proportion to its long, needlelike body. But the two colorful expressions yielded to the shorter *darning needle* over the years. Another colorful Americanism was *devil's riding horse* for the praying mantis. It was also called the *cheval du diable, devil's horse, devil's mare, devil's rear horse,* and *devil's war-horse.*

devil's footsteps See quote. ". . . a series of marks called the 'Devil's footsteps.' These were patches of sand in the pasture where no grass grew." (Oliver Wendell Holmes, *Professor at the Breakfast Table,* 1860)

devil's half acre A term used in the past for a rough section of town noted for its drunken brawls.

devil's picture book, the A colorful, little-known term for *playing cards* that was used by the Puritans, who considered it sinful to play cards or even have a deck of cards in the house. In fact, not until the mid-19th century were playing cards deemed permissible in devout New England homes. Long before this, however, 16th-century clergymen issued playing cards bearing scriptual passages. Cardinal Mazarin taught France's Sun King (Louis XIV) history, geography and other subjects by printing instructive text on "educational" playing cards.

devil to pay and no hot pitch, the See HELL TO PAY AND NO PITCH HOT.

Dewey Decimal System The famous library classification system invented by Melvil Dewey was first used in the Amherst (Mass.) College Library in 1873.

Diana An early New England grape variety developed from Catawba grape seed by Mrs. Diana Crehore of Milton, Massachusetts, in the mid-19th century.

dicker A bargaining. "He's always the best man in a dicker." The expression did not originate in New England. Deriving from *decem,* "ten," *decuria* was the Latin word for the bundle of ten animal hides that Caesar's legions made a unit of trade in Britain and elsewhere; this word eventually was corrupted to *dicker.* On the frontier in America the haggling and petty bargaining over *dickers* of pelts became the meaning of the word itself.

diddledees An unusual word Nantucketers and other New Englanders use for fallen pine needles. It may derive from the Falkland Island shrub called the *diddledee,* which was a source of kindling for whalers, the name transferred to Nantucket pine needles, which also were used as kindling. "In some sections [of New England] a big hogshead of 'diddledees', the name given to the brown evergreen [pine] needles, was always kept well filled in the woodshed [for kindling]." (Hayden Pearson, *New England Flavor,* 1961) Such pine needles have been called *pins, shats, spills, straws, tags,* and *twinkles* in other sections of the country.

didn't go to Didn't intend to. "Didn' go to, Sir." (Oliver Wendell Holmes, *Elsie Venner,* 1861)

dido A slash in the top of a pie crust to let out steam while the pie is baking.

dight A dab, a little bit. Also *a little dight.* "Give me a little dight of butter, will you?"

dingclicker Something or someone exceedingly pleasing. "That's a real dingclicker of a carriage." Given as a common expression in George Allen England, "Rural Locutions of Maine and Northern New Hampshire," *Dialect Notes,* Vol. IV (1914).

dingdie A Maine term for *dingus, doodad, thingamagig.* "You just have to tighten that dingdie near the carburetor."

dinging Used on Isleboro, off the Maine coast, for *nagging.* "Stop dinging me."

dingle cabin See quote. "A dingle cabin is two log camps set end to end. with a roofed-over open space between." (*Saturday Evening Post*, April 5, 1941)

dinglefuzzie Mainers use this term for someone whose name they can't remember, like *whatshisname* or *whatshisface*.

Dingley A high protective tariff proposed by Maine Congressman Nelson Dingley and enacted into law in 1897.

ding-toed Pigeon-toed, but often applied to anyone awkward on his or her feet.

dirty water Water difficult to sail due to many rocks, shoals and other obstructions. "We went through a stretch of dirty water."

dishwater diarrhea A joking term for an imaginary ailment one fabricates as an excuse for not doing the dishes after dinner or any other chore.

District of Maine Until 1820 the area that is now the state of Maine was a part of Massachusetts known as the *District of Maine*. "His fame went abroad through all the county round about, that is, the District of Maine—for that was long before it was a State—and even to the farthest corner of New England." (Anonymous, "Father Moody," quoted in May Lamberton Becker, *Golden Tales of New England, 1931*)

dite A bit, a few. " 'One mustn't be too hard on the newcomers / But there's a dite too many of them for comfort . . .' " (Robert Frost, "The Generations of Men," 1914)

divinity A soft homemade candy or fudge for which there are a number of New England recipes.

dock A pronunciation commonly heard in Boston for *dark*.

doctoring Giving medical treatment to. ". . . He thinks I'll be all right / With doctoring . . ." (Robert Frost, "A Servant to Servants," 1914)

dod blast ye to Hilshibub A colorful old Yankee oath that, according to Burgess Johnson in *As Much As I Dare* (1937), "seems to avoid both hell and Beelzebub [the Devil], but gains strength from each."

doesn't amount to a fiddle of sticks Used to describe someone worthless, lazy. "He doesn't amount to a fiddle of sticks."

doesn't know beans Boston, home of the "bean eaters," "home of the bean and the cod," may be behind the phrase. Walsh, in his *Handbook of Literary Curiosities* (1892), says that the American expression originated as a sly dig at Boston's pretensions to culture, a hint that Bostonians knew that Boston baked beans were good to eat, that they were made from small white "pea beans"—even if they knew nothing else. The American phrase also may be a negative rendering of the British saying "he knows how many beans make five"—that is, he is no fool, he's well informed—an expression that probably originated in the days when children learned to count by using beans. But *he doesn't know beans*, "he don't know from nothing," possibly has a much simpler origin than either of these theories. It could refer to the fact that beans are little things of no great worth, as in the expressions *doesn't amount to a hill (or row) of beans* and *not worth a hill (or row) of beans*.

do for To care for. " 'The doctor don't want I should be left without anybody to do for me,' she said in her flat whine." (Edith Wharton, *Ethan Frome*, 1911)

dogan-headed Heard on the Maine coast for *thick-headed, dense*; origin unknown.

dog barking navigator, a A humorous derogatory description of a poor navigator who hugs the shore making his or her way by landmarks rather than navigation, or one who knows where he or she is by the barks of various dogs known along the shore.

dogberry Another name for the poison ash or sumac (*Pyrus arbutifolia*).

dogfish See SUMMER COMPLAINT.

dog's age A long period of time. The phrase was first recorded in early 19th-century New England and then spread countrywide. "I haven't seen you in a dog's age."

dogwatch Originally a seafaring term meaning the two watches between 4 P.M. and 8 P.M., properly called the first and second dogwatches. On the New England coast it came to be applied to the evening hours of 4 P.M. and 8 P.M.

doin' for oneself Taking care of oneself. "[He] would soon get tired of living alone and 'doing for himself.' " (Dorothy Canfield, "Old Man Warner," in *Raw Material,* 1925)

dollar bugs A nickname for the whirligig beetle (of the family *Gyrinidae*), because an old story holds that if you catch one in your hand, you'll find a dollar in it. Called *lucky bugs* for the same reason.

dollar-fish An old name in Maine for what is called *butterfish* (*Poronotus triacanthus*) in Massachusetts and other places.

dolphin striker Another name for the *martingale* spar on a sailing ship. This spar would plunge into the water in rough weather, and old salts would tell landlubbers aboard that the "dolphin striker" often speared dolphin fish for supper.

donkey's breakfast Borrowed from seafaring usage, this old expression means a straw-filled mattress. "I slept good all night on my donkey's breakfast."

don't See quote. "The use of don't [for doesn't, as in 'He don't care'] is the most common grammatical error current in Vermont, possibly defensible as it was sanctioned by the highest classes in the 18th century." (Charles Edward Crane, *Let Me Show You Vermont*, 1937) *Don't* is commonly used this way throughout New England, especially in rural areas.

don't bust your biler (boiler) Don't be too eager, overindustrious.

don't drown the miller Don't water the whiskey.

don't have enough sense to pound sand Has no sense at all, can't even do a simple thing such as pounding sand with a hammer.

don't know as I know See quote. "Dunnow'z I know: the nearest your true Yankee ever comes to acknowledging ignorance." (James Russell Lowell, *The Biglow Papers*, 1867)

don't know enough to lap salt To have no common sense, to be thoroughly stupid. Cited as a common expression in George Allen England, "Rural Locutions of Maine and Northern New Hampshire," *Dialect Notes*, Vol. IV (1914).

don't know enough to pound sand in a rat hole Extremely stupid. Given as a common expression in George Allen England, "Rural Locutions of Maine and Northern New Hampshire," *Dialect Notes*, Vol. IV (1914).

don't know enough to pour water out of a boat Has no common sense at all.

don't know no more than a goose knows God Said of someone completely ignorant, who knows nothing at all about anything.

don't know whether he's (she's) afoot or ahorseback Is very confused or very stupid. "He's not got much up there; he don't know whether he's afoot or ahorseback."

don't like the cut of his jib The cut of the jib, or triangular headsail of a ship, indicates the ship's character to a sailor. *Jib* also means face in sailor's talk. Thus *don't like the cut of his jib*, a nautical phrase that probably came ashore in New England a century ago, translates as "I'm suspicious of him; I don't like the expression on his face."

don't look no higher than his (her) head fer my savior He or she is all the world to me, my whole life. Cited as a common expression in George Allen England, "Rural Locutions of Maine and Northern New Hampshire," *Dialect Notes*, Vol. IV (1914).

don't need it any more than a dog needs two tails Given as a Vermont expression in Charles Edward Crane's *Let Me Show You Vermont* (1937).

don't need it any more than a pig needs a wallet Has no use at all for something.

don't plant corn until the bobtail whistles An old New Hampshire planting saying, *bobtail* being the New England word for *quail*.

don't strain your pooper Don't work too hard; heard on Isleboro, off the Maine coast.

don't take any wooden nutmegs See YANKEE PEDDLER.

don't that beat all get out! An old-fashioned exclamation of surprise or amusement.

door dung A colorful old term for *manure* taken from the backyards of farm dwellings.

door rock A term, rarely used anymore, for a door stone or step of a house.

dooryard call A short visit by friends or neighbors made outside the house in the dooryard, that is, on the grounds of a house, not inside.

Dorr's rebellion An 1842 insurrection led by Thomas Dorr (1805–1854) in Rhode Island seeking to extend suffrage to more people.

doss over more often Come again, stay with us again soon, *doss* meaning a bed or to sleep. "As we left, making our way toward the car, he shouted, 'Doss over more often.!' "

doted Decayed. "That wood got doted."

do tell! Recorded as early as 1815 for *really! indeed! is that so!* " 'Dew tell, naow!' " (Oliver Wendell Holmes, *Elsie Venner,* 1861) The expression still has some currency regionally and nationally.

do they climb when he walks? A Maine expression that asks if an animal has been castrated. " 'My daughter's got a cat . . .' 'Do they climb when he walks?' 'I beg your pardon?' 'He still got his balls or has he been fixed?' "

do trading To shop. "He paid spot cash for what he bought in his semiyearly trips to the village to 'do trading,' as our [Vermont] phrase goes." (Dorothy Canfield, "Old Man Warner," in *Raw Material,* 1925)

double-barrel A four-lane highway with a dividing strip. Also called a *double-barrel road*.

double house A house with rooms off each side of a main entrance hall.

Dover An eggbeater invented in Dover, New Hampshire about 1866. "The Dover eggbeater has two revolving flat loops on different shafts, each passing alternately inside the other, gathering the egg towards the center of the bowl and whirling it in cross currents." (Edward Knight, *Knight's American Mechanical Dictionary,* 1883)

down See HOUSE.

down along See quote. "No one has ever been able to locate just where this popular destination is located in Nantucket. The North Shorer, the Upper Main Streeter, or the Chicken Hiller means when he says 'I'm jest going down along' that he is going downtown. The New-towner . . . uses it to express a port in the opposite direction . . ." (William F. Macy, *The Nantucket Scrap Basket*, 1916)

down bucket! See quote. "When two Marbleheaders meet, they say to each other, 'Down bucket!' or else they say, 'To hell I pitch it!' Why they say it, or how they began, the Marbleheaders themselves can't tell you." (Jeremiah Digges, *Cape Cod Pilot*, 1937) May have originally been a warning that a chamber pot was being emptied out a window. See DRAWN BUCKET.

down by the head A person bowed by old age; the old expression, not much heard anymore, derives from a nautical term for a ship with its bow too deep in the water.

down cellar Down into the cellar. See GO DOWN CELLAR.

down East (1) The New England region, especially northeastern New England. (2) Maine, but see quote.

> . . . Maine people are indisposed to accept without challenge the name so universally applied to them of Down Easters. We do not say *down to the North Pole*, and we do say *down South*. The higher latitude we make northwardly the farther down we get. Nevertheless, disposed as I avow myself to present the case fairly, the people of Maine uniformly say "up to the westward", when speaking of Massachusetts. Of one thing I am

persuaded—Down East is nowhere in New England." (Samuel Adams, *Nooks and Corners of the New England Coast*, 1875)

Some authorites say the term *down East* derives from early ships sailing out of Boston with the northeasterly winds toward Maine. "There are three towns lying in a line with each other as you go down East,' each of them with a *Port* in its name." (Oliver Wendell Holmes, *Elsie Venner*, 1861)

Downeaster (1) From the end of the Civil War to the early years of this century any large ship built in Maine was called a *Downeaster*. (2) A person hailing from Maine. (3) A New Englander.

downhill side of March The last part of March, when spring begins.

down on one's uppers The *upper* in this phrase, meaning to be in bad financial condition, is the upper part of a shoe. Anyone walking down on his or her uppers then would be someone very needy indeed.

down street In town, down town. "He's down street to the dentist."

down to the heel Often heard instead of *down at the heel* for *poor, seedy-looking*.

doze Wood with rot in it, usually but not always firewood. Sometimes called *dozey wood*.

dragging anchor Used to describe someone who has no control over him- or herself, who is drifting to disaster like a ship whose anchor isn't holding and is drifting toward rocks or the shore. "He's been dragging anchor for the last year or so."

dragoness plant An old name for *wild lily of the valley* (*Convellaria borealis*).

drail See quote.

> The drail is made of heavy metal, is bright and shiny and has the hook rigidly set in its after end. I mention the "rigidly" because the hook attached to a feather bait usually swings loose from a ring. Pulled—or "hauled"—through the water . . . [the drail] looks like a rapidly swimming sand eel or "shiner" and the bluefish darts to snap it. (Joseph C. Lincoln, *Cape Cod Yesterdays*, 1935)

drastic Adventuresome. "He was feeling drastic and went on the bungee jump."

draw Drag, pull. "We drawed in a load of wood."

draw lots of water A nautical term for a ship loaded down in the water with cargo; on land the expression came to mean an important person, one who carries a lot of weight. "He draws lots of water up in the capital."

drawn bucket A greeting heard in Marblehead, Massachusetts when one sees a friend. One theory has it that the words originated in the old days as a warning when chamber pots were being lowered from windows to the street. But the warning could be nautical in origin. The reply to the greeting "Drawn bucket" is usually "Up for air." See DOWN BUCKET, a variation on the term.

dreadful Often used for *dreadfully*. "Life is dreadful uncertin." (Oliver Wendell Holmes, *Elsie Venner,* 1861)

dressing An old term for *horse manure*. "He added some dressing from the milkman's horse to the compost heap."

dribs and drabs A little at a time. "He gave us the money in dribs and drabs." The expression is now national in use.

drift whale A term early New Englanders used for a dead whale that drifted near shore.

drinked Drank. "He drinked a lot of it."

drive Throw. "Did you drive a rock at them?"

driver (1) Said of someone who is always a very hard worker. "I'd hire her anytime, she's a real driver." (2) A Maine lumberman whose job consisted of guiding floating logs downstream.

drizzly-drazzly Foggy with a drizzling rain. "It's sure been drizzly-drazzly weather."

drop a stitch To have a sharp sudden pain in the back. "He stamped his foot on the ground, dropped a stitch and couldn't move."

drop of, a A drink of, considerably more than a drop. " 'We'll have the game, / Assuredly,' said Isaac; 'and I think / That I will have a drop of cider, also.' " (Edward Arlington Robinson, "Isaac and Archibald," *Captain Craig,* 1902)

dropped egg A term used only in New England for *poached egg.*

drowsy cape, the See the LANGUID CAPE.

drunkards The young leaves of the checkerberry plant or the wintergreen (*Gaultheria procumbens*), probably because they were once used in brewing beer.

druv An old-fashioned way of saying *driven.* "He's been druv around all day."

dry as a prune Very witty, usually said of someone with a dry wit.

dry bridge An overpass that doesn't cross over water.

dry goods cart A specialized New England peddler's cart in days past carrying clothes of all kinds, ranging from calicos to silks.

dry-goods store Stores that may take their name from stores run by New England shipowners, many of whom were merchants in colonial times.

Their two chief imports were rum and calico, which usually were displayed on opposite sides of the store—a wet-goods side containing the rum, and a dry-goods side containing the calico.

dry-ki Driftwood in a lake or river. "We made a fire from the dry-ki we found along the shore."

dry salvages, the A small group of rocks, with a beacon, off the coast of Cape Ann, Massachusetts. *Salvages* here rhyme with *assuages,* perhaps because "the dry salvages" is a corruption of *les trois sauvages.* "The Dry Salvages" is the title of a famous poem by T.S. Eliot.

dry skin (1) A whale without much blubber. (2) A person who died without leaving much of an inheritance.

dub around Putter, tinker. "He dubbed around with his car all day."

dubersome A word used for *doubtful* a century ago.

Dublin Once used as a name for the section of towns where people of Irish descent live.

duff (1) To work hard. "I'm beat. I've been duffing here all day." (2) A pudding made from flour, water and raisins or other fruit. (3) A staple on New England whaling ships, said to have been made with flour dampened with seawater, then mixed with lard and yeast into a sticky dough that was boiled in a bag until it could be dropped from the topgallant cross-tower without breaking.

dull To make a bad or stupid mistake. "She sure dulled when she married him." Given as a common term in George Allen England, "Rural Locutions of Maine and Northern New Hampshire," *Dialect Notes,* Vol. IV (1914).

dull as a hoe Heard in Massachusetts for *very dull.* "That party was dull as a hoe."

dumb Betty A washing machine or any other household appliance; the term is first recorded in 1766 and was used in 1820 for a washing machine.

dumb-fish An old term once used for the dunfish, a thick codfish salted, dried and kept until it became mellow, or "dumbed."

dummy A term for a *traffic circle* used in Connecticut.

dunderfunk A hash made with molasses; the word dates back to colonial times.

dunderment Astonishment, confusion. "You never see'd a fellow in such dunderment in your life." (Thomas C. Haliburton, *The Clockmaker,* 1835)

dunnow Don't know. "Well then, it's Granny speaking: 'I dunnow! / Mebbe I'm wrong to take it as I

do . . .' " (Robert Frost, "The Generations of Men," 1914)

dunstable A type of woman's straw hat made at Foxboro, Massachusetts and popular in New England during the 19th century.

dursn't Dare not. " '. . . I dursn't go nigh him.' " (Louisa May Alcott, *Little Women,* 1868)

dust as high as a cat's back An old Nantucketism for a big fight, quite a row.

dust bunnies See quote. " '. . . dust bunnies. You know what I mean: those little balls of dust that collect under beds and behind doors and in corners. Look sort of like milkweed pods, they do.' " (Stephen King, *Dolores Claiborne,* 1993). This term and *dust kittens* is now used throughout the U.S.

Dutch cap See HAYCAP.

Dutch cheese See COTTAGE CHEESE.

Dutchman's anchor Derived from an old tale of a Dutch sea captain who lost his ship because he forgot to bring along his anchor. The story gives us this term meaning anything important that has been forgotten.

dying man's dinner, a An expression used when a bite to eat instead of a meal is served when work is going on in a house; originally a nautical term.

E

eaceworm A term used in Rhode Island and Massachusetts for *earthworm*.

each tub must stand on its own bottom An old proverb stressing New England self-reliance.

eastard A pronunciation of "eastward."

eastern hemlock *Tsuga canadensis*, a common New England tree with feathery foliage and coarse wood.

eastern parts, the A term once used in Massachusetts for the area that is now Maine.

eastern white pine *Pinus strobus*, the state tree of Maine.

East India captain, an Used to describe an excellent sailor, one as good as the captains of old who sailed their ships to the East Indies and brought home valuable cargos.

easygoing as old Tilly A simile heard in New England meaning very relaxed.

eating tobacco A once-common regional name for *chewing tobacco*.

eaves spouts The channels or gutters along the edge of a roof for carrying off rainwater are most often called *eaves spouts* or *eaves troughs* in New England.

eelgrass A word commonly heard in New England, Long Island, New York and the coastal area of New York City for the marine grass *Zostera marina*, called *grass-wrack* in Europe.

eelspear A long spear with three or more barbed prongs used for spearing eels in the mud.

eel stifle A stew made of eels, onions, potatoes and salt pork. Imogene Wolcott's excellent *New England Yankee Cookbook* (1939) calls it *Martha's Vineyard eel stifle*.

eenamost An old-fashioned way to say "almost" that is rarely, if ever, heard anymore.

ef A rural pronunciation of "if." "Ef he can ketch him, he will."

egg pop An eggnog drink popular in New England in the 19th century, the term first attested in 1776.

ehyuh See AYUH.

Eighteen-hundred-and-freeze to death Clifton Johnson in his *New England* (1931) gives this as a humorous name in Maine for 1817, when an unusually cold winter was followed by a cold spring, and the weather continued to be so unseasonable that many crops failed. Other sources put the years as 1816–1817 and include the summer of 1816 as a very cold one when crops failed.

elastic A rubber band. "Put an elastic on it."

election cake Also called *Dough Cake, Hartford Election Cake, 'Lection Cake,* and *March Meeting Cake,* this delicious cake is said to have originated in Hartford, Connecticut, over 150 years ago. An old story says it was served only to those who voted the straight ticket.

election pink A pink rhododendron or azalea (*Rhododendron prinophyllum*) that blooms in June in New England, around the time of the old election day.

elegant A synonym for *excellent.* "That pie was sure elegant."

Eli A name for a Yale student or graduate since the late 19th century; after early Yale benefactor Elihu Yale (1648–1721), for whom the school is named.

Elm City See quote. "New Haven in Connecticut is known as . . . Elm City from the number and magnificent size of the elm trees that adorn its public squares." (Maximilian Schele De Vere, *Americanisms,* 1871) Since then elm disease has destroyed the trees.

Emmanuelism The use of both mental and moral healing and modern medical practices to cure nervous diseases; named after the Emmanuel Protestant Episcopal Church in Boston, where its originators introduced the healing method in 1906.

emptyin's The yeasty settlings in beer barrels.

end for about The other way around, or inside out; originally a nautical term. "You've got the front for the back, you've got it end for about."

English elementary school An obsolete term for a public school that also has been used in proper names, such as Boston's English High School.

English monkey A cheese dish poured over toast or crackers that is similar to Welsh rabbit or rarebit, a humorous play on the old name.

enjoyin' dretful poor health Cited as a humorous Vermont expression in Charles Edward Crane's *Let Me Show You New England* (1937).

enough sight A lot. "It was enough sight better than being cooped up in the shop." (Mary Wilkens Freeman, *A New England Nun and Other Stories,* 1891)

enough to gag a maggot Said of someone or something very dirty, filthy. "It's enough to gag a maggot the way he keeps that place."

entire wheat bread An old-fashioned term for *whole wheat bread.*

eperlans French-speaking New Englanders use this name for the small fish generally known as smelts.

essence peddler (1) A Yankee peddler of potent medicines. "He was not exclusively an essence peddler, having a large tin box, which had been filled with dry goods, combs, jewelry, etc. . . ." (Nathaniel Hawthorne, *American Notebooks,* 1838) (2) See quote. "Essence-peddler: a skunk." (James Russell Lowell, *The Biglow Papers,* 1867)

every hair a rope yarn Heard in New England for a rugged seaman. The complete old nautical phrase is *Begotten in the galley and born under a gun, every hair a rope yarn, every tooth a marline spike, every finger a fishhook, and all his heart's blood good Stockholm tar.*

everything's drawing An affirmative reply, nautical in origin, to the greeting "How are you?" It originally referred to a ship sailing well.

every which way All over the place. "[It] set off briskly for so slow a thing / Still going every whichway in

the joints, though." (Robert Frost, "The Witch of Coos," 1923)

ex Heard for over a century in New England for *axle.* "The car sank to its exes in the mud." Often written as *X* in the past.

exercised Upset, angered. "She was right exercised when she lost her job."

extry An old-fashioned rural pronunciation of "extra." "A dollar extry." (Edith Wharton, *Ethan Frome,* 1911)

eye of America, the An old nickname for *Boston* because of its intellectual and cultural leadership.

eyes like two burned holes in a blanket Used to describe someone very ill, his or her eyes standing out prominently in a pale drawn face.

eyestone A small piece of chalky material that is moistened and put in the eye to absorb and remove foreign matter such as cinders.

ey-uh A common pronunciation of "air" on Cape Cod.

F

faculized An old-fashioned usage meaning good at many things, versatile. "He's the most faculized person I know."

faculty See quote. ". . . the Potters had that trait which conquers the world far more surely and subtly than grit,—'faculty,' i.e., a clear head and a quick wit, and capacity of adaptations . . ." (Rose Terry Cooke, "Grit," in *Huckleberries Gathered from the New England Hills,* 1891)

failed up Failed; gone bankrupt. "He lost everything when the bank failed up."

faint at the stomach Nauseated. "I'm awful faint at my stomach." (Mary Wilkins Freeman, "Gentian," 1887)

faint away See GOOD LAND!

fair (1) Excellent, terrific, the best of its kind. "That's a fair chowder you made." (2) Quite. "She was fair foolish about it."

fall afoul of See RUN AFOUL OF.

fallen away Wasted away, usually from illness. "He's really fallen away since we last saw him."

fallen away to a cartload Thin, wasted, sickly looking. "He looks delicate to her! All fallen away to a cartload, as the Maine saying goes." (Robert Tristram Coffin, *Captain Abby and Captain John,* 1939)

fallow Said of land recently cleared of trees and brush. "He walked up in the fallow." Sometimes pronounced *follow.*

Fameuse Long a leading New England apple variety; the name is French for "famous."

fancy work Needlework, crocheting. "She does her fancy work every evening by the fire."

Faneuil Hall Pronounced FAN-ul or FAN-yul; a historic building in Boston, Massachusetts. An old rhyme instructs how to pronounce this famous landmark:

> When you speak of the market
> That's known as Faneuil,
> Kindly pronounce it
> To rhyme with Dan'l.

See GRASSHOPPER.

fannie daddies A name for fried clams on Cape Cod and in other places, according to Imogene Wolcott's *The New England Yankee Cookbook* (1939).

far piece A long distance. "It's a far piece from here to Boston."

farrow cow A cow that doesn't produce milk, or one that is unable to conceive.

farziner A humorous word used a century ago for *as far as I know*.

facinator A fancy head scarf. ". . . the lively young man . . . drew forth a girl who already wound a cherry-colored 'fascinator' about her head . . ." (Edith Wharton, *Ethan Frome*, 1911)

fast To tie, make secure. An old New England saying had it: "A woman ties a horse, a man hitches him, but a sailor makes him fast."

fast as a cat in a gale A simile heard in New England meaning very fast.

fast day (1) A day of fasting and prayer formerly widely celebrated in New England and now observed in New Hampshire on the fourth Monday in April, according to *Yankee Magazine* (February 1969). (2) Once common in New England for spring days designated for various religious observances.

faster than a cat lapping chain lightning Cited in *The Old Farmer's Almanack* (1946) as a common Yankee saying.

fat as a butterball Used to describe a plump, healthy animal. "Teeth are good and she's fat as a butterball. Good mare, Bessie . . ." (Hayden Pearson, *New England Flavor*, 1961)

fat as a doe Pleasingly plump. "I was fat as a doe but still pretty spry."

father God and Sonny Jesus! An exclamation heard in Maine. " 'And you shoulda heard him. Loud? Father God and Sonny Jesus!" (Stephen King, *Dolores Clairborne*, 1993)

father longlegs An old New England name for the insect commonly called *daddy longlegs*.

Father of His Country, the Long before being applied to George Washington, this title was given to Governor John Winthrop of the Massachusetts colony.

fatter'n a settled minister Very fat. Given as a common expression in George Allen England, "Rural Locutions of Maine and Northern New Hampshire," *Dialect Notes*, Vol. IV (1914).

fat up Fatten up. "A few months of home cooking and she'll fat up."

fay A once-common word meaning to fit in, fill in, agree. "That piece doesn't fay with the rest of the puzzle."

fearnaught A humorous term for a winter jacket made of a very heavy woolen fabric. "You have to put on your fearnaught in this kind of weather."

Feast of Shells A festival held until about 1806 to honor the founding of the Massachusetts colony. It was probably so called because the early settlers subsisted to a large extent on shellfish.

feather white (1) A sea wind-whipped and full of whitecaps. (2) A very angry person. "He made her all feather white."

feel bluer'n a whetstone, to A Vermont saying meaning to be in a very low or blue mood.

feeling stones Stones worn very smooth from the water and a small pleasure to hold in the hand.

feetings An old word for *woolen stockings*. "She was knitting feetings for them." Also *footings*.

feller Fellow. Besides its usual meaning, a *feller* has long been a young woman's sweetheart, a meaning that has spread from New England to other regions of the country. To a young woman in the past, *her feller* was the young man who was "sparkin'" her, her "stiddy company."

fell flat on his floot Fell down hard, often used figuratively. "He lost by ten points, fell flat on his floot." The origin of *floot* here is unknown.

fence viewer A New England official who inspects fences to see that they have been erected and maintained according to the law. "Non-New Englanders often regard appointments to these seemingly antiquated posts as amusing; yet fence viewers officiated only very recently in Portsmouth, New Hampshire." (*American Notes and Queries*, November 1944)

fer An old-fashioned pronunciation for "for." "Ninepence a day fer killin' folks come kind o' low fer murder." (Words of a "Private in the Massachusetts Regiment") (James Russell Lowell, *The Biglow Papers*, 1846)

fetched Gave. "He fetched the dog a kick."

fetched up (1) Brought up. "That's the way I was fetched up." (2) To end up in a certain place, or come to a sudden stop. "His ship fetched up on the rocks."

fiddlehead ferns The finest fiddlehead ferns come from Maine. The delicious greens, which taste something like a combination of asparagus, broccoli and artichokes, are so named because their delicate fronds resemble the head of a fiddle. Legend has it that when Adam and Eve were banished from the Garden of Eden, the Archangel Gabriel guarded the gate through which they left to earn their bread by the sweat of their brows in the wilderness. Stepping aside to let them pass, Gabriel brushed a wing against a boulder and a feather dropped to the ground. The feather took root and grew into the fiddlehead fern, which has ever since been sacred to the archangel.

fiddleheading Gathering fiddleheads. "We arrived in time to get fiddlehead ferns for supper . . . Someone had been 'fiddleheading' before us." (William O. Douglas, *My Wilderness,* 1961)

fiddlesticks! A once-common exclamation roughly meaning nonsense. " 'Fiddlesticks!' returned Jo, slamming the door." (Louisa May Alcott, *Little Women,* 1868)

field driver See TOWN POUND.

fierce (1) Agitated. "She was some fierce." (2) Eager, excited. "That dog was fierce to get outside." (3) "The New England *ferce* for *fierce,* and *perce* for *purse,* are also Norman [pronunciations]." (James Russell Lowell, *The Biglow Papers,* 1867)

filer's two inches Because poorly filed chainsaws were turning out bolts of wood that could run an inch or so over or under the traditional 48-inch lengths, buyers in Maine demanded 50-inch lengths so that they could be sure they got at least 48 inches of wood. These *filer's two inches* came to mean a gratuitous extra amount.

Filene's bargain basement A Boston institution in Filene's department store famous for its bargain merchandise. "She wanted to buy her shoes in Filene's Shoe Salon on the third floor instead of in the bargain base-

ment . . ." (Joyce Kornblatt, "Offerings," 1985)

Filliloo bird An imaginary bird of Maine fables that flies backward to see where it's been or to keep the wind out of its face.

fillit A word used by Maine fishermen for *filet.* "He fillited some haddock with his fillitin' knife."

fill to the north To take a last drink in a bar before leaving. Among sailors it was considered lucky if the sails were filled initially to the northward.

find the devil's golden tooth, to A saying once common in Massachusetts that refers to a story about the pirate Captain Kidd, who was fabled to have stolen the devil's eyetooth, which gave one the power of changing all metals into gold.

finest kind The very best, used to describe anything from one's health to the weather. "Have the finest kind of day." Also *the finest kind of pork,* as in "That's the finest kind of pork."

finnan haddie See quote.

> Finnan haddie [smoked haddock] is, strictly speaking, a Scotch and not a Yankee dish. It gets its title from the reputation of the haddock cured around Findon (or Findhorn), a fishing village near Aberdeen, Scotland. Once our American supply was almost entirely imported, but now the great bulk of it, and some of the very

finest, comes from New England. (Imogene Wolcott, *The New England Yankee Cookbook*, 1939)

fin out Badly injured, close to dying. The old expression is nautical in origin, first referring to a dying whale that rolls over, showing its fin. "She's near ninety and just about fin out."

fire balloon A paper fireworks device (outlawed because it caused fires) that contained kerosene and was ignited, causing hot air to fill the balloon and make it rise into the dark sky.

fire hangbird A name for the Baltimore oriole because of the male bird's orange color and the hanging nests orioles make.

fireroom Once a common term for any room in a house with a fireplace.

fire trumpet A brass trumpet or megaphone that old-time fire officers used to shout instructions to their men.

first (1) Sometimes pronounced "furst." " 'I'll see y' darned furst!' " (Oliver Wendell Holmes, *Elsie Venner*, 1861) (2) Used in the past to mean eager. "He was quite first to get there."

first along At first. "First along, I thought he'd easily win the race."

First Fathers The first or early settlers of New England; also called *Pilgrim Fathers*.

fish (1) In New England nautical language, *fish* can mean to repair or mend a spar, usually by splinting it. The word sometimes is used on shore to mean "to repair something": "Will you fish that cabinet for me today?" (2) A term of historical interest meaning to fertilize land with fish or fish parts, a practice the first European settlers in this country learned from the Indians: "He fished the corn ground."

fish ball Shredded fish and mashed potatoes rolled into little balls, dipped in egg and fried until golden brown in deep fat. "Eating fish balls for Sunday morning breakfast is part of Boston's tradition, like reading the *Transcript* or taking visitors to see the glass flowers." (Imogene Wolcott, *The New England Yankee Cookbook*, 1939)

fish, cut bait, or go ashore Do something or leave the premises. This was originally an order to Yankee fishermen working on dories on the Grand Banks who had to either be fishing with their lines or cutting bait for their hooks, otherwise the captain would set them ashore. The expression is heard often as *fish or cut bait* in Maine and elsewhere.

fish draft A curious home remedy that was said to draw (draft) fever or infection from a patient by tying a salt fish to the sole of each foot.

fisherman farmer See quote. "Said of such persons as alternate farming and fishing at different periods, especially such as customarily farm in one, and fish in another part of each year [on the] seacoast of Massachusetts." (John Bartlett, *Dictionary of Americanisms*, 1877)

Fisherman's Monument A famous monument honoring New England fishermen in Gloucester, Massachusetts.

fish hash A New England dish of dried, soaked codfish chopped up with boiled potatoes.

fish pea A term heard in Maine for *roe, caviar, fish eggs,* especially when they are massed together.

fish warden An official, often of the town, who enforces local fishing regulations.

fit Fought. "They fit and fit and he finally won."

fit like a Mediterranean pass, to A 19th-century Nantucketism no longer heard that means to fit very well. A *Mediterranean pass* was a pass issued to sailing vessels for a fee. It was severed in two pieces by the issuing government so that the two pieces fit exactly when placed together, to prevent counterfeits.

fitout An outfit of clothing. "Go-ashore jackets and trousers [were] got out and brushed; pumps, neckerchiefs, and hats overhauled . . . so that among the whole each one got a good fit-out." (Richard Henry Dana, Jr., *Two Years Before the Mast,* 1840)

fits like a shirt on a beanpole Fits very poorly, is much too large. Given as a common expression in George Allen England, "Rural Locutions of Maine and Northern New Hampshire," *Dialect Notes,* Vol. IV (1914).

fitting An old-fashioned expression meaning the moving of a household to a new home. "These mysterious fittings roused a suspicion." (Sara Orne Jewett, "The Gray Mills of Farley," 1898)

fit with a Yankee jacket, to To tar and feather someone. "He commanded some of the crew to furnish the d——d English rascal with a good *Yankee jacket,* which in plain English is a quantity of tar besmeared over the human body, upon which an abundance of feathers is immediately strewn." (Seine Painter, *The Emigrants Guide, or a Picture of America,* 1816)

five-fingers A starfish with five arms. "She [found] several five-fingers." (Nathaniel Hawthorne, *The Scarlet Letter,* 1852)

fizzy Another name for the American scoter (*Melanitta nigra*), a diving duck found in New England.

flacket An expression once heard down east for a woman whose clothes hang off her too loosely.

flake (1) Heard in Massachusetts for a piece, a part, a section. "They put it together flake by flake." (2) A platform on which fish are dried.

flamigigs Affectations, airs. "She put on flamigigs for his benefit." Given as a common term in George Allen England, "Rural Locutions of Maine and Northern New Hampshire," *Dialect Notes,* Vol. IV (1914).

flaming falls Autumns with especially colorful foliage, which are the rule rather than the exception to it. "New England has brief summers and long, cold winters, sudden springs, and long, 'flaming falls.'" (Robert P. Tristram Coffin, *New England,* 1951)

flapdoodle Foolish talk, nonsense. "The whole speech was nothing but flapdoodle."

flapjack The preferred word for *pancake* or *griddlecake,* though these are also heard, as is *flatjack.*

flared Mentally deranged or disturbed. "She's kind of flared."

flatjack See FLAPJACK.

flat out, to See quote. "Generally, disappointed and broken down men are those who have failed in trade . . . or to use an expressive Yankee phrase, have flatted out in a calling or profession." (Josiah Holland, *Plain Talk,* 1865)

flax out To become weary, exhausted. "These dretful, smart, handsome folks are just the ones that flax out sometimes." (Mary Wilkins Freeman, *A New England Nun,* 1891)

fleet Once said in Massachusetts of dishes that are shallow. "Put out one of those fleet dishes."

Fletcherize To masticate food thoroughly; after Horace Fletcher (1849–1919), a Lawrence, Massachusetts nutritionist who advocated 32 chews to each bite of food for better health. His slogan was: "Nature will castigate those who don't masticate."

flew An obsolete word for *flowed* noted in James Russell Lowell's *The Biglow Papers* (1866). "The stream flew down the hill."

flicker A detective. " 'Are you a flicker?' . . . In France 'flic' is a police detective; the word must have crossed the Channel, entered the slang of the Englsh underworld, and had probably been imported to Newport [Rhode Island] by Henry himself." (Thornton Wilder, *Theophilus North,* 1973)

flicker up Heard on Cape Cod for *failing.* Also *flicker.*

flint corn See JOHNNYCAKE.

flipper Another term for *flapjack.*

flirt o' snow A very light sprinkling of snow. "We had a flirt o' snow last night."

flop To flap. "The bird flopped its wings."

Flora's paintbrush A name in Maine for the beautiful orange hawkweed (*Hieracium aurantiacum*).

Floridy A pronunciation of "Florida," especially in Maine.

flow Flood. "They flowed the cranberry bogs every spring."

flower-pot judge A humorous term for an associate judge once commonly used in New England, the term suggesting that such judges just sit on the bench for show.

flume (1) A narrow ravine worn or cut out by a stream. (2) Capitalized, the name of a famous flume in New Hampshire's White Mountains. "Nobody could help laughing at the child's notion of leaving a warm bed and dragging them from a cheerful fire, to visit the basin of the Flume— a brook, which tumbles over the precipice, deep within the Notch." (Nathaniel Hawthorne, "The Ambitious Guest," 1835) See NOTCH.

flummery A sweet cornstarch pudding made with fruit and served with cream and sugar.

flummydiddle An old-fashioned term meaning nonsense. "That's a lot of flummydiddle."

flush-to-bung town! Reported as a colorful New Hampshire Yankee oath by the Federal Writer's Project in 1937.

flushration An expression, coined in the early 19th century, for a state of frustration. Also *flusteration*.

fly off one's jib A Nantucketism meaning to become old or be in poor health. "He's not long for this world, he's flyin' off his jib."

fly off the handle To lose one's self-control or head, like an ax head flying off its wooden handle. The expression may have been invented by 19th-century humorist Thomas C. Haliburton, who wrote of the itinerant Yankee peddler Sam Slick in many books. The saying is now commonly used throughout the United States.

flying axhandle A humorous old name for an attack of diarrhea; alluding to the fact that a wild flying axhandle can't be controlled and can land anywhere.

fodder corn Field corn; that is, corn grown for fodder, feeding animals, rather than for human consumption.

fog mull (1) A heavy fogbank without wind but usually accompanied by a drizzle of rain. (2) Sometimes used to describe drunkenness: "He's in a fog-mull."

fogo A bad smell; an unusual word of unknown origin rarely if ever used anymore. ". . . he had to take out his handkerchief, all scented with muck, to get clear of the fogo of it." (Thomas Haliburton, *The Clockmaker*, 1840)

fog's so thick you kin hardly spit A Maine saying recorded in John Wallace, *Village Down East* (1943).

folks Can be used in Maine to mean "friends" and even one's wife, as in

"How's your folks?" "She ain't feel-in' very well."

folksy Gregarious. " 'I'm real folksy; grasshoppers ain't no neighbors to me. I want to be amongst them that'll talk back to me." (Rose Terry Cooke, "Town Mouse and Country Mouse," 1891)

fool An English dessert made of fruit, cream and sugar that has long been popular in New England. Its name is of unknown origin.

foolhead An old-fashioned expression heard in Massachusetts for a fool. "You old foolhead, that's not how you do it!"

foolish (1) A term once common for the orange file fish (*Alutera Schoepfic*) in southern New England because of what fisherman considered its absurd way of swimming. (2) Another name for the eel-back flounder, which bites at any bait, including a rag on the hook. (3) Sometimes used to describe a feeble-minded person, someone not of normal intelligence.

foolkiller A character of folklore who kills fools. "Whenever he heard of the death of somebody he didn't like, he'd say, 'Well, the Fool-Killer's come for so-and-so,' and sort of smack his lips." (Stephen Vincent Benét, *Tales Before Midnight,* 1939)

fool plover Another name for the bird commonly called the dowitcher (*Limnodromus griseus*).

foopaw A mistake, the word a corruption of the French *faux pas.* Cited in William F. Macy, *The Nantucket Scrap Basket* (1916).

footin' around Doing needless work, fussing, fooling around. "Stop your footin' around."

footins Heavy winter stockings.

footstove A small tin box with small holes in it that was filled with hot coals and taken to the unheated church to keep one's feet warm during services.

forceput Heard along the Maine coast for *necessary.* "Theirs was a force-put marriage."

fore-and-after (1) A square dance once popular in New England. (2) Heard in Maine for something trim, alluding to a fore-and-aft rigged ship.

foredoor A name dating back three centuries or more for the front door to a house.

foreigner A word used in New England meaning someone not born in a town or area, even if he or she has lived there for many years.

forefather's cup The pitcher plant (*Sarracenia purpurea*); also called *forefather's pitcher.*

Forefather's Day A New England holiday, celebrated mostly in Massachusetts on December 21, that commemorates the Pilgrims landing at Plymouth in 1620. Traditionally, samp porridge is served on this day, which is not a legal holiday. The annual holiday was first celebrated at Plymouth, Massachusetts in 1769.

forehanded Said of someone foresighted and prudent. "Regular habits, forehandedness (if I may use the word) in worldly affairs, and hours reclaimed from indolence and vice . . . follow in the wake of the converted man." (Richard Henry Dana, Jr., *Two Years Before the Mast,* 1840)

forelay A nautical expression meaning both to lie in wait for and to plan in advance. "You'd better forelay for a cold winter."

foreroom Once commonly used for the living room or parlor of a house, where people were entertained.

fore-royal The first morning cup of coffee on a ship or on shore in some coastal areas of New England; the expression takes its name from the foremast sail on sailing ships.

Forest City Portland, Maine has had this nickname for over a century and a half due to the many trees in its vicinity. Cleveland, Ohio and Savannah, Georgia share the name.

for goodness-goodness Agnes! An old exclamation of surprise, usually a pleasant surprise.

fort An old pronunciation of "fault." "Well, Mister, if you don't understand plain English, that isn't my fort." (David Humphreys, *A Yankey in England,* 1815)

forth-putting Used to describe a badly behaved, arrogant, forward person. " 'I'd ha' got my ears took off if I'd been so forth-putting when I was little.' " (Sara O. Jewett, "Lost Lover," 1878)

Fortino See quote. "Fortino (for aught I know). This remarkable specimen of clipping and condensing a phrase approached the Indian method of forming words. The word is very common throughout New England, Long Island, and the rest of New York." (John Bartlett, *Dictionary of Americanisms,* 1848) *Fortino* is now an obsolete expression of historical interest only.

forty eleven A large amount. "She put up forty eleven kinds of fruits and vegetables."

fourcorners A name given to any crossroads, especially in Maine.

fourpence ha'penny This term is not important because it meant a Spanish half real worth about five cents but because the pronunciation *fourpence ha'penny* was a Yankee shibboleth in the early 19th century. If you said fourpence ha'penny you were set down as a New Englander. Most others said *four pence half penny.*

fowl An old hen or chicken, tough and chiefly used for stewing. "Never use fowl to make fried chicken."

fowy Rancid, spoiled. "The butter she used was fowy." The word was once common for anything inferior in quality, especially wood that is spongy or brittle.

Foxes An old name for residents of Maine. According to Walt Whitman, writing in the *North American Review* (November 1885): "Among the rank and file [in the Civil War] . . . it was very general to speak of the different States [men] . . . came from by their slang names. Those from Maine were called Foxes; New Hampshire, Granite Boys; Massachusetts, Bay Staters . . ." Whitman gives no reason for the names.

fox grape A wild purplish-black grape (*Vitis labeusca*) common in New England. " 'Now you know how it feels,' my brother said / 'To be a bunch of fox grapes, as they call them . . ." (Robert Frost, *Wild Grapes*, 1923)

foxy granpas See BOSTON BAKED BEANS.

frappé (1) What is called a milkshake—a drink made of milk, flavored syrup and ice cream—in some places is often called a frappé in New England, where a *milkshake* is made of milk and syrup. "Just south of Boston, ordering a milkshake would get you milk mixed with flavored syrup; no ice cream was included. 'Frappé' was the order if ice cream was included . . . Incidentally, the French ending of frappé . . . was never pronounced; it came out 'frap.' " (William Safire, *On Language*, 1980) (2) Chilled, iced; from a French word meaning artificially chilled. "The air you drink is frappé." (James Russell Lowell, *My Study Windows*, 1871)

free belt See BANKING.

Freestone State A nickname for Connecticut since the early 19th century because of the state's freestone quarries. More frequently called the *Nutmeg State*.

freeze down To stick closely, become established. "I friz down right where I wus, married the Widder Shennon." (James Russell Lowell, *The Biglow Papers*, 1862)

freezy A Mainism for *cold*. "Sure is a freezy morning."

Frenchers A historical term for Frenchmen. ". . . he is appointed of the escort to bring the captivated Frenchers and Indians home to the province jail." (Nathaniel Hawthorne, "The Wives of the Dead," 1832)

Frenchman The most common term in Maine for *people of French descent*. See P.I.

fresh cook A cook who uses very little salt. Said to be used commonly in Portsmouth, New Hampshire, according to Frederic D. Allen, "Contributions to New England Vocabulary," *Dialect Notes*, Vol. I (1890). A *heavy cook*, or *heavy-handed cook*, according to the same source, is one who uses a lot of salt.

freshet A word Mainers use for a stream caused by heavy rain.

freshwater clam A bivalve of the family *Uniosidae* found in inland waters; sometimes called the *freshwater mussel.*

freshwater lobster The preferred name for *crayfish* found in New England inland waters.

fret Worry. " 'The next time you'll know better'n to fret like this.' " (Edith Wharton, *Summer,* 1917)

frettish An old-fashioned word for *fretful.* Also *fretty.*

fried pie A name used in New England and the South for a fruit-filled turnover fried in deep fat.

fried pudding Fried leftover cornmeal mush; called *fried mush* in other regions.

frig around Putter around, fool around. Though the term may once have been a euphemism for *fuck around,* the word *frig* has no sexual connotations in Maine (as it does in other places) and is used in mixed company. "I frigged around on my car all morning." See FUB.

frock A denim work jacket, any outer coat; the word is heard mainly in northern New England. Often *barn frock.*

frog it (1) To jump or hop like a frog from place to place, especially over puddles or across swampy areas. (2) To walk a canoe through shallow water.

frolic Another name for the bees (gatherings), such as apple-cut bees or quilting bees, that used to be common in New England. "Every one has heard of the 'frolic' or 'bee,' by means of which the clearing of lots, the raising of houses, the harvesting of crops is achieved [with all the neighbors working together]." (Harriet Martineau, *Society in America,* 1837)

from away Used to describe anyone residing in Maine who doesn't hail from the state. Heard in one tourist center: "He's from away, she's from away—sometimes it seems the whole state's from away."

front parlor The parlor near the front of the house. "She awoke on the horsehair sofa in her own front parlor. The air was musty, for the room was unused and unloved." (Susan Dodd, "Rue," 1984)

front room The living room, which is usually nearest the front of the house; frequently heard along the Maine coast.

front yard fence A picket fence, often with sharp pickets.

frostbird Chiefly the golden plover (*Pluvialis dominica*), but the name is given to several other birds as well, including the black-legged kittiwake and the red-backed sandpiper.

frost blow The aster *Aster ericoides,* because it often flowers after the first frost in autumn.

frostfish The tomcod or whiting (*Microgadus tomcod*), so called because it is plentiful in early winter after the first frost.

frost flower Asters (of the genus *Aster*) in general, because many of them bloom into late fall, after the first frost.

frost heave Bumps in the road caused by very cold weather; often indicated by small orange signs reading "Frost Heaves."

frothed up Angry. "She was all frothed up about it."

frouch An apparently obsolete old word meaning botch. "He frouched up the job."

frowzy Ill-smelling, partly decomposed. "He never got queer and frowzy and half-cracked." (Dorothy Canfield, "Old Man Warner," in *Raw Material,* 1925)

frozen Yankee Doodle A famous saying by Thomas G. Appleton about the Boston Art Museum, torn down in 1908. Appleton said that if architecture was "frozen music," this building was "frozen Yankee Doodle." Called "the first conversationalist in America" by Emerson, the rich, worldly Appleton, Longfellow's brother-in-law, was according to Van Wyck Brook's in *New England: Indian Summer* (1940) "the only man who could ride over Holmes and Lowell and talk them down." He also coined the now-familiar phrases, *mutual admiration society* and *All good Americans go to Paris when they die,* the latter of which often is attributed to Oliver Wendell Holmes and Oscar Wilde.

fry pan *Fry pan* and *frying pan* for a skillet were once New England regionalisms, but both are now in general use.

fub Usd in Maine and New Hampshire to mean "putter or fuss about doing unworthwhile things." "He fubbed around with his car all day and it still won't start." See FRIG AROUND.

fuddy-duddy A derogatory term describing someone very fussy or unmanly. "He's an old fuddy-duddy."

full Sometimes used instead of "much" in comparisons. "He's full smarter'n you are."

full chisel An old-fashioned expression meaning full speed. "He driv into the yard, full chizel, with his pig." (Harriet Beecher Stowe, "The Minister's Housekeeper," 1871)

full stick Same as FULL CHISEL.

fulled up Shrunk. "My socks fulled up when I washed them."

full of ginger Peppy. "The plump horse was full of ginger as I drove to Johnson's sawmill." (Hayden Pearson, *New England Flavor,* 1961)

full of weasel juice Full of vim and vigor; the quick movements of the weasel inspired the phrase.

funkify An obsolete term meaning to frighten or alarm someone.

funny eye Heard in Maine and other areas for the round opening in a lobster pot. Also called *funny hoop*.

furrow out To make a furrow or trench and plant potatoes and other crops in it.

fush out To play out, die out, fail. "This wind should fush out by morning."

fusspot Someone who is fussy or finicky.

fust A pronunciation of *first*. "That's the fust thing I thought of."

fuzzle To act in a confused or aimless way. "They fussed and fuzzled till they'd drinked up all the tea." (Harriet Beecher Stowe, "The Minister's Housekeeper," 1871)

G

gad A small whip used for livestock, or the stock of a whip without the lash.

gaffle Used chiefly in northern New England to mean "seize hold of and carry." "He gaffled the hay into the barn." Also *gaffle up*. "He gaffled up the anchor."

gahd A common Boston pronunciation of "guard."

galamander A large-wheeled wagon with a derrick once used to lift large blocks of granite. The term's origin is unknown but perhaps is based on *salamander*.

gal boy An old New England term for *tomboy*.

gale wind A redundancy for *gale*.

gallied, gallyied Rattled, frightened and excited; the word originally applied to whales. Cited in William F. Macy, *The Nantucket Scrap Basket* (1916).

gallus An old-fashioned term New Englanders used for a suspender or an overall strap. *Galluses* is the plural. "He wore overalls, with only one arm through a gallus."

galvanized Yank Used in the South during the Civil War for a Southerner who was pro-Union.

gam No one knows the origins of this word for a sailor's bull session, or chat, or conference, although it appears to have been first recorded in reference to a sociable visit between two whaleships at sea. Herman Melville used and defined the word in *Moby Dick* (1850), which owed much to Melville's personal experiences and to whaling chronicles of the day. Melville defined the word as "A social gathering of two (or more) whale-ships, generally on a cruising-ground; when, after exchanging hails, they exchange visits by boats' crews; the two captains remaining for a time on board of one ship, and the two chief mates on the other." *Gam* was later used ashore, as in "I had a long gam with John yesterday," and the author heard it employed a year or so ago to describe two police patrol cars in Connecticut "gamming at the side of the road." Some etymologists suggest that the word *gam* for a pod of whales is the source, while others opt for the obsolete English word *gammon*, meaning animated talk or chatter.

gambrel roof A ridged roof with two slopes on each side, with the lower side having the steeper pitch. John Bartlett's *Americanisms* (1848) says the roof is "so called from its resemblance to the hind leg of a horse which by farriers is termed the gambrel."

gambrel stick A redundancy for *gambrel*.

gander (1) A rubberneck, one who ganders at people. (2) An awkward gangling person.

gander party See quote. "Gander-party: a social gathering of men only." (James Russell Lowell, *The Biglow Papers,* 1867)

ganging The twine used to make fishing line. Pronounced *gan-jing.*

gannet-gutted Someone with a voracious appetite, one like that of the gannet, a bird that knows no limit. "He's a gannet-gut if I ever saw one."

ganted out Gaunt, wasted. "She's been workin' too hard. All ganted out."

gansey Heard down East for a sweater; a corruption of *guernsey.*

gap-and-swallow A humorous term for *soft food* such as cornmeal mush or crackers and water. " 'Gap and swallow' was another venerable emergency dish, not unlike Hasty Pudding." (Imogene Wolcott, *The New England Yankee Cookbook,* 1939). *Gap* here is a variation of "gape."

gape Sometimes used in New England and other regions for "to yawn." "He stretched up his arms and gaped."

garb up To dress. "It's cold out, you'd best garb up good."

garden hash An old-time term for *compost* from the compost heap.

garden sass (1) Fresh vegetables grown in the home garden. "Garden sass always was the most of my living, and there's some tailoring to be did . . ." (Rose Terry Cooke, "Town Mouse and Country Mouse," 1891) Sometimes heard as *garden sauce.* (2) Another name for *rhubarb.*

gaum (1) To move clumsily. (2) A clumsy oaf. (3) To act in a stupid, bungling way. "He really gaumed that job." Also *gorm.*

gaumy Clumsy, stupid. "Of all the gaumy cusses I know, you take the cake." Also *gauming.*

gaunted up Thin. "The gaunted-up long-legged animals." (Oliver Wendell Holmes, *Elsie Venner,* 1861)

gaup To gape or stare. "Stop gauping at me."

Gawdfreediamonds! A euphemistic exclamation heard on Isleboro, off the coast of Maine.

gawky An old-fashioned term for *fool, simpleton.* "She's a regular gawky."

gawnicus This synonym for *dolt* is given by James Russell Lowell in *The Biglow Papers* (1867).

gee-bucking Children hitching a ride on a horse-drawn sled by attaching the rope of their smaller sleds to it.

gee whittakers! An old-fashioned euphemistic exclamation.

general court A name for the legislative assembly in New Hampshire and Massachusetts; in early times these bodies had judicial as well as legislative powers.

gentleman cow An old euphemism for *bull*; also called a *gentleman* and a *gentleman ox*.

gent's walk See LADIES WALK.

gerrymander Above editor Benjamin Russell's desk in the offices of the *Centinel*, a Massachusetts Federalist newspaper, hung the serpentine-shape map of a new Essex County senatorial district that began at Salisbury and included Amesbury, Haverhill, Methuen, Andover, Middleton, Danvers, Lynnfield, Salem, Marblehead, Lynn and Chelsea. This political monster was part of a general reshaping of voting districts that the Democratic-Republican–controlled state legislature had enacted with the approval of the incumbent governor, Elbridge Gerry. The arbitrary redistricting would have enabled the Jeffersonians to concentrate Federalist power in a few districts and remain in the majority after the (then-yearly) gubernatorial election of 1812 and was of course opposed by all Federalists, although it was a fairly common practice of the times. When the celebrated painter Gilbert Stuart visited the *Centinel* offices one day before the elections, editor Russell indignantly pointed to the monstrous map on the wall, inspiring Stuart to take a crayon and add head, wings, and claws to the already lizardlike district. "That will do for a salamander," the artist said when he finished. "A *Gerry*-mander, you mean," Mr. Russell replied, and a name for the political creature was born, *gerrymander* coming into use as a verb within a year.

get a wiggle on it Heard in Isleboro, off the Maine coast, for *hurry up*.

get done To be fired, laid off a job. "I'm going to get done down at the store next Friday."

get one's dander up, to Many of the early Yankee humorists—such as Seba Smith, Charles Davis and Thomas Haliburton—used this Americanism for *to get angry*, and it is found in the *Life of Davy Crockett*. It is one of those expressions with a handful of plausible explanations. The most amusing is that the *dander* in the phrase is an English dialect form of *dandruff* that was used in the Victorian era; someone with his dander up, according to this theory, would be wrathfully tearing up his hair by the fistful, dandruff flying in the process. Another likely source is the West Indian *dander*, a ferment used in the preparation of molasses, which would suggest a rising ferment of anger. The Dutch *donder*, "thunder," also has been nominated, for it is used in the Dutch phrase *op donderon*, "to burst into a sudden rage." And then there is the farfetched theory that *dander* is a telescoped form of "damned anger." And if these aren't enough, we have the possibilities that *dander* comes from an English dialect word for *anger*; from the Scots *danders*, "hot embers"; and from the Romany *dander*, "to bite."

get one's goin'-home-acryin', to To get one's comeuppance. "He started the fight and got his nose broken, got his goin'-home-acryin!"

get onto yourself and ride the jackass Get up and get moving; an old saying heard in Massachusetts.

get out! *Bartlett's* (1848) gives this as a mid-19th-century New Englandism meaning Leave me alone!

gets up so early he (she) meets himself (herself) going to bed Said of a very early riser. Recorded in Ernest Poole, *The Great White Hills of New Hampshire* (1946).

getting up the wood See quote. " 'Getting up the wood.' That was a term we always used [in New Hampshire] for hauling the wood from the wood lot to the yard behind the house and starting it, ready for the saw rig.' " (Hayden Pearson, *New England Flavor*, 1961)

get your bait back An expression heard in Maine meaning to catch just enough fish to cover your expenses for bait. "I didn't catch enough to get my bait back."

gibraltar A hard candy often flavored with peppermint or lemon, long a favorite in New England. See BOSTON BAKED BEANS.

gill-ver-the-ground A folk name for ground ivy (*Nepeta glechoma*).

gimp Courage, guts, spirit. "She's got lots of gimp." The word possibly derives from the fishing line strengthened with wire called *gimp*.

gin Once used as a past-tense form of "give." "He gin me ten dollars."

ginger! An old-fashioned euphemistic exclamation, usually in the form of *by ginger!*

ginger plum (1) The berry of the wintergreen (*Gaultheria procumbens*). (2) The plant itself. Also called *ginger berry*.

ginger water A refreshing New England homemade drink of water, molasses and a little vinegar and ginger.

girling A Mainism describing a boy courting a girl. "He went girling."

gism Heard in Rhode Island for *strength, genius, talent*.

git A pronunciation of *get* in Maine and other places. See quote under MORE'N COMMON STUPID.

git a holt A synonym in Maine and New Hampshire for *take hold of*. "You watch out or I'll git a holt on you."

give a turn Startle, upset. " 'George! You gave me such a turn.' " (Thornton Wilder, *Our Town*, 1938)

give a whaling to Give a beating to. Many etymologists believe this phrase should be *give a waling to,* as a *wale* is a mark raised on the flesh by the blow of a stick or whip. But the key word in the phrase has been spelled with an *h* ever since it first appeared, over a century ago. This suggests that a *whaling,* "a terrible beating," was one given with a whalebone whip, though the wales it raised may have contributed to the phrase, making it more vivid. In the past riding whips were commonly made of whalebone. *Whalebone,* incidentally, is a misnomer: It's not made from the bones of a whale but from a substance found in the whale's upper jaw. *Whaling* is first recorded in Harriet Beecher Stowe's *Uncle Tom's Cabin* (1852): "How did yer whaling agree with yer, Tom?"

give her honest measure, but don't kick the salt An old saying meaning be honest but don't cheat yourself. A merchant who kicked the salt container would settle the salt and the customer would get too much for his or her money.

give one's eyeteeth for To give one's most prized possessions for. "I'd give my eyeteeth for a horse like that."

give the very Jesse To curse someone out vehemently. "She gave him the very Jesse."

give Yankee Doddle An old expression meaning to give hell to. "They gave him Yankee Doddle and then some."

giving down Used especially in Maine for a cow producing milk. "The cow was unhappy . . . She wasn't 'giving down.'" (John Gould, *It Is Not Now,* 1993)

glare Bright, smooth and slippery ice. "The roads were glare and slippery." (Mary Wilkens Freeman, *A New England Nun and Other Stories,* 1891) The word *glare* in this sense dates back to the 16th century. *Glare ice,* an Americanism coined in about 1825, is ice having a smooth glassy surface that reflects sunlight.

glauackus The name of an imaginary monster first reported in Connecticut in 1939, when a wire service story told of a mysterious beast variously resembling a lion, panther or boar, among all sorts of descriptions, that terrified the people of Glastonbury. It has been sighted since by all sorts of people except skeptics.

glinning up Said when a bright streak breaks through the clouds in the sky. "It's glinning up in the east."

glorit Heard in New Hampshire and Maine for *to glory.* "They glorited in their victory."

Gloucester Pronounced GLOSSter; a Massachusetts town. See BOUND.

glow-shoes An old way of saying galoshes. ". . . the necessity of the young man providing a certain number of superfluous glow-shoes, and umbrellas . . . before he dies?"

(Henry David Thoreau, *Walden,* 1854)

glut An old Maine and New Hampshire word for a fresh, impertinent reply to a question. "Don't glut me like that."

go around Robin Hood's barn To go in a circuitous way. The expression originated in England centuries ago. "Her way of going round Robin Hood's barn between the beginning of her story and its end." (Sara Orne Jewett, "Miss Debby," 1883)

go ashore to windward To go wrong or fail with no excuse for it. Cited in William F. Macy, *The Nantucket Scrap Basket* (1916).

go bag yer head! Shut up. Given as an angry exclamation in George Allen England, "Rural Locutions of Maine and Northern New Hampshire," *Dialect Notes,* Vol. IV (1914).

go-billy An old-fashioned term for any four-wheeled vehicle.

Goddams Cape Cod fishermen of Portuguese descent often bestowed nicknames on each other and used the nicknames so consistently that they virtually replaced the surnames of the families concerned after several generations. One family, for example, became known as the *Codfishes,* another as the *Rats.* The most extreme example recorded is the *Goddams.* Captain Joseph Captiva explained this oddest of surnames to Alice Douglas Kelly of the Federal Writers' Project and she recorded it in *Living Lore of New England* (1938): "That's cause the old lady she couldn't speak English so good and she'd call the children when they was little: 'You come here, goddam,' 'Don't you do that, goddam.' So they call 'em the 'Goddams'." Many readers have heard comedian Bill Cosby's routine in which the child thinks his name is "Damnit" because his father so often summons him with a "Commere, damnit!"—there's truth behind every fiction! More examples of this odd custom can be found in Jeremiah Diggs, *Cape Cod Pilot* (1937).

godfrey! A euphemistic exclamation meaning roughly *By God!*

godfrey dorman! Same as GODFREY!

godfrey lijah! Same as GODFREY!

godfrey's might! An exclamation heard on Cape Cod that is a euphemism for *God almighty!*

godfrey mighty! Same as GODFREY.

Godlike A nickname for New England statesman Daniel Webster. "Black Dan, alias the Godlike, as he has been cognomened by his especial admirers, is a sort of intellectual hippopotamus." (Quincy (Ill.) *Whig,* Nov. 3, 1850)

God made the food, but the devil made the cook Said of a poor cook; the expression is of nautical origin. Cited in William F. Macy, *The Nantucket Scrap Basket* (1916).

go down cellar Go down into the cellar. "And Archibald, with a soft light in his eyes, / Replied that if he chose to go down cellar, / There he would find eight barrels . . ." (Edward Arlington Robinson, "Isaac and Archibald," *Captain Craig*, 1902)

God rock Any small pure white stone a child finds and keeps in his or her pocket as a treasure.

God's amount (amint) Heard in Maine for a large amount. "They's God's amint o' woodchucks in them woods."

God sometimes shows his contempt of wealth by giving it to fools An old New England saying.

go fry some ice Get out of here, don't bother me; an expression heard in Massachusetts.

going around Robinson's barn Doing something in an involved, complicated way. A New England, chiefly Maine version of the much older *going round Robin Hood's barn*.

going down to salt water An expression once used by inland farmers to describe an outing to the seashore. "We're going down to salt water tomorrow."

going full stick Going very fast.

going greening Going to gather wild greens for the table.

going out on a flink Going out for a good time; *flink* here may be a corruption of "fling." Cited in William F. Macy, *The Nantucket Scrap Basket* (1916).

go it, Sal! An old-fashioned exclamation meaning roughly go ahead!

goldarn! A euphemism for *God damn* heard in New England and other regions.

golly-wopper bird An extraordinary imaginary bird that figures in New England folklore.

go 'long! An old-fashioned command to a horse meaning Get up!

gone by (1) Said of old tough vegetables. "They're gone by carrots not even fit for a stew." (2) Dead. "He's gone by ten years now."

gone goose, a Someone "lost past recovery," as *Bartlett's* (1848) puts it, someone sure to lose.

goneness Extreme weariness, complete exhaustion. "I feel a goneness I've never felt before."

gone to his long home Has died, gone to his final resting place, the "long" indicating the duration of his stay. "He's gone to his long home three years now."

goney An old, perhaps obsolete, term for a *stupid person*. See GOONEY.

good Often used in New England and other parts of the Northeast for *best.* "[It was] her good dress." (Edith Wharton, *Ethan Frome,* 1911)

good earth and seas An old-fashioned rural exclamation. "But good airth an' seas, he'd saw that fiddle all up into tunes." (Rowland Robinson, "A Paring Bee," 1900)

good fences make good neighbors An old saying that became associated with New England poet Robert Frost, who used it in his famous poem "Mending Wall" (1914).

good holding ground A place where one can stay even when conditions are bad. Originally a nautical term referring to a place offshore where an anchor could catch and hold fast even when the sea was rough and the wind was blowing hard.

good land! A common old-fashioned exclamation. " 'Good land, Luella, how you look! You'll faint away." (Mary E. Wilkins, "Life-Everlastin'," 1891)

good land a mercy! Once a common euphemistic exclamation.

good morning, damn you See the following quote from a story based on Bronson Alcott's idealistic community Fruitlands. "One youth [a member of the community] believing that language was of little consequence if the spirit was only right, startled newcomers by blandly greeting them with "Good-morning, damn you," and other remarks of an equally mixed order." (Louisa May Alcott, "Transcendental Wild Oats," 1876)

good pear or apple costs no more time or pains to rear than a poor one, a See quote. "It is commonly said by farmers, that a good pear or apple costs no more time or pains to rear, than a poor one; so I would have no work of art, no speech, or action, or thought, or friend, but the best." (Ralph Waldo Emerson, "Nominalist and Realist," 1844)

good riddance to bad rubbish An old saying, still occasionally heard, that dates back to at least 1815 and is used in other regions as well.

Goody A polite form of address for a "goodwife," a good woman of humble means in old New England. " '. . . my broomstick hath strangely disappeared, stolen, as I suspect, by that unhanged witch Goody Cory, and that, too, when I was all anointed with the juice of smallage and cinque-foil and wolf's-bane—' " (Nathaniel Hawthorne, "Young Goodman Brown," 1835)

go-off The start, the beginning. "He was doomed from the go-off."

gooney Any awkward, stupid person, a fool or simpleton, the word an English dialect term that is first recorded in New England in the early 19th century: "If the feller has been such a ravin' destracted gooney, I hope they will hang him." (Thomas Haliburton, *The Clockmaker,* 1838)

go on with your bird's-egging An expression little heard today meaning get on with your story, say what you have to say and get it over with.

go pleasurin! Take a pleasure trip. "Virgil asked us to go 'pleasurin' down to one of the islands [in Maine] for a Sunday picnic . . ." (John Gould, *It Is Not Now,* 1993)

gorby bird A Maine and New Hampshire term for the woodland Canada jay (*Perisoreus canadensis*), which is considered a good-luck omen. The bird also is called the *camp thief,* after its habit of stealing bright objects and food.

gore A long narrow piece of land that is often triangular in shape, roughly resembling a cow's horn. Such pieces of land, frequently worthless and unwanted, often are found between the boundaries of farms, towns and counties.

go right along out See quote. "She laughed at him . . . and told him to 'go right along out' and leave her to see to things." (Edith Wharton, *Ethan Frome,* 1911)

gorm A gooey mess. "He had a gorm of worms on his hook."

gorming Used to describe a stupid, clumsy person or animal, or even an inanimate object that is in one's way. "Move aside, you great gorming lummox." Given as a common expression in George Allen England, "Rural Locutions of Maine and Northern New Hampshire," *Dialect Notes,* Vol. IV (1914). The word, however, can be used in a less offen-sive way, as in the following quote. "I asked her how her little grand-daughter Dorry was. 'Little?' say she . . . she's a great big gormin' girl now.' That 'gormin' did bring back old times and pa. He always applied that term to me when I was growin' up, and it's a scrumptious word. I do lot on words that pictur' things out like that." (Annie Trumbull Slosson, "A Local Colorist," 1912)

go-round The action of going around and around, like a merry-go-round. "All this go-round [to find someone lost]." (Mary Wilkins Freeman, *A New England Nun,* 1891)

gorry! A common Maine exclamation. " 'Gorry! What makes some men so *dumb?*' " (Stephen King, *Dolores Claiborne,* 1993)

go sandpaper the anchor Get out of here, go do any foolish thing so long as you leave. Usually said to children underfoot.

gosh all fish-hook! A euphemistic oath meaning God Almighty!

gosh all hemlock! An old exclamation that is a euphemism for *God almighty!*

goshfrey mighty dorman! Reported as a colorful New Hampshire oath by the Federal Writers Project in 1937.

go snucks Share the expenses of something. "They went snucks on the candy."

go to Ballyhack! Go to hell. "*Go to Ballyhack!*—a common expression in New England. I know not its origin. It savors in sound, however, of the Emerald Isle." (John Bartlett, *Dictionary of Americanisms*, 1859) *Bally* and *hack* are old English dialect words for *town* and *hell*

go to grass! An old-fashioned expression meaning get out! begone with you!

go-to-hell Said of someone who has no concern for what anyone else thinks of him or her. "Rake looked like the original go-to-hell dory fisherman—leathery face, dirty cap, dirtier deck shoes, and flannel shirt stuffed into trousers so dirty you could chop them up for chum." (William Martin, *Cape Cod*, 1991)

go-to-meetin's A humorous term often used in the past for one's best clothes, those worn to Sunday church meetings.

Go to poodic! An Indian name for a point of land on the Maine coast; it translates as "Go jump in the bay!" Cited in George R. Stewart, *Names on the Land* (1945).

go us Last us. "We've got enough food to go us the week."

governor's meat Deer and other game shot out of season.

Governor Winthrop A combination desk-bookcase like one owned by Governor John Winthrop (1588–1649) of the Massachusetts Bay Colony.

gownd, geound A once-common pronunciation of "gown." "The Yankee, who omits the final *d* in many words, as do the Scotch, makes up for it by adding one in *geound*." (James Russell Lowell, *The Biglow Papers*, 1866)

gracious evers! A euphemistic exclamation, like the more common *gracious me!*

gracious me! See GRACIOUS EVERS!

gra'ma'mam An old form of "grandmother."

grammy A form of "grandmother" or "grandma" heard mostly in Maine.

gramp, grampy, grandser, granther Synonyms for *grandfather*; the last three are old-fashioned terms.

grandsir Grandfather. "I can make out old Grandsir Stark distinctly—/ With his pipe in his mouth and his brown jug / Bless you, it isn't Grandsir Stark, it's Granny . . . (Robert Frost, "The Generations of Men," 1914) Also *grandsire*.

grange supper See CHURCH SUPPER.

Granite boys See FOXES.

Granite City An old nickname for *Boston, Massachusetts.*

Granite State, the A nickname for *Vermont.* It is said that Vermont's granite industry was established as a result of Vermonters drilling for salt. In 1827 Montpelier citizens drilled hole after hole searching for precious salt, only to give it up as a bad job upon striking layer after layer of granite. Soon after, they decided to mine the granite.

granite insides An iron constitution. "She was a little widow, with granite insides, a native of Whiteridge [New Hampshire]." (Bliss Perry, *"By the Committee,"* 1899)

granny (1) A nickname for any old woman or crone in times past. "Granny Gordon, so she was familiarly denominated . . . thin and withered away in person . . . bore no small resemblance to a newly exhumed mummy, and to all appearance promised to last as long as one of those ancient dames of Egypt." (Nathaniel Hawthorne, "The Haunted Quack," 1831) (2) Sometimes used in Maine for a fussy, officious man.

granny knot A poorly tied knot that often comes loose; though it is a nautical term referring to a landlubber's knot, *granny knot* is heard on land as well in New England and New York, including New York City (and wherever else, I would guess, that seamen have introduced it).

grass about the bows A humorous term for *whiskers,* or for the beginnings of a beard. "He's got some grass about the bows." Originally nautical in use.

grassing Lovemaking outdoors. "Remember us grassin' down by the lake?"

grasshopper All true Bostonians know that this is the creature represented on the weather vane on the cupola of Faneuil Hall. Faneuil Hall, "the Cradle of Liberty," was erected as a public market in 1742 by merchant Peter Faneuil.

graveyard Often the preferred word for *cemetery* among older speakers.

greasy luck Good luck. A local Nantucket expression that first arose among whalemen trying out oil from whale blubber on the decks of whaleships. The decks became very slippery at such times, and this was considered lucky because it meant a more prosperous voyage. Well-wishers often wished departing whalemen *greasy luck* when they embarked on a voyage. Cited in William F. Macy, *The Nantucket Scrap Basket* (1916).

great Heard in Maine and other parts of New England for a great amount. "I guess she won't be troubled no great with 'em." (Sara Orne Jewett, "White Heron," 1886)

Great Awakening A religious revival that began in New England in 1734.

Great Carbuncle See quote.

There are few legends more poetical than that of the "Great Carbuncle" of the White Mountains. The belief was communicated to the English settlers, and is hardly yet extinct, that a gem, of such immense size as to be seen shining miles away, hangs from a rock over a clear, deep lake, high up among the hills. They who had once beheld its splendor, were enthralled with an unutterable yearning to possess it. But a spirit guarded that inestimable jewel, and bewildered the adventurer with a dark mist from the enchanted lake. Thus, life was worn away in the vain search for an unearthly treasure, till at length the deluded one went up the mountain, still sanguine as in youth, but returned no more. On this theme, methinks, I could frame a tale with a deep moral." (Nathaniel Hawthorne, "Sketches from Memory," 1835)

Hawthorne did later write "The Great Carbuncle" (1837), noting that the tale was based on an "Indian tradition."

great Keezer's ghost! An exclamation heard in Maine.

great sufficiency, a Ample, more than enough. "More pie, Ezra?" "No thanks, had a great sufficiency."

green corn (1) Growing corn plants or corn plants cut green for feed. (2) Corn picked when it is milky but before it is completely mature.

green front A Maine state liquor store; so called because such stores once had green fronts. Also *Dr. Green's.*

greenhead (1) See quotes. "And the first greenhead found them. This is a fly that breeds in the salt marshes. It is born with an enormous green head, a taste for salty flesh and a sting like a hot needle." (William Martin, *Cape Cod,* 1991) "Not only mosquitoes and midges and gnats but a curious plentitude of ticks and greenheaded, bloodthirsty flies breed in the marshes and the winding saltwater channels." (John Updike, "Wildlife," in *The Afterlife,* 1994) (2) A name given to the American golden plover (*Pluvialis dominica*) in Massachusetts.

Green Mountain A popular New England potato variety named after Vermont's Green Mountains.

Green Mountain boy A nickname for a Vermonter; originally a member of the Vermont militia organized in 1771.

Green Mountain City A nickname for *Montpelier,* the capital of Vermont.

Green Mountaineer A nickname for a Vermonter.

Green Mountain State A nickname for *Vermont* since the early 19th century. The word Vermont comes from the French for "green mountain."

green sauce Vegetables. "*Green sauce* for *vegetables* I meet in Beaumont and Fletcher . . . and elsewhere." (James Russell Lowell, *The Biglow Papers,* 1867)

green snake A name given to two green snakes (*Opheodrys aestivus* and

Opheodrys vernalis) found in New England.

green to green All's well, there's clear sailing. Originally a nautical term referring to the port and starboard lamps on a sailing ship.

Greenwich Commonly pronounced GREN-itch, or GRIN-itch, but sometimes pronounced GREEN-witch; a Connecticut town.

greezy A pronunciation of "greasy." See GREASY LUCK.

gret Often a pronunciation of "great." "He's got a gre't cur'osity t' see ye . . ." (Oliver Wendell Holmes, *Elsie Venner*, 1861)

griddlecake A pancake or flapjack.

grinder Used chiefly in New England, especially Boston, for what is called *submarine sandwich, hero, hoagie, torpedo, poor boy, Cuban sandwich, wedgy, guinea grinder* and *Dagwood* in other regions. The sandwich filling consists of meats, cheese, lettuce and tomato, when cold, but can be filled with hot meatballs and sauce, eggplant parmigana, and so on. It is made of split loaves of Italian bread. The sandwiches are called grinders because you need a good set of grinders (teeth) to chew them. See WEDGY.

grind one's own bait Do one's own work, do as one pleases, be independent. "I don't want to work for anyone else, I want to grind my own bait."

griping of the gizzard An attack of diarrhea. "He went home with a griping of the gizzard."

groaner (1) A foghorn, because foghorns make a groaning noise; (2) A whistling buoy whose whistles sound like groans.

Groton The Connecticut city's name is properly pronounced *Graton*.

ground bird Heard in Massachusetts for the field sparrow (*Spizella pusilla pusilla*), the song sparrow (*Melospiza melodia melodia*) and the vesper sparrow (*Pooedetes gramineus*), all of which often make their nests on the ground.

grounded out Used in seacoast towns to describe a vessel grounded in the mud at low tide and unable to sail until higher water comes.

ground hemlock Though a misnomer, this is a synonym for the common yew (*Taxus canadensis*), which is not native to the region.

Groundhog Day February 2, when the groundhog is supposed to come out of its hole to evaluate the weather. If it sees its shadow winter will last six weeks more; if it doesn't there will be an early spring.

ground swamp robin Heard especially in Maine as a name for the hermit thrush (*Turdus pallasi*), which often frequents the undergrowth of secluded woods.

grouties, the A general feeling of discomfort, illness. See GROUTY.

grouty Surly, cross, sullen. "Old Black Hoss was awfully grouty about Miry's refusin' Tom Beacon." (Harriet Beecher Stowe, *Sam Lawson's Fireside Stories*, 1872)

Grover's Corners A fictional place in New England often cited as a typical rural town. From Thornton Wilder's play *Our Town* (1938). In the play one character refers to a letter addressed to "Jane Crofut; The Crofut Farm; Grover's Corners; Sutton County; New Hampshire; United States of America . . . Continent of North America; Western Hemisphere; the Earth; the Solar System; the Universe; the Mind of God . . ."

growthy weather An old-fashioned rural term for *good growing weather*. " 'At any rate,' he said, 'it's growthy weather for grass!' " (Annie Trumbull Slosson, "A Local Colorist," 1912)

grue Heard in Maine for a shiver. "It give me a grue."

grunt A fruit pudding or dumpling made with apples or various berries. Said to be so named after the satisfied grunts of those who eat them, or because of the sound the dough makes when it steams.

gudgeon A name given to several little fish of the Cyprinidae family called *golden shiners, silvery minnow* and *killifish* elsewhere.

guess Think, suppose, calculate, reckon. "The northern word 'guess'—imported from England, where it used to be common—is little used among Southerners. They say 'reckon'," wrote Mark Twain in an 1883 letter. Observed James Russell Lowell in *The Biglow Papers* (1867):

> I have never seen any passage adduced where *guess* was used as the Yankee uses it. The word was familiar in the mouths of our [English] ancestors, but with a different shade of meaning from that we have given it, which is something like *rather think,* though the Yankee implies a confident certainty by it when he says, 'I guess I du!' "

gull (1) A pronunciation commonly heard in Boston for *girl*. (2) To gulp food down ravenously, as a gull does. "He gulled his meal in a minute."

gull hunter The jaeger, a smaller bird that attacks large gulls in midair and steals their food, forcing them to drop it as they dive down and then catching the food as it falls.

gullup A belch, or to belch; the word derives from *gulp*. Also *gollup*.

gummer A Maine term for a person who collects spruce gum (used as a chewing gum) in the woods.

gump This word meaning a fool, a stupid person, is recorded in James Russell Lowell's *The Biglow Papers*

(1867) and accounts for the last name of the early comic strip character Andy Gump as well as the last name of the eponymous hero of the 1994 film *Forrest Gump*.

gumption Courage, nerve, guts. "He sure has a lot of gumption."

gumshoe A term heard among older people for *overshoes, galoshes* and *rubbers*.

gum tickler A humorous early expression for a draft of rum or other spirits.

gundalow A kind of scow or barge long used along the New England coast for hauling lumber, salt-marsh hay, coal and other freight, propelled by the tide, poles and a square sail. Few, if any, gundalows operate today. The word is a corruption of "gondola" first recorded in 1733. Also *gundalo*.

gunkhole A *gunkhole* is just a mudhole, in Maine. The word *gunk* is an old Scottish one meaning to hoax or fool. According to the "Sayings of the Oracle" column in *Yankee Magazine* (October 1971), "likely someone once thought they could walk on the mud and it let 'em down."

gunning season The hunting season, when the gunners come out in force, usually in the late fall.

gunshot wedding A synonym for a shotgun wedding, that is, a marriage people are forced into because a child has been conceived.

gurnet Heard chiefly in Maine and Massachusetts for an ocean inlet. No one knows the word's origins, and it is sometimes found in place-names such as *Simons Gurnet* in Maine.

gurried up To be in a mess, all messed up. A figurative use of GURRY.

gurry (1) The remains of fish after cleaning them; fish oil. "He cleaned the fish as he caught them and used the gurry as chum." The origin of the word, first recorded in 1776, is unknown. (2) Refuse or dirt in general.

guyascutus One of the earliest New Englandisms, this amusing Vermont term described a cow with short legs on one side so that it could better walk around the steep Vermont hills. The pronunciation is generally *guy-as-cut-as*.

guzzle A term used in Cape Cod for a small channel between two sandbars of a stream through a marsh.

H

H A letter burned on the hand in early New England for the crime of heresy. See A.

Haavaad accent See the Introduction and HARVARD.

habbage A word that apparently originated in Newfoundland for a rough, cruel dishonest person; possibly a corruption of *savage*.

hackmatack A New England name for several conifers; the name is a corruption of an American Indian designation for the trees. "Here and there was a larch or hackmatack whose roots were used in the old days as knees in building ships and tree nails or wooden pegs." (William O. Douglas, *My Wilderness*, 1961)

hacking and hammering Vacillating, backing and filling; said of someone who won't take a stand on an issue.

Haddam A Connecticut town. Of literary interest because Wallace Stevens in *The Letters of Wallace Stevens* (1966) remarked about its use in his poem "Thirteen Ways of Looking at a Blackbird" (1923): "I just like the name. It is an old whaling town, I believe. In any case, it has a completely Yankee sound."

hadn't oughter Shouldn't. "I hadn't oughter go."

had out Took out. "He had her out last night."

had the pork Gotten in bad trouble. "He knew he had the pork when the game warden showed up."

hagdon A shearwater (of the genus *Puffinus*); a fulmar (*Fulmarus glacialis*). This name for the birds derives from an old British word, its origins unknown.

hahnsome A frequent pronunciation of "handsome." Also *harnsome*.

hail (1) Heard in New England for a catch of fish, the word an old form of "haul." "We caught a good hail of mackerel." (2) A vessel's home port. "Her hail was painted on the stern after her name: Pequod—New Haven." (3) Any address. "He carved his name and hail on the wood." (4) A telephone call. "Give me a hail tomorrow."

haint An old-fashioned rural contraction of "have not." "I haint gone there yet."

haired up Very angry or excited. "He's all haired up."

hairlegger A name, its origin unknown, that early New England fishermen used for *farmer*. New England farmers, in turn, called fishermen *herring chokers.*

hairpin An early term for *crook, liar,* or *cheat.* "That hairpin would cheat his own mother."

hake See MERLAN.

half hours See BOSTON BAKED BEANS.

half the bay over Drunk, though not completely. "He's half the bay over—a few more drinks he'll be over the bay."

Halfway Rock A famous rock formation halfway between Boston Light and Cape Ann onto which fishermen bound for the Grand Banks used to cast pennies for good luck.

Hampton boat A dory-type sailboat often used in lobstering and probably named for Hampton, New Hampshire. "It is the Hampton boat, the reach-boat, the backbone of the profession of lobstering, which is the boat that now most means Maine." (Robert P. Tristram Coffin, *The Yankee Coast,* 1947)

Handkerchief Moody The nickname of eccentric York, Maine pastor Joseph Moody (1700–1753), who for 20 years preached with his back to his congregation. Moody wore a crepe mask when in public. Upon his death it was revealed that he had once accidentally killed a man and was ashamed to be seen. Nathaniel Hawthorne based his short story "The Minister's Black Veil" (1836) on Moody: ". . . [his] face is dust; but awful is still the thought that it mouldered beneath the Black Veil!"

handle A newborn male child is said to have a handle (in reference to its penis). "They put a handle to this one."

handsome Once common for *best clothes.* "I wore my handsome Sunday."

handy as a pocket in a shirt Quoted as a contemporary saying in James Russell Lowell's *The Biglow Papers* (1867).

hangbird The Baltimore oriole, because its nest hangs from the trees.

hanging around This expression meaning to idle or loiter about is possibly the ancestor of "hangout," a place for hanging around, and today's popular phrase *hanging out,* idling about. The *Dictionary of American Slang* gives its origin as the late 19th century, but it is definitely older than this for Oliver Wendell Holmes uses it as a New England expression in his novel *Elsie Venner* (1861), putting it in quotes: "He had been 'hangin' 'raown' Alminy."

hang on by one's eyelids To be in a precarious situation. "I tarred down all the head-stays, but found the rigging about the jib-booms, martingale, and spritsail the hardest. Here you have to hang on with your eyelids and tar with your hands." (Richard Henry Dana, Jr., *Two Years Before the Mast,* 1841)

hang up your boots To die, or to retire from work. It's said that in early times the boots of a riverman who died on the job would be hung on the cross over his grave.

ha'n't Haven't. "Ha'n't I tol' y' a dozen times?' " (Oliver Wendell Holmes, *Elsie Venner,* 1861)

happy as a clam at high tide Very happy and content, like a clam with high water covering it so that most of its enemies can't reach it. Clams are usually dug at low tide. Also *happy as a clam* and *happy as a clam in the mud*. The expression is first recorded in 1834 and is now used throughout the United States. Wrote an anonymous poet over a century ago:

> Happy as a clam, sez you—
> It surely gives me jitters,
> To think my happiness will end
> On a blue plate full of fritters.

happy as a pig in mud Very contented; heard in Massachusetts, but used in other regions as well.

happy as bean water Once a common New England simile, but rarely, if ever, heard anymore.

hard day's work makes a soft bed, a An old New England saying.

hard fisted A synonym for *tightfisted*; stingy, mean, cheap.

hardhack *Spiraea tomentosa,* a flowering plant also called *steeple-bush*.

hard pushed Hard-pressed, pressured, short of money. "I'm hard pushed for cash this month."

hardscrabble A bread pudding made from brown bread, butter and cream. Imogene Wolcott's *The New England Yankee Cookbook* (1939) also calls it *brown bread brewis*.

hardshell clam The common quahog (*Venus mercenaria*); from Narragansett Bay eastward it is usually called the *quahog*.

hard wood In days past, woods that decayed relatively quickly, such as beech, birch and maple, were called *hard wood* in Maine, while they were called *light wood* in the South and West. Oak, generally considered a hard wood today, wasn't so regarded at the time.

hark! Be still, keep quiet, listen. "Hark, hark, the dogs do bark!" as my grandmother used to say.

harker Someone or something fine or strong. Given as a common expression in George Allen England, "Rural Locutions of Maine and Northern New Hampshire," *Dialect Notes,* Vol. IV (1914).

harness bull A bull trained to pull a buggy, so that his owner could drive him to the animal's well-paid matings with cows.

harness cask A wooden barrel once used on sailing ships for preserving salted meat. "Before any of the beef is put into the harness-cask, the steward comes up, and picks it all over, and takes out the best pieces." (Richard Henry Dana, Jr., *Two Years Before the Mast*, 1840) The black hoops on the barrels resembled harness straps, giving them their name, or they may be so named because each barrel was attached to the deck through four horseshoes nailed to its side. The meat in them may have been called *salt-horse* because of these associations with horses.

harry wicket The yellow-shafted flicker *Colaptes auratus,* because the bird's cry sounds like *harry wicket, harry wicket.*

harsh See HASH.

Harvard Frequently pronounced Hahvard. "He was a real Hahvard, by which we outlanders meant graduate of Harvard College with a broad *a.*" (William Alexander Percy, *Lanterns on the Levee*, 1941) Harvard, the first institution of higher learning in North America, has since 1637, three years after its founding, borne the name of John Harvard (1607–1638), an English minister who lived for a time in Charlestown, Massachusetts and later willed the fledgling university half his estate and his library of over 400 books. Cambridge, Massachusetts, where Harvard University is located, was named for England's Cambridge University. It was originally called Newe Towne. See the Introduction.

Harvard accent A name sometimes given to the Boston and New England accent. See the Introduction.

Harvard beets *Harvard beets,* often called pickled beets, are made from sliced beets cooked in sugar, cornstarch, vinegar and water. There is no record that the dish was invented at Harvard University, but it is said that the unknown chef who did invent it named it after the resemblance of color of the deep-red beets to the crimson jersies of the then-vaunted Harvard football team.

Harvard University See HARVARD.

Harwich Pronounced HAR-witch or, less formally, HAR-itch; a town on Cape Cod, Massachusetts.

has a screw loose Is crazy, eccentric; apparently this common saying had its origins in New England, as perhaps did the similar expressions in the following quote. "They have different names for sech folks. They say they're 'cracked', they've 'got a screw loose,' they're 'a little off,' they 'ain't all there,' and so on." (Annie Trumbull Slosson, *A Local Colorist and Other Stories*, 1912)

has no more suavity than a swine Recorded as a Maine expression in Marion Nicholl Rawson, *From Here to Yender,* 1932.

hash A frequent pronunciation of "harsh."

has his sitting britches on Used to describe someone who won't go home, or won't go on about his or her business, who sits and sits and talks and talks, often while he or she drinks and drinks.

haslet The viscera (heart, liver, etc.) of a slaughtered pig. Also *harslet*. Sometimes used in the threat "I'll bust yer haslet out."

hasn't got a snowball's chance in hell Has no chance at all; heard in other regions as well.

hassock A small hump of thick grass growing in a marsh or swamp. *Hummock* is used more often.

has too many shingles to the weather Such a person is trying to do too many things at one time.

hasty pudding John Bartlett in his *Dictionary of Americanisms* (1859) defines this as "Indian meal stirred into boiling water until it becomes a thick batter or pudding . . . eaten with milk, butter, and sugar or molasses." It is mentioned in a verse of the Revolutionary War song "Yankee Doodle": "Father and I went down to camp, / Along wi' Captain Goodin, / and there we see the men and boys, / As thick as *hasty puddin'*." But its most famous mention is in Joel Barlow's mock epic *The Hasty Pudding* (1793), which the poet wrote in a Savoyard inn in France when he was served a dish of boiled Indian meal that reminded him of Connecticut. Part of it goes:

Thy name is Hasty Pudding! thus
  our sires
Were wont to greet thee fuming
  from their fires;
And while they argued in thy just
  defence,

With logic clear they thus explain'd
  the sense:
"In *haste* 't is serv'd; and then in
  equal *haste*,
With cooling milk, we make the
  sweet repast."
Such is thy name, significant and
  clear,
A name, a sound to every Yankee
  dear.

hatchway doors Sloping cellar doors on the outside of a house.

Hat City of the World, the An old name for Danbury, Connecticut, where numerous hat factories were located and many "mad hatters" suffered from the tremor known as the *hatter's shakes*, caused by the mercury used in the making of felt hats.

hatter's shakes See HAT CITY OF THE WORLD, THE.

have a brick in one's hat To be drunk. According to Mainer Timothy W. Robinson (*American Speech,* April 1948): "At the time [matches] were made so that one using them had to have a brick to scratch them on, and the saying was that he carried a brick in his hat, so when anyone had been to the store [for liquor] and walked a little crooked, the boys would say 'he had a brick in his hat.' " This may or may not be the origin of the New England expression, but it is an old one—Longfellow used it in his poem *Kavanagh* (1849).

have a great good mind to To have a strong inclination to. "I have a great good mind to leave you here by yourself."

have an edge on To be drunk. Pronounced *aidge* in Maine.

haven't seen you in an age of years Haven't seen you in a very long time.

haven't seen you since the Concord fight Haven't seen you for a very long time. The reference is to the Battle of Concord and Lexington on April 19, 1775, when the American Minute Men, with local Yankee militia, fired the shot heard round the world at the British Redcoats.

have one's head in a bucket, to To be led by the nose, easily controlled. From the practice of putting a pail over the head of pigs to ease them on freight cars.

have one's high-heeled shoes, to An expression commonly used a century ago for a conceited woman; to be conceited, stuck-up. "To say of a woman that she 'has on her *high-heeled shoes* is to intimate that she sets herself up as a person of more consequence than others allow her to be . . . that she is 'stuck up.' " (John Bartlett, *Dictionary of Americanisms,* 1859) Infrequently said of men as well. Also *to have on one's high-heeled slippers.*

have one's nose broke, to An old-fashioned expression used to describe a child who has to relinquish his or her place as the youngest in a family when a baby is born to his or her parents.

Haverhill Pronounced HAY-vril, or HAY-vir-ill; towns in Massachusetts and New Hampshire.

have the horrors An old expression meaning to be in low spirits, have the blues.

have the luck of Hiram Smith A historical expression meaning very unlucky; after Hiram Smith, the only soldier killed in the Aroostook War of 1836 to 1839.

have the stouts An old expression meaning to be conceited, too cocksure.

Hawkins' whetstone See quote. "Hawkins's whetstone: rum; in derision of one Hawkins, a well-known temperance lecturer." (James Russell Lowell, *The Biglow Papers,* 1867)

haycap A covering for haystacks or formerly, other crops as well. Also called a *Dutch cap.* "The white haycaps, drawn over small stacks of beans or corn in the fields on account of the rain, were a novel sight to me." (Henry David Thoreau, *The Maine Woods,* 1864)

hayfield lobsterman A farmer who works at lobstering.

hayburner A humorous term for a horse, especially an old nag.

haystack A term used in whitewater canoeing for a dome-shaped wave created by the rush of the water and the topography of the riverbed.

heared Sometimes used for *heard*. "I've heared a good deal of talk." (Oliver Wendell Holmes, *The Professor at the Breakfast Table*, 1860)

hearn Once common in rural areas for *heard*. "I hearn that he's selling his place."

heater piece The New England name for the corner piece of land that results when two streets intersect at an acute angle, so called because its three-sided shape resembles that of a flat iron (or heater piece). "They slipped [the small house] along as if it had been a handsled . . . and left it settin' there right on the heater piece." (Sara Orne Jewett, "Miss Debby," 1883)

heave and haul See quote. ". . . down our way, in August and September and early October, to 'heave and haul' means to cast for bluefish from the beach with a hand line and it does not mean anything else." (Joseph C. Lincoln, *Cape Cod Yesterdays*, 1935)

heavens to Betsy! An exclamation of surprise, joy or even annoyance.

Possibly the phrase was known in Revolutionary War days, but I doubt it. Nor do I think, as some friends have suggested, that it pertained in any way to the maker of the first American flag, Betsy Ross. It is much more likely to have been derived in some way from the frontiersman's rifle or gun which, for unknown reasons, he always fondly called Betsy. However, despite exhaustive search, I am reluctantly forced to resort to the familiar lexicographical locution, 'Source unknown.' " (Charles Earle Funk, *Heavens to Betsy and Other Curious Sayings*, 1955)

In his book Mr. Funk devotes a full two pages to the expression's possible origins.

heavy cook See FRESH COOK.

heavy dictionary Used to describe a big or unabridged dictionary. "He opened the heavy dictionary."

heavy water The main current in a body of water.

he (she) couldn't carry a tune in a basket A Maine expression meaning someone can't sing.

he-cow An old euphemism for *bull*; also called *he-creature*.

hedgehog A term heard frequently in New England for *porcupine*, because the European hedgehog has quills similar to those of the North American porcupine.

he doesn't know beans when the bag's untied He's really stupid or ignorant, can't identify beans when he sees them.

he (she) don't know whether he's afoot or ahossback He or she is very puzzled, is in a quandary, or doesn't have any common sense.

heel tap The end slice of a loaf of bread, the heel.

hellbent for election Very fast. " 'Then I tore out of his fist and pelted into the brambles, hellbent for election.' " (Stephen King, *Dolores Claiborne,* 1993)

hell-bent n' crooked In a quick, excited and disorderly way. "He lit out after him hell-bent and crooked." Given as a common expression by George Allen England, "Rural Locutions of Maine and Northern New Hampshire," *Dialect Notes,* Vol. IV (1914).

hell to pay and no pitch hot A fouled-up situation, a bad predicament. Originally a nautical term referring to a bad leak in a boat when there was no hot pitch to patch it with. Also *the devil to pay and no hot pitch.*

help Used mostly in New England to refer to a hired laborer or servant, but is heard in other regions as well.

helpkeeper Once commonly used for *housekeeper.*

hen-hussy A derogatory name common a century ago for a man overly concerned with household duties.

hennery A henhouse. Also called *hen roost.*

hen roost See HENNERY.

hen tight See COW-TIGHT.

he (she) pries up the sun with a crowbar Said of someone who rises long before sunrise each morning. Cited as a common New England saying in *The Old Farmer's Almanack* (1946).

her Sometimes used for "she." "Him and her has the prettiest baby."

herdie A historical term for a small horse-drawn carriage invented in about 1880 by American Peter Herdie and often used as a taxi.

herd's grass A New England name for Timothy grass (*Phleum pratense*) and redtop (*Agrostis stolonifera major*); possibly named after someone named Herd.

here This place. "Do you like here?"

here's to swimmin' with bowlegged wimmin Is this a humorous New England toast? Possibly. It is given by Captain Quint in the movie version of Peter Benchley's *Jaws,* set in New England.

hermit A chewy homemade cookie often filled with raisins and dates.

hern Hers. "His heart kep' goin' pitypat, but hern went pity zekle." (James Russell Lowell, *The Biglow Papers,* 1866)

Herod all handsaws! A euphemistic oath meaning "God Almighty!"

herring bird The phalarope (*Boreal phalaropes*).

herringbone fence A rail fence made of split rails.

herring-choker A name applied to Prince Edward Islanders in Maine and New Hampshire, and a derogatory term for Scandinavians in other regions. Also applied to any French Canadian and to those from all the Maritime provinces. The name was given to these people because they were said to eat so many herring that they choked on the bones. Cited as a common term in George Allen England, "Rural Locutions of Maine and Northern New Hampshire," *Dialect Notes*, Vol. IV (1914).

he's got short arms and long pockets Heard by the author on one occasion in Connecticut as a description of someone very cheap, whose arms don't reach the pockets where he keeps his money.

he's (she's) got an unfinished attic Used in Massachusetts to describe a stupid person.

he's (she's) so contrary he (she) could float upstream A Vermont description of a very stubborn person.

he's (she's) the whole team and the little dog under the wagon He's (she's) a one-person operation, the whole show. Cited as a Vermont expression in Charles Edward Crane's *Let Me Show You Vermont*, 1937, but the term had had wide currency throughout New England and was cited as a New England saying in James Russell Lowell's *The Biglow Papers* (1867).

hickory An adjective old-timers in Massachusetts and Martha's vineyard use for *rough, tough*. "He's all hickory."

hide and coop An old name for the children's game *hide and seek* in New Hampshire.

hidey-hole Hiding place. " '[We] could play hide-and-go-seek the whole day long, and not use the same hidey-hole twice.' " (George V. Higgins, *The Mandeville Talent*, 1991)

highbush blueberry Any cultivated blueberry species, as opposed to species growing in the wild. So called because the cultivated varieties are much taller.

high check rein behavior Behavior that is snobbish, pretentious. Refers to check reins, a part of the reins that forces a horse to hold its head very high.

high hook The angler among a group of fishermen who catches the most fish or the largest fish. "The three of us went out at dawn and Tom was the high hook with a four-pounder." Also used on commercial fishing vessels.

highlander A word used chiefly by Maine fishermen for *farmer* or *woodsman*.

high time Long overdue, the time to do something before the best time for doing it passes forever. "It was high time / Those oats were cut, said Isaac . . ." (Edward Arlington Robinson, "Isaac and Archibald," *Captain Craig*, 1902)

highty tighty Said of someone pretentious or haughty. Pronounced hoity toity in the rest of the country. " 'Highty tighty,' said the elder matron, '[some people] remember when the hull family [ate] out of airthenware [earthenware] bowls . . ." (Rowland Robinson, "The Paring Bee," 1900)

highway patrol A Maine road repair gang.

hill countryman A name old rural New Hampshire residents often called themselves. " 'The cities are all right for them who want them . . . But I'm a hill countryman . . . I've had my life and I've spent it among these hills and it's here among them I'm going to sleep. It's hard to say what I feel, but men who like the hills will know what I mean." (Hayden Pearson, *New England Flavor*, 1961)

him (her) and wuk (work) has had a fallin' out Said of a very lazy person. Given as a common expression in George Allen England, "Rural Locutions of Maine and Northern New Hampshire," *Dialect Notes*, Vol. IV (1914).

hinder See INSTEAD.

hindside Once heard on Cape Cod for *behind*. "It's hindside the shed."

hind side to A euphemism for *ass-backward*.

hinny The buttocks or backside.

hired money An old expression dating back to the 18th century meaning to borrow money, paying interest. "You hired the money, you'll have to pay it back."

his (her) head looks as if it has worn out two bodies Said of someone old and wrinkled. Given as a Vermont expression in Charles Edward Crane's *Let Me Show You Vermont* (1937).

his name is Dennis He is finished, has had it, is fired. The old term, rarely used anymore, derives from the whaling expression *Dennis* that meant a harpooned whale spouting blood and likely to be taken. Why such whales were named Dennis is not known.

hist Hoist. "Grandmother histed the cover off the dish."

hist-a-boy! An exclamation used in setting a dog on an animal. "And cry Hist-a-boy to every good dog." (Ralph Waldo Emerson, "Illusions," 1841)

hit between the face and the eyes The preferred expression in Maine for *hit squarely in the face*.

Hitchcock chair Any style chair designed or made by Lambert Hitchcock (1795–1852) in his Barkhamsted, Connecticut factory. Hitchcock chairs come in a variety of designs and sizes, but were characterized by strong legs, curved-top backs and seats that were wider in the front than in the back. The chair maker won such renown that Barkhamsted renamed itself Hitchcocksville in his honor, although the town changed its name again to Riverton in 1866.

hitch horses To get married. "An' so we fin'lly made it up, concluded to hitch horses." (James Russell Lowell, *The Biglow Papers,* 1862)

hitch your wagon to a star Set your goals high. Famous words written by Ralph Waldo Emerson in *Society and Solitude* (1870).

hit the felt Go to sleep. Felt once was widely used for blankets in lumber camps.

hither an' yen See quote. "The Yankee says 'hither an' yen' for 'to and fro.' " (James Russell Lowell, *The Biglow Papers,* 1867)

hoarsed up Hoarse. "A cold had me all hoarsed up."

hobby A hobby horse or a pet project or idea. "Each member [of Bronson Alcott's Fruitlands community] was allowed to mount his favorite hobby and ride it to his heart's content. Very queer were some of the riders, and very rampant some of the hobbies." (Louisa May Alcott, "Transcendental Wild Oats," 1876)

ho-cake Not a cake made on a hoe, but a meal of parched corn made in New England since colonial times. It derives from the Indian name *noke-hick* for the parched corn.

hoe out To clean out a room or anyplace. "I want you to hoe out that room by noon."

hog age A Nantucketism of old meaning between boyhood and manhood.

hog Howard A colonial town official in New England whose duty it was to collect stray pigs. Also called *hog-reeve* or *hog-ward.*

hog Latin Pig Latin, a simple secret language long used by children to confuse others. It usually consists of the addition of *ery* preceded by the hard *g* sound to each word; thus *Wiggery youggery gogerry wiggery miggery* means "Will you go with me?"

hog's back son-of-a-bitch A name, probably nautical in origin, for a dish of boiled salt codfish topped with pork scraps. It is no relation to the Western dish *son-of-a-bitch stew.*

hog-tied & weary A nickname for the HT&W railroad, whose initials actually stood for the Hoosac Tunnel and Wilmington Railroad. Variations were the *Hoot, Toot & Whistle* and the *Hot Tea & Whiskey.* Noted in

Archie Robinson, *Slow Train to Yesterday* (1945).

hog walnut A synonym for the pig walnut of the pignut hickory tree (*Carya glabra*). It is not the walnut but the hickory nut that is a favorite of pigs.

hold her, Newt! An expression used when anyone (a Jim, Phil, Carol, Irene, etc.) is trying to keep something under control, especially a horse, wagon or car. Who the original Newt was, if there was one, is anybody's guess.

hold one's tongue Be quiet, not speak. An old New England expression widely used today. " '. . . I don't see's there's much difference between the Fromes up at the farm and the Fromes down in the graveyard; 'cept that down there they're all quiet, and the women have got to hold their tongues.' " (Edith Wharton, *Ethan Frome,* 1911)

hold the thought To make a mental note of something that can't be acted upon or discussed immediately. "Hold the thought, we'll talk about it later."

hole A small deep bay, such as Wood's Hole, Massachusetts or any deep place in the water.

holiday A spot missed in painting or other jobs such as dusting; the spots are called *holidays* because the painter, duster or whomever did not work on them.

hollow See CORNER.

holt Hold. "I got a holt on it and pulled it toward me."

Holyoke The place-name is pronounced HULL-yoke by local residents, but HOLY-oke elsewhere in Massachusetts.

holy old mackinaw! A common expletive among loggers in the Maine woods.

holy poke Bread dough formed into large, round balls and deep fried. Imogene Wolcott in *The New England Yankee Cookbook* (1939) says that holy pokes are called *huff jiffs* in Maine and *Baptist bread* in other parts of New England.

holy sailor, call the water! An old exclamation of surprise whose origins are unknown.

home correction Wife or child beating.

"No one calls it home correction anymore—the term has passed right out of conversation, so far as I can tell, and good riddance—but I grew up [in the 1940s] with the idear that when women and children step off the straight n' narrow, it's a man's job to herd them back onto it. I ain't tryin' to tell you that just because I grew up with the idear, I thought it was right, though . . ." (Stephen King, *Dolores Claiborne,* 1993)

homely as a stone fence A simile heard in Vermont and New Hampshire.

homely enough to stop a down train
Very ugly. Mainly a Vermont saying, with variants such as *homely as hell is wicked* and *homely as a stone fence*.

home of the bean and the cod Boston, from the poem by John Collins Bossidy given as a toast at the Holy Cross Alumni Midwinter Dinner in 1910: "And this is good old Boston, / The home of the bean and the cod, / Where the Lowells talk to the Cabots, / And the Cabots talk only to God."

honeypot Used chiefly in Maine for a mucky hole in the ground that one can sink down deep into, or for a soft clay spot under the sand on a beach. "Most of them . . . dyke marshes have what you call 'honey pots' in 'em; that is a deep hole . . . where you can't find no bottom. Well, every now and then, when a feller goes to look for his horse, he sees his tail a stickin' right out . . . from one of these honey pots, and wavin' like a head of broom corn . . ." (Thomas Haliburton, *The Clockmaker*, 1838)

honeysuckle A name for *red clover*, whose blossoms people sucked for nectar, though the name is applied to other clovers as well.

honeysuckle apple A fungus that grows on the branches of the false honeysuckle (*Rhododendron nudiflorum*) and has the crisp cool juicy taste of an apple but is not sweet or flavorful.

honey wagons A truck used to empty cesspools. "[He] leaned against the truck, one of those big red tankers with a shit-covered hose squirming like a tail out the back and a smell that seemed to be rusting the paint from the inside. On Cape Cod they called them honey wagons." (William Martin, *Cape Cod*, 1991)

honk To move along rapidly; probably after the sound of a car's horn. "She was honking on down the road."

honker Another word for *anything large*. "That was some honker of a deer."

honor jar A jar put out at country farmstands whose operators trust customers to pay for produce on their own. The system usually works well, customers even honestly making change for themselves from the jar.

hooby A name used chiefly by Irish Americans around Boston for a large rock too heavy to be lifted by one person.

Hoodsie A trademarked name for a paper cup of ice cream sold in the Boston area since the 1920s by H.P. Hood and Sons dairy. "We all bought Hoodsies and ate them on the bus."

hoojee An old term used on the Maine coast for a really dirty or frightening tramp.

hook Jack To play hookey; used mainly in the Boston area, the term dates back to the 1860s. "As often as we could we boys played hook Jack from school."

hooraw's nest Said of anything very disordered, disorganized. Originally a sea term whose origin is unknown. "Your room is a regular hooraw's nest."

hoper See quote. "We are not 'hopers,' Irish who go to bed hoping that when they wake up they will be Yankees." (Alice Hennessy, vice president of the West Roxbury, Massachusetts Historical Society, as quoted in the *New York Times,* July 22, 1986)

hope to die and cross my throat To swear, to affirm that one is telling the truth. " 'No, honest now, twant nothin' but jest that,' affirmed Plupy, 'hope to die and cross my throat,' he added, drawing his fingers crosswise over his skinny neck, which with the boys was then and may possibly be now the most solemn oath possible." (Henry A. Shute, *Plupy,* 1910)

horned gentleman, the An old name for *devil.* "Uplifting his ace, he hit the horned gentleman such a blow on the head, as not only demolished him, but the treasure-seeker also . . ." (Nathaniel Hawthorne, "Peter Goldthwait's Treasure," 1838)

horning A noisy mock serenade for newlyweds; used mainly in western New England.

horns Often used to mean "a deer's antlers."

horribles See ANTIQUES AND HORRIBLES.

horrt A pronunciation of "heart." " 'Here's Flud Oirson, fur horrd horrt, / Torr'd an' futherr'd an corr'd in a corrt / By the women o' Morble'ead.' " (John Greenleaf Whittier, "Skipper Ireson's Ride," 1828)

horse clogs Four round pieces of hardwood attached to a horse's hooves enabling the animal to walk better on soggy soils such as marshes.

horse corn The tough field corn fed to livestock.

horse dressing A euphemism for *horse manure.*

horsefeathers! Another euphemism for *horseshit!* A statement expressing disbelief, this word has been around at least since 1925. It may or may not be related to the term *horsefeathers* once used in carpentry, which were the large feathering strips used in roofing and siding houses. How these *horsefeathers* came to be a euphemism for "horseshit!" is not clear—unless it came easily to some roofer's tongue when he had half said "horseshit" and a lady abruptly appeared upon the scene. On the other hand, *horsefeathers* may have first been a synonym for "nonsense," originating with a saying such as "That's nonsense, that's like saying horses have feathers!"

horsefoot See HORSESHOE CRAB.

horse-mackerel A name heard in New England for *bluefin tuna,* which is nicknamed the "chicken of the sea."

horseshoe crab A name used in New England, New York and other areas for what is less frequently called the king crab (*Linulus polyphemus*), which is not a true crab but a relative of the spider. An old New England name for the horsehoe crab is the *horsefoot crab.*

horsehoe violet The bird's-foot violet (*viola pedata*) of Massachusetts.

hosey To claim or reserve something. The term is used chiefly in Maine and in the Boston area. "I hosey that chair."

hot (1) A Mainism for drunk or half drunk. "It's only noontime and he's hot already." (2) A pronunciation commonly heard in Boston for *heart.* "He had a bee-ad (bad) hot."

hot as a red wagon Very drunk. Given in George Allen England, "Rural Locuations of Maine and Northern New Hampshire," *Dialect Notes,* Vol. IV (1914).

hot ass A guessing game played among lumberjacks in which a circle was formed and a blindfolded person put in the middle. He was swatted hard on the rear end and had to guess who in the circle hit him, remaining in the circle until he did; thereupon the identified swatter took his place. Also called *hot back.*

hot as the Devil's kitchen Extremely hot. Quoted as a contemporary saying by James Russell Lowell in *The Biglow Papers* (1867).

hot cross bun A sweet bun filled with raisins and marked on the top with a white frosting cross. Imogene Wolcott's A *New England Yankee Cookbook* (1939) says they go "good at church suppers." Such Lenten buns were, of course, not invented in New England; they date back to 16th-century England.

hot-me-tot A term used in Maine meaning someone who is always in a state of agitation; the expression possibly derives from *hot-to-trot.* "He's what we call a hot-me-tot."

hotter'n a skunk (1) Very drunk. See HOT. (2) Said of very hot weather or anything extremely hot.

hotter'n love in hayin' time Extremely hot. Cited as a common expression in George Allen England, "Rural Locutions of Maine and Northern New Hampshire," *Dialect Notes,* Vol. IV (1914). See HOT.

hotter than a Methodist Hell About as hot as it can get; an expression used chiefly in Maine.

hot-top To pave with asphalt. "If it was up to you . . . you'd fill the cracks and hot-top the beach." (William Martin, *Cape Cod,* 1991)

house Often pronounced *haouse* in Maine, Vermont and other areas, just as *round* is pronounced *raound* and *down* is pronounced *daown*. "I suppose this vowel twisting was a direct inheritance from certain counties in England where it can still be noted; but I think to some extent our twisting has been deliberate—a sort of contemptuous effort of the Yankee to show he was not of the aristocracy, but good common folk." (Charles Edward Crane, *Let Me Show You Vermont*, 1937)

housen An ancient Cornish word for *house* said to be used commonly in 19th-century Cape Cod, according to Shebnah Rich's *Truro-Cape Cod* (1884).

house names In *Memories of My Boyhood Days in Nantucket* (1923), Joseph Farnum writes of the "unique, catchy, original and forcefully cute titles . . ." given to many of the old houses there by "a hardy farmer and fishermen people of days long agone." He remembers, among many others, such house names as *Takitezie, In and Out, Bigenough, Nonetoobig, House of Lords, Seldomin, Thimble Castle* and *Waldorf Astoria, Jr.*

house with lungs, the See quote. "There's a [Newport, Rhode Island] house [the Wyckoff House] that the famous Italian architect, Dr. Lorenzo Latta, has called the most beautiful house in New England—and the healthiest. Built in the nineteenth century, too. He called it 'The House That Breathes,' 'The House With Lungs.' " (Thornton Wilder, *Theophilus North*, 1937)

hovel A shed for cows or chickens.

how? See quote. "Haow?—said the divinity-student. He coloured . . . A country-boy . . . caught a little too old not to carry some marks of his earlier ways of life . . . Gentlemen in fine linen, and scholars in large libraries, taken by surprise, or in a careless moment, will sometimes let slip a word they knew as boys in homespun and have not spoken since that time—but it lay there under all their culture. That is one way you may know the country-boys after they have grown rich or celebrated—*haow* means *what*." (Oliver Wendell Holmes, *The Professor at the Breakfast Table*, 1860)

how are they crawlin'? Fish "run" but lobsters "crawl" in Maine. A lobsterman wanting to know how good the lobstering is in a certain area will ask, "How are they crawlin'?"

how be you? Heard in Maine and other areas for *how are you?*

how much tobacco have you got? See quote. ". . . a notorious romancer is often interrupted [by the whalers] in the midst of a thrilling story, with the inquiry, 'How much tobacco have you got?' meaning, 'How much can you give us to believe it? We'll believe anything, if you've got tobacco enough to put it through.' " (William Hussey Macy, *There She Blows*, 1877)

how they actin'? How are the fish biting?

Hub, the A nickname for *Boston*. The name possibly originated from all the roads leading into the city like spokes to the hub of a wheel. However, in *The Autocrat of the Breakfast Table* (1858), Oliver Wendell Holmes writes of a young man who told him he had heard that "Boston State-House is the hub of the solar system." Holmes replied that to the residents of every other town or city, "the axis of the earth sticks out visibly through the center of each." He concludes that "Boston is just like other places of its size—only, perhaps, considering its excellent fish market, paid fire-department, superior monthly publications, and correct habit of spelling the English language, it has some right to look down on the mob of cities . . ." Also *hub of the universe*.

hubbard squash A noted squash variety named for Mrs. Elizabeth Hubbard, the Massachusetts woman who first cultivated it over a century ago.

hubbly Used to describe rough uneven dirt roads with frozen ruts. "The road was all hubbly."

hubbub The word *hubbub* used to mean "loud noise or din" probably comes from a Celtic word meaning the same, but the word also was used by New England colonists to describe a Native American game:

Chiefs who have seen eighty snows look on stoically while the young men strike on the beach a wooden bowl containing five flat pieces of bone, black on one side and white on the other; as the bones bound and fall, white or black, the game is decided; the players sit in a circle making a deafening noise—*hub, hub,* "come, come", from which it was called hubbub. (Katherine M. Abbott, *Old Paths and Legends of New England,* 1904)

hub of the universe See HUB.

huck A word used by Mainers for *foot* or *shoe*. "My huck got stuck in the muck."

huckabuck towel A linen or cotton towel with a rough surface and of a special weave. "[It was] a huckabuck towel." (Edith Wharton, *Ethan Frome,* 1911)

huddle An old-time name for *dance* or *ball* cited in William F. Macy, *The Nantucket Scrap Basket* (1916).

huddup Giddup, to a horse or cow. " 'Huddup! said the parson. Off they went." (Oliver Wendell Holmes, "The Deacon's Masterpiece," 1858)

huff-puffs The Maine name for small balls of raised bread dough fried in deep fat; they are called *holy pokes* in Connecticut and *Baptist bread* elsewhere.

huge paw A colorful term for *laborer* or *farmer* that is said to have been coined by Daniel Webster.

hugger Disorderly, jumbled. "Till having failed at hugger farming / He burned his house down for the fire insurance." (Robert Frost, "The Star-Splitter," 1923)

hull A pronunciation of "whole." ". . . the hull town can hear the yelling and screaming from those schoolyards.' " (Thornton Wilder, *Our Town*, 1938)

Hullahwee tribe, the A name given by Maine natives to out-of-state hunters, fishers and campers.

hulled corn Called *hominy* in the South, this is dried corn kernels with the hulls removed and boiled until ready to eat. Also called *samp*.

hull koboodle, the The whole caboodle, the whole thing, entire group. Variations on the old-fashioned expression are *the hull kit and bilin'* and *the hull kit an tolie*.

Hull-yoke See HOLYOKE.

hum A pronunciation of "home" heard primarily in Maine. "He hummed 'Hum sweet Hum.' "

humbug A peppermint-flavored taffy candy dating back to the early 19th century.

humbugs See BOSTON BAKED BEANS.

humdurgan A large stone tied in the crotch of a tree on shore to serve as a boat's anchor. Also called *killick*.

humility (1) A name for the wilet (*Symphemia semipalmata*), perhaps because of its bowing movements. The name is also applied to several other birds. (2) A nickname given to the snipe (*Gallinago gallinago*) for over three centuries in New England, because of the long-billed bird's bowing habit or because it "probes for worms in the humble mud," as one ornithologist put it.

hummock Used in New England and other regions for *small hill* or *knoll*.

hummer Any bad guy or generally unworthwhile person with some saving grace, such as a sense of humor.

hungry as a graven image Quoted as a contemporary saying in James Russell's Lowell's *The Biglow Papers* (1867).

hungry enough to eat a boiled owl Starving, hungry enough to eat almost anything.

husband Once used aboard New England sailing ships for the man in charge of all business affairs.

hurrup! A command for a horse to start moving or go faster. A corruption of "hurry up!"

husher A crocheted piece fitted over a chamber pot cover so that the chamber pot could be used quietly, especially at night.

hush-up-with-you Be quiet, shut up. " 'Ma, I hate that dress.' 'Oh, hush-up-with-you.' " (Thornton Wilder, *Our Town,* 1938)

husking A party held at harvest time to strip ears of corn from their husks. Also called a *husking bee*.

hyper Hurry, move quickly. " 'I mus' hyper about an' git tea.' " (James Russell Lowell, *The Biglow Papers,* 1866)

hyper out-a there Run, go quickly. Given as a common expression in George Allen England, "Rural Locutions of Maine and Northern New Hampshire," *Dialect Notes,* Vol. IV (1914). Also *hiker out-a there.*

I

I Those convicted of incest in colonial New England were sentenced, according to a 1734 law, to wear a capital *I* "two inches long and of a proper proportionate bigness, cut out in cloth of a contrary color to his coat, and sewed upon his upper garment on the outside of his arm, or upon his back in open view."

I bought his thumb An old-fashioned expression meaning that someone is sure a storekeeper was cheating by pressing his or her thumb on the scales when weighing something.

Ichabod A name given to Daniel Webster by John Greenleaf Whittier in his 1850 poem of that title, which expresses the Abolitionists' disappointment with Webster's support of the Compromise of 1850. "Ichabod" means inglorious in Hebrew. Webster figures in much New England history, including Stephen Vincent Benét's famous story "The Devil and Daniel Webster."

icebound A word used to describe a cold, reserved person unable to care or show emotion. *Icebound* was the title of a 1922 Pulitzer Prize-winning play by Maine playwright Owen Davis about the tight-lipped, "icebound" Jordan family in Veazie, Maine.

ice-cream shot In summer hunting camps, ice cream was made in large wooden tubs filled with ice and salt. After use, this ice and salt was dumped in the woods, and often attracted deer. Deer occupied with such treats made easy targets, and shots taken at them came to be called *ice-cream shots,* a term soon applied to any easy shot.

ice storm A winter storm in which rain freezes on and bejewels all it touches, though often causing trees or tree limbs to break and fall. "We have days in January, after an ice-storm, when living in Maine is living inside a diamond with all the walls cut and polished so they flame." (Robert P. Tristam Coffin, *Yankee Coast,* 1947)

idear Heard along the New England coast as a pronunciation of "idea."

idee Often heard since early times as a pronunciation of "idea."

if you don't like the New England weather, just wait a minute A saying referring to the mercurial nature of New England weather attributed to Mark Twain, who despite his many years in the region, never got used to the weather.

if you're a mind If you care to, if you feel like it or want to. " 'You come over, if you're a mind.' " (Stephen King, *Pet Sematary,* 1983)

I guess Often used to mean "without a doubt." "Do you like her?" "Like her? I guess. No one compares."

I guide The state motto of Maine.

I just ate chagrin A Maine saying expressing embarrassment over a faux pas; recorded in Marion Nicholl Rawson, *From Here to Yender* (1932).

I'll be blowed! An old-fashioned euphemistic exclamation.

I'll be buggered! A common curse that probably originated among seamen.

I'll be danged! A euphemism for *I'll be damned!*

I'll be dinged! Another euphemism for *I'll be damned!*

I'll be jiggered! An old-fashioned exclamation not heard much anymore.

I'll be vummed! Still another euphemism for *I'll be damned!*

I'll bust yer haslet out! A violent threat; *haslet* means intestines or guts. Given as a common expression in George Allen England, "Rural Locutions of Maine and Northern New Hampshire," *Dialect Notes,* Vol. IV (1914).

ill news flies fast See quote. " 'Ill news flies fast, they say,' thought Dominicus Pike; 'but this beats rail-roads." (Nathaniel Hawthorne, "Mr. Higginbotham's Catastrophe," 1834)

I'll take the longboat and go ashore An old nautical expression used by mariners wanting to back out of an argument or other difficult situation.

I'm doing nicely I'm doing very well, thank you; I've no complaints.

improved Once a common synonym for an occupied house, an unoccupied house being *unimproved.*

improvement The conclusion of a sermon, especially a long-winded one.

in a bit of a tight Being in trouble. "He had . . . come across to see if he could help when it seemed they were 'in a bit of a tight.' " (Stephen King, *Pet Sematary,* 1983)

in a pucker Heard in Maine for *mad, angry.* "He's still in a pucker over what she did last month."

in a terrible wacket A Mainism meaning in an awful hurry.

in a tickle Heard in Isleboro, off the Maine coast, for in a happy mood.

in a tight place See SHADE.

Indian (1) Used historically to describe participants in the Boston Tea Party, who disguised themselves as

Indians. (2) Once common for *Indian corn*. "The newcomer from another part of the country, when he first crosses the Connecticut River, is startled at being asked by an innocent-looking girl waiter in a village tavern if he will have some fried Indian." (*Century Magazine,* April 1894)

Indian barn A colonial term for a hole in the ground where corn is stored. The hole is covered with bark and then dirt.

Indian Bible A Bible translated by John Eliot into a Massachusetts Indian dialect and published in 1663.

Indian corn Sweet corn, which, of course, the Indians showed the first European New Englanders how to grow. In his famous poem "The Hasty Pudding," Joel Barlow wrote that all his "bones were made of Indian corn." Also *Indian*.

Indian dog See quote. "The Indian dog is a creature begotten 'twixt a wolf and a fox, which the Indians . . . bring up to hunt the deer with." (John Josselyn, *New England Rarities Discovered,* 1674)

Indian-named New England places These include Connecticut, Housatonic, Kennebec, Massachusetts, Merrimack, Narragansett, Passamaquoddy, Pawcatuck, Penobscot and Quinneoug, among many many others.

Indiany A term once heard on Cape Cod for *like an Indian*. "He's Indiany looking."

in good case In good condition, healthy. "Those pigs were in good case when I sold them."

inheaven Boston transcendentalists invented this word, which is explained in the following excerpt from a sermon from about 1850: "The One circumflows and inheavens us. The infinite Father bears us in his bosum, shepherd and flock."

Injun See quote. "Our people say *Injun* for *Indian*. The tendency to make this change where *i* follows *d* is common. The Italian *giorno* and French *jour* from *diurnus* are familiar examples." (James Russell Lowell, *The Biglow Papers,* 1867)

injun bannock An early name for the JOHNNYCAKE.

inna Heard in Boston for *in the*, which can be used by the same speaker, depending on the emphasis. " 'I go inna Men's, Walmsley said. 'Nothing there. I go in the Women's, and also nothing there.' " (George V. Higgins, *Outlaws,* 1987)

innards The entrails of a butchered animal. See LIGHT PIE; LIVER AND LIGHTS.

in one's naked bed To be in one's sickbed. Cited as a common expression in George Allen England, "Rural Locutions of Maine and Northern New Hampshire," *Dialect Notes,* Vol. IV (1914).

in primlico order In good, neat or prime order. Said to be commonly used in Portsmouth, New Hampshire, according to Frederic D. Allen, "Contributions to New England Vocabulary," *Dialect Notes,* Vol. I (1890)

instead See quote. "While the New Englander cannot be brought to say *instead* for *instid* (commonly *'stid* where not the last word in a sentence), he changes the *i* into *e* in *red* for *rid, tell* for *till, hender* for *hinder, rense* for *rinse.*" (James Russell Lowell, *The Biglow Papers,* 1867)

inter A pronunciation of *into.* "I went inter the house."

interestin' A pronunciation of *interesting.* "This, however, made him look more interesting, or, as the young ladies at Major Bush's said, 'interestin'.'" (Oliver Wendell Holmes, *Elsie Venner,* 1861)

intervale Once a common distinctive term in New England for a narrow tract of low-lying land, especially a piece so situated along a river, *intervale* still has some use in the region. The word is a combination of *interval* and *valley* or *vale.*

in the Cape Ann stage An old, obsolete expression meaning to be drunk; after Cape Ann in northeast Massachusetts.

in the name of the Great Jehovah and the Continental Congress The traditional words attributed to Vermonter Ethan Allen when he demanded the surrender of New York's Fort Ticonderoga by the British commander during the Revolutionary War. There is another story, however. According to John Pell in *Ethan Allen* (1929): "Professor James D. Butler, of Madison, Wisconsin, has informed me that his grandfather Israel Harris was present and had often told him that Ethan Allen's real language was, 'Come out of here, you damned old rat.' "

in the seeds In the midst of things, in the swim. "He's right in the seeds of things."

in the wood Destined, fated. "It wasn't in the wood for it to happen."

into Sometimes used to mean "in." "It had a big crack into it."

Ipswitch sparrow A songless sparrow (*Passerculus princeps*) first sighted and recorded near Ipswitch, Massachusetts in 1868.

Irish turkey Heard in Boston for *corned beef and cabbage.*

iron men and wooden ships Old New England salts said this of the old days: "When I went to sea there were iron men and wooden ships; now there are iron ships and wooden men."

irregardless Often used in Maine as a synonym for *regardless.* "He's going to do it, irregardless."

Isleboro An island off the Maine coast that has a distinctive vocabulary; an excellent collection of these

Isleboroisms is given by Darrel A. Roberson in *Yankee Magazine* (Jan. 1977).

I snum! Once a common euphemism for *I swear!*

I swan! / I swanny! / I swow! / I swum! Old euphemisms for *I swear!* An anonymous 19th-century poet wrote: "The Yankee boy, with starty eyes, / When first the elephant he espies, / With wonder swums, and swoons and cries."

Italian sandwich Used in Maine as the designation for the many-named sandwich also known as the *Cuban sandwich, grinder, guinea grinder, hero, hoagie, hooker boy, poor boy, submarine* and *torpedo*, among other names.

it blows so hard it takes two men to hold one man's hair on Said of gale-force winds. Cited in William F. Macy, *The Nantucket Scrap Basket* (1916).

it's a poor back that can't press its own shirt Cited as a Vermont expression in Charles Edward Crane's *Let Me Show You Vermont* (1937).

it's as thick as marsh mud Used to describe a thick fog.

it's raining pitchforks and barn shovels A colorful Maine term for a very heavy rain. See TREE-BENDER.

it's some hot today It's a very hot day; *some* takes the place of *very* here.

it takes a voyage to learn Experience is the best teacher; a saying quoted in William F. Macy, *The Nantucket Scrap Basket* (1916).

I vowny! A century ago this expression was used to mean "I swear," "I vow!"

I vum! Old-fashioned for *I swear!* "Well, I vum!" Also *I vummy!*

ivy An old term for *mountain laurel* (*Kalmia latifolia*). Often pronounced *ivory*.

Ivy League The colleges referred to as the *Ivy League* are Harvard, Yale, Princeton, Dartmouth, Cornell, Brown, Columbia and the University of Pennsylvania. They are all "old-line institutions," with thick-vined, aged ivy covering their walls, and the designation at first applied specifically to their football teams. Sportswriter Caswell Adams coined the term in the mid-1930s. At that time Fordham University's football team was among the best in the East. A fellow journalist compared Columbia and Princeton to Fordham, and Adams replied, "Oh they're just Ivy League," recalling later that he said this "with complete humorous disparagement in mind."

I want to know! An exclamation of surprise meaning Really! Do tell! You don't say!

I wish I had a neck as long as a cart-rut New Hampshire praise for a good drink recorded in Marion Nicholl Rawson, *From Here to Yender* (1932).

I wouldn't know him from Adam's off ox The *off ox* in this national expression is the ox in the yoke farthest away from the driver. The expression probably began life as the Nantucketism *I wouldn't know him from God's off ox*, the *Adam* substituted as a euphemism.

I wouldn't touch it with an eleven-foot pole A variation heard in Maine of the old expression *I wouldn't touch it with a ten-foot pole*.

J

jack Fun, mischief, as in *full of jack.* "Mr. Holmes and James Lowell were full of jack, chaffing each other and going on." (Sara J. Hale, *Letters,* 1919)

Jackson balls See BOSTON BAKED BEANS.

jag *Bartlett's* gives this as a 19th-century term for a load or large quantity of something. "He's got a jag of corn on the wagon."

jam A 19th-century term for a party or other social gathering; possibly derives from GAM.

jeeroosely Big, enormous, mighty. "That's a jeeroosely tree he cut down." Rarely used today, but given as a common term in George Allen England, "Rural Locutions of Maine and New Hampshire," *Dialect Notes,* Vol. IV (1914).

jeezly cold Used in Maine to describe very cold weather. "It's jeezly cold out."

jeezly-crow An old Maine exclamation. " 'Jeezly-crow, you ain't *never* shook the ants out of your pants, have you?' " (Stephen King, *Dolores Claiborne,* 1993)

Jerusalem cherry Another name for the tomato when it began to be widely used in New England in the 19th century.

Jerusalem crickets! An old-fashioned exclamation. "Jerusalem crickets, ain't it hot today!"

jest A pronunciation of *just.* "Jest look at the picters!" (Oliver Wendell Holmes, *Elsie Venner,* 1861)

Jesus to Jesus and eight hands around! An exuberant exclamation of astonishment that may have had its origin among lumbermen describing a huge tree.

jibbers Heard among hunters for *small game* such as rabbits; from the French *gibier,* meaning the same.

Jill-o'er the ground A New England flower. "Jill-o'er-the ground is purple blue, / Blue is the quaker-maid, / The alder-clump where the brook comes through / Breeds cresses in its shade." (William Vaughn Moody, "Gloucester Moors," 1901)

jill-poke Any log stuck in the mud. Cited as a common term in George Allen England, "Rural Locutions in Maine and Northern New Hampshire," *Dialect Notes,* Vol. IV (1914).

133

jimmies A name given in New England to the candy flecks, often chocolate, that ice-cream cones are dipped into. They are called *dots, nonpariels, shots, sparkles* and *sprinkles* in other regions.

Jim-slicker Said of anything excellent. "That's a real Jim-slicker of a car."

Jim Whittiker! An old-fashioned rural exclamation.

jingled Drunk. "He was half jingled by noon."

jizzicked Said of something worn out and beyond repair. "When are you going to get rid of that jizzicked stove?"

Joe Booker A hardy stew famous in Boothbay Harbor, Maine; named after a long-forgotten Joe Booker.

Joe Frogger A cookie made of molasses and ginger, baked and sold in Marblehead, Massachusetts, said to be invented by and named for a black Gay Head Indian called Black Joe who lived during colonial times near a local pond inhabited by many frogs.

Joe-Pye weed A weed, according to the old saying, is only an uncultivated flower. Sometimes a weed also has beneficial properties. The Joe-Pye weed (*Eupatorium purpureum*) for instance, may have been named for an Indian medicine man of that name because he "cured typhus fever with it, by copious perspiration." This tall, common plant, with clusters of pinkish flowers (also called purple boneset), might well be the only weed ever named after a real person. Records from 1787 reveal the existence of a Josephy Pye, or Shawquaathquat, who was possibly a descendant of the original Salem, Massachusetts healer, but the colonial Joe Pye has not been unequivocally identified yet.

johnnycake (1) "New England corn pone," someone has dubbed this flat corn bread once cooked on a board over an open fire. Most scholars agree that the cakes are not named after a cook named Johnny who had a hand in inventing the bread. *Johnnycake* is usually traced to *Shawnee cakes,* made by the Shawnee Indians, who even in colonial times were long familiar with corn and its many uses in cooking. Not everyone agrees, though. One popular theory holds that *johnnycake* is a corruption of *journeycake,* which is what early travelers called the long-lasting corn breads that they carried in their saddlebags. However, *johnnycake* is recorded before *journeycake* in the form of *jonnikin,* "thin, waferlike sheets, toasted on a board . . . eaten at breakfast with butter," a word still used for griddle cakes on the eastern shore of Maryland. The word apparently progressed from *Shawnee cake* to *jonnikin* and *johnnycake,* and then to *journeycake.* When people no longer needed to carry the cakes on journeys, *johnnycake* probably became popular again. Today there is a Rhode Island Society for the Propagation of Johnnycakes and an annual Usquepagh, Rhode Island Johnnycake Festival. The bread is properly made of white Indian corn called *flint corn*. " 'Your Johnnycakes are getting cold,' he said. 'Eat.' " (Susan Dodd, "Rue," 1984) (2) A New Englander. "I've been through the mill, ground and bolted, and come out a regular down-east johnnycake." (Richard Henry Dana, *Two Years Before The Mast*, 1840) See JONNY-CAKE.

John R. Braden, a A winner, any sure thing; after a Maine horse who won almost all his harness races in the early 1900s.

John Yankee An 18th-century American equivalent of England's John Bull.

join the great majority To die. "He's joined the great majority."

jo-jeezly Used to describe someone or something stubborn, ornery. "He's so jo-jeezly he'll never admit he did it wrong."

jolly Flirt with. ". . . he felt as heavy and loutish as in his student days, when he had tried to 'jolly' the Worcester girls at a picnic." (Edith Wharton, *Ethan Frome*, 1911)

Jonathan A nickname the British gave to a New Englander and finally to any American; the word in this sense is first recorded in 1765, and its origin is unclear.

jonny-cake See quote.

[Do not] describe the name of Rhode Island's chiefest luxury with an "h" sticking up in the middle of it . . . [its] original spelling . . . was "journey-cake" . . . that of "jonny" substituted in its place [at the close of the Revolutionary War] in honor of [Connecticut] governor Jonathan Trumbull, the honored and trusted friend of General Washington, who always addressed the sterling patriot with the affectionate pet name of Brother Jonathan . . ." (Thomas Robinson Hazard, *The Jonny-cake Papers of "Shepherd Tom,"* 1915) See JOHNNYCAKE.

jorum Old-timers used this term for a large mug, especially one containing hard cider or another alcoholic beverage.

joual A French dialect heard in Quebec and Maine that takes its name from a regional pronunciation of *cheval* (horse). *Joual*, also spelled *jooal*, borrows many words from English and has its own grammar. It is perhaps the least-known dialect speech in the United States.

jucket This word apparently derives from the surname *Jacquet* and is used to describe a poor uneducated person, often one who marries within his or her family; by extension it means anything inferior.

Judas Priest! An old-fashioned exclamation of surprise or disapproval.

judge See U.

jumped like a cat out of the wood box Cited as a Vermont expression in Charles Edward Crane's *Let Me Show You Vermont* (1937).

jumping around like a pea in a hot skillet Used to describe someone very active, even antsy.

jumpin' gehosephatt! An old-fashioned euphemistic exclamation.

jumping jings! An exclamation of surprise not much heard anymore. "Jumping jings, I never expected to see you!"

junction A small town that grew in a place where two railroads meet. Also called *crossing*.

junk A chunk. "Throw that junk of wood on the fire."

just staggerin' around A humorous Maine reply to "How are you?" Cited in E.K. Maxwell, "Maine Dialect," *American Speech* (November 1926).

K

Kancamagus Pronounced kan-cah-MAWG-us; a noted highway in the White Mountains of New Hampshire.

katouse Din or tumult. "What a katouse you people made last night!"

kaybecker A Maine name for a Canadian from the province of Quebec.

kedge An old-fashioned, perhaps obsolete, way to say "in good health or spirits." "I'm feeling pretty kedge today."

kedgeree There's an interesting story behind this delicious dish of rice, fish, milk and eggs often made in Connecticut. Originally this was an Armenian dish called *kidgeri*. New Englanders not only changed the spelling to *kedgeree* but substituted eggs for the eggplant that the Armenian recipe calls for, as at the time they were not familiar with that vegetable.

kedidoes Tricks or pranks. The word is recorded in Maine and New Hampshire.

keeled up Disabled, laid up with illness or injury. "He's keeled up with a broken leg."

keep (1) To stay at a house. "Where do you keep these days?" (2) A name for New England herdsmen in colonial times. (3) Maintain. "Well I know where to hie me—in the dawn, / To a slope where the cattle keep the lawn." (Robert Frost, "The Vantage Point," *A Boy's Will*, 1913)

keep an eye to windward Be prudent. Cited in William F. Macy, *The Nantucket Scrap Basket* (1916).

keeper See SHORTS.

keeping room Parlor or sitting room. "Nobody ever went away unconsoled from Miss Eunice's 'keeping-room'." (Rose Cooke, "Uncle Josh," 1857)

keeping vegetables Vegetables such as potatoes and onions that can be harvested and kept over the winter, unlike parsnips and other vegetables that are better left in the ground to "sweeten" over the winter.

keeps Mainers use this word in the sense of "operates" or "functions" in referring to the school system. "When school keeps again at the end of summer, things'll be back to normal."

Keezer's ghost! Cited as a common exclamation in George Allen Eng-

137

land, "Rural Locutions of Maine and Northern New Hampshire," *Dialect Notes,* Vol. IV (1914). Also *Great Keezer's Ghost.* Both expressions apparently are variations of the widespread exclamation *Great Caesar's ghost!*

kelp A valuable seaweed of the family Laminariaceae, often used for fertilizer, that is abundant along the New England coast.

Kennebecker A term used for *packsack*; named after Kennebec, Maine.

Kennebec turkey See quote.

> I know there is a Yankee joke in this name for herring . . . But there is substance and truth behind the joke. For any Kennebec [Maine] man would rather have a slab of that dark meat that grows in the sea than one off the best speckled and bearded bird that ever blushed and gobbled on a Vermont hill. And herring is a foundation stone of Maine life and character . . ." (Robert P. Tristram Coffin, *Kennebec, Cradle of Americas,* 1937)

ketch Catch. " '. . . let Jotham Powell drive me over with the sorrel in time to ketch the train at the Flats.' " (Edith Wharton, *Ethan Frome,* 1911)

kick and stram Said of a child having a temper tantrum. "He kicked and strammed for an hour."

kicked to death by cripples A contemptuous expression, as in "You ought to be kicked to death by cripples!" Cited as a common saying in George Allen England, "Rural Locutions of Maine and Northern New Hampshire," *Dialect Notes,* Vol. IV (1914).

kicking the dashboard The dashboard on a buggy protected the driver from the horse pulling the vehicle, but sometimes the horse kicked up its heels, refusing to go forward, its heels hitting the protective shield. From this derived the phrase *kicking the dashboard* to describe a difficult, stubborn person. "We can't reason with him, he's just kicking the dashboard."

kill-devil A colorful word for *liquor.*

killhag A wooden trap used by hunters in Maine; according to *Bartlett's* (1859), it derives from an Indian word.

killick (1) A stone anchor. Also *killock, kellock.* (2) See HUMDURGAN.

Kilroy was here No catchphrase has ever rivaled *Kilroy was here* since it appeared on walls and every other surface capable of absorbing it during World War II. It was first presumed that *Kilroy* was fictional; one graffiti expert even insisted that *Kilroy* represented an oedipal fantasy. But word sleuths found that James J. Kilroy, a politician and an inspector in a Quincy, Massachusetts shipyard, coined the slogan. Kilroy chalked the words on ships and crates of equipment to indicate that he had inspected them. From Quincy the phrase traveled on ships and crates all over the world, copied by GIs wherever it went, and Kilroy, who died in Boston in 1962, at the age of 60, became the most widely published man since Shakespeare.

> On December 5, 1941, I started to work for Bethlehem Steel Company, Fore River Ship Yard, Quincy, Mass., as a rate setter (inspector) . . . I was getting sick of being accused of not looking the jobs over and one day, as I came through the manhole of a tank I had just surveyed, I angrily marked with yellow crayon on the tank top, where the tester could see it, "KILROY WAS HERE." (James J. Kilroy, *New York Times Magazine*, January 12, 1947)

kinder Sort of, kind of. "He kinder choked." (Edith Wharton, *Ethan Frome*, 1911)

kinder sorter Somehow, rather. "I kinder sorter think so." (Thomas C. Haliburton, *Nature and Human Nature*, 1855)

kindling wood wagon A peddler's wagon of days past that carried pine kindling door to door.

King's English See the Introduction.

kiss my back cheeks A Maine euphemism for *kiss my ass*. ". . . no high-steppin' kitty like Vera-Kiss-My-Back-Cheeks Donovan was going to listen to a plain old country doctor.' " (Stephen King, *Dolores Claiborne*, 1993)

kitchen closet An old-fashioned term for *pantry*. Also *closet*.

kittencornered Diagonal, catercornered.

kittens Balls of dust under a bed or other furniture. Also *kitties*. See DUST BUNNIES.

kiver A common old pronunciation of "cover."

kivy Once commonly used as the name for an ocean *sunfish* (*Mola mola*).

knee-high to a scupper Said of someone very short or very young. "She was knee-high to a scupper when she learned to ride.' The *scupper* on a ship is an opening at deck level that allows water to run off.

knockabout The first *knockabouts* were pleasure boats built in Marblehead, Massachusetts in 1892. They had no bowsprit and were rugged ships, hence their name. Soon after, fishing schooners were so rigged.

knock galley-west No one has been able to explain why a ship's galley or the compass point west have anything to do with this expression meaning to knock into smithereens. They may not. The words may be a corruption of the English dialect term *collyweston*, which in turn derived from the town of Colly Weston in Northamptonshire, a town reportedly given to excessive violence. Colly Weston itself may have been named for a local, violent troublemaker of the same name. In any case, the expression still is used in New England. "He stopped so abruptly that the second man banged into him, scattering the dream galley west." (John Cheever, *Falconer*, 1977)

knowed Often used by rural old people for "knew." "He knowed she was there."

kof A frequent regional pronunciation of "cough."

kub A pronunciation of "curb," especially in rural areas.

kyat A common pronunciation of "cat."

L

"L", the See quote.

> I saw then that the unusually forlorn and stunted look of the house was partly due to the loss of what is known in New England as the "L": that long deep-roofed adjunct usually built at right angles to the main house, and connecting it by way of storerooms and toolhouse, with the wood-shed and cow-barn. Whether because of its symbolic sense, the image it presents of a life linked with the soil . . . or whether merely because of the consolatory thought that it enables the dwellers in that harsh climate to get to their morning's work without facing the weather, it is certain that the "L" rather than the house itself seems to be the center, the actual hearthstone of the New England farm. (Edith Wharton, *Ethan Frome,* 1911)

laborin' oar Someone who works very hard. "He's a real laborin' oar."

labrador tea An evergreen shrub (*Legum groenlandicum*) common in New England and used to make a tea substitute during the Revolutionary War.

lace-curtain Irish A name given to successful people of Irish descent by the CODFISH ARISTOCRACY.

lace curtains An old term often used in Maine for any kind of curtains, regardless of the material they are made of.

Ladies Walk A euphemism for the women's privy (bathroom) in days past. The men's privy was called the *Gents Walk.*

Lake Webster The body of water with the longest name is located near Webster, Massachusetts and is called Lake Webster by almost everyone. But its official, Indian-derived name is of 40 letters and 14 syllables, translating into English as "You fish on your side, we fish on our side, nobody fish in the middle." For those who want to try pronouncing this Indian name, its Lake Chargogagogmanchaugagogchaubunagungamamaug.

lalock An old pronuncation and spelling of "lilac." Also *layback.*

lamb A name Mainers give to venison poached out of season.

land! An old-fashioned exclamation. "But, land! victuals and drink ain't the chief o' my diet." (Rose Terry Cooke, "Town Mouse and Country Mouse," 1891)

Land of Baked Bean A humorous nickname for *New England.* Also *Land of Baked Beans and Hard Cider.*

141

Land of Johnnycake New England. "This was the mystery connected with his visit to the land of johnnycake and wooden nutmegs." (James Russell Lowell, *Lowell Offering*, 1844)

Land of Lumber A nickname for *Maine,* due to its vast forests and lumber companies.

Land of Pork and Beans A nickname for *Massachusetts.*

Land of Punkins A nickname for *New England.* "The most confirmed drunkard we ever knew, was an old man in the land of Punkins." (*Boston Transcript*, February 20, 1832)

Land of Steady Habits (1) A nickname for *Connecticut,* in reference to the strict morals encouraged by its early Blue Laws. (2) A nickname for all New England, for much the same reason as above.

Land of the Wooden Nutmegs New England, after the sharp Yankee traders who were said to have sold carved wooden nutmegs (and hams, pumpkin seeds, etc.) for the real thing. "A Yankee mixes a certain number of wooden nutmegs, which cost him 1–4 cents apiece, with a quantity of real nutmegs, worth 4 cents apiece, and sells the whole assortment for $44; and gains $3.75 by the fraud." (James Hill, *Elements of Algebra*, 1859)

landshark A merchant or boardinghouse proprietor who cheated sailors. As an old whaling song went:

They send you to New Bedford,
  that famous whaling port
And give you to some landsharker
  to board and fit you out . . .

land sakes alive! An old-fashioned euphemistic exclamation. Often lands sake alive.

Languid Cape, the Cape Cod. "Ransom had heard that the Cape was the Italy, so to speak, of Massachusetts; it had been described to him as the drowsy Cape, the languid Cape, the Cape not of storms, but of eternal peace." (Henry James, *The Bostonians,* 1886)

Lapland rosebay A flowering mat-forming evergreen (*Rhododendron lapponicum*) that is found on the peaks of higher New England mountains such as Mount Washington, New Hampshire.

lap tea See quote. "A few phrases not in Mr. Bartlett's book which I have heard include: *Laptea*; where the guests are too many to sit at table." (James Russell Lowell, *The Biglow Papers,* 1866)

lard eaters A Maine nickname for *French Canadians* noted in Robert P. Tristram Coffin, *Kennebec, Cradle of Americans,* 1937.

large as life We owe this popular phrase to one of Thomas C. Haliburton's Sam Slick tales, *The Clockmaker* (1837), in which Sam Slick of Slicksville says of another character: "He marched up and down afore the street door like a peacock, as large as life and twice as natural." Sam's words became a popular catchphrase in America and still survive in both the original and abbreviated versions.

larrigan A boot or "shoe pac" made of leather with a long leg that reaches above the knee. The origin of the word, used mostly in Maine, is unclear.

larruping A beating. "Gerald gave him a good larrupin'."

last rose of summer A name in New England for the late-blooming New England aster (*Aster nova angliae*), a field flower that the Indians called *It-brings-the-frost.*

la suz See DEAR ME SUZ.

later Used in Maine as a synonym for *good-bye.*

laundress An old-fashioned, decidedly politically incorrect term heard in Maine for *one's wife*, though usually said in a humorous way.

law and order This term was used long before present times in New England, notably by the Rhode Island Law and Order Party, which opposed various insurrections in the state in 1844.

law is off, the Refers to the open season for hunting in Maine; when the hunting season ends, *the law is on.*

law sakes alive An old-fashioned exclamation. " 'Law sakes alive, S'manthy [after] twenty year, I guess

he c'n stan' one evenin's catousin.' " (Rowland Robinson, "A Paring Bee," 1900)

law suz See DEAR ME SUZ.

lawsy! Once a common exclamation. "Lawsy! we can get in good enough,' said Melinda, alertly climbing over the hind wheel . . ." (Rose Terry Cooke, "Town Mouse and Country Mouse," 1891)

lay An old term for *price*. "I got the goods at a good lay."

lay away Put away. "The book is completed / and closed like the day / And the hand that has written it / Lays it away." (Henry Wadsworth Longfellow, "Seaweed," 1849)

lay by! Pull up close to, save. "Sailed away from a sinking wreck, / With his own town's-people on her deck! / 'Lay by! lay by!' they called to him. / Back he answered, 'Sink or swim!' " (John Greenleaf Whittier, "Skipper Ireson's Ride," 1828)

lay off To take off one's clothes or coat. "Come on in and lay off your things."

lazy dog A log situated so that it has to be rolled uphill. Loggers originated the pun *slope up = slow pup = lazy dog.*

leewardly A word nautical in origin that means very clumsy or stupid, even unlucky.

left holding the bag To be made a scapegoat (also the one who's forced to suffer the consequences of a group's deeds). First recorded in Royall Tyler's *The Contrast* (1787), the first comedy written by an American. In the play Jonathan, the trusty Yankee retainer of the serious-minded American Revolutionary War officer Colonel Manley, is a servant full of homespun shrewdness, regional sayings and downeast dialect. After referring to Shay's Rebellion, a 1786 revolt of Massachusetts farmers against high land taxes, Jonathan says: "General Shay has sneaked off and given us the bag to hold."

leg stretcher An early 19th-century expression meaning a drink. So named after passengers in coaches going into a tavern for a drink with the excuse "I think I'll stretch my legs for a while."

Lemon Fair River This Vermont river's name is the subject of several stories. One claims it derives from the old English phrase *lemon fair*, meaning mistress fair. Another says an Indian massacre occurred on the stream's banks and the massacre was called *the lamentable affair*, which over the years was corrupted to *lemon fair*. George R. Stuart, in *Names on the Land* (1945), says "the most likely explanation is that the strange name is only a Vermonter's attempt to render *Les Monts Verts* (The Green Mountains)."

Leominster Pronounced LEM-in-ster; a Massachusetts town.

let on Pretended. "He let on like he was ailing."

let's talk turkey Let's get down to real business. According to an old story, back in colonial days a white New England hunter unevenly divided the spoils of a day's hunt with his Indian companion. Of the four crows and four wild turkeys they had bagged, the hunter handed a crow to the Indian and took a turkey for himself, then handed a second crow to the Indian and put still another turkey in his own bag. All the while he kept saying "You may take this crow and I will take this turkey," or something similar, but the Indian wasn't as gullible as the hunter thought. When he had finished dividing the kill, the "ignorant savage" protested: "You talk all turkey for you. You never once talk turkey for me! Now I talk turkey to you." He then proceeded to take his fair share. Many scholars believe that from this probably apocryphal tale, first printed in 1830, comes the expression *let's talk turkey*.

liar's bench The bench in front of a country store where men gathered in good weather to swap news and stories and do a bit of trading.

liberty tea A substitute tea made of four-leaved loosestrife (of the family Lythraceae) popular in New England during the American Revolution.

liberty tree, liberty elm A tree in Boston from which effigies of unpopular people were hanged during the protests over the Stamp Act in 1765. The ground under the tree became known as Liberty Hall. In 1775 the British cut the venerable elm down, and for a time it became known as the *Liberty stump*. Soon after liberty trees were being planted all over New England and in other regions, some say in almost every American town.

lickety larrup Same as LICKETY WHITTLE.

lickety split Bartlett's *Dictionary of Americanisms* (1859) defines *lickety split* as "very fast, headlong; synonymous with the equally elegant phrase 'full chisel.'" Today *lickety split* is heard only infrequently, and it is folksy rather than "elegant." The *lick* in the phrase probably is associated with speed because of the rapidity with which the tongue moves in the mouth, and *split* perhaps is associated with "split second." The Puritans used the phrase, but it wasn't very popular until the mid-19th century. *Lickety brindle, lickety click, lickety cut, lickety liver,* and *lickety switch* are variations on the expression.

lickety whittle Very fast, at great speed. "She got there lickety whittle."

licking good Very tasty, excellent. "That pie's licking good!"

lief An old form of "leave" still heard in New England. "I'd just as lief stay home."

lie like a tombstone Used to describe a great liar; the comparison is with the tombstones of old, whose inscriptions often exaggerated the good qualities of those who lay beneath them. "He lies like a tombstone."

life-everlasting See quote.

> No native son [of New England] needs a description of the plant . . . At the height of summer, life-everlasting lies along pasture slopes and in sunny hollows like patches of snow. Looking closely, the blossoms have a tidy look of artifice, clusters of miniature roses with petals of straw. They seem to demand that something be done with them . . . (Mary Lamberton Becker, *Golden Tales of New England,* 1931)

The flowers (of the genus *Anaphalis*) are used to make bouquets and wreathes. In times past, women filled pillows with them to relieve asthma sufferers, as Mary E. Wilkins mentioned in *A New England Nun*, 1891.

life-of-man (1) A New England name for the medicinal spikenard plant (*Aralia racemosa*), also called *pettymorel*. (2) Another name for the stonecrop plant (*Sedum telephium*), also called *live-for-ever*.

lifted Hit. "He lifted him so hard he knocked him into the next county."

light and shut Used to describe weather where the sun comes out at intervals; the expression apparently derives from the New England maxim *Open and shet's a sign of wet*. Cited in Frederic D. Allen, "Contributions to the New England Vocabulary," *Dialect Notes,* Vol. I (1890) as a common Portsmouth, New Hampshire term.

light pie A pastry containing the innards of a slaughtered animal, which were usually thrown away; in days past this dish was often a hard-times meal. See LIVER AND LIGHTS.

lights See LIVER AND LIGHTS.

like (1) See quote. "The [New England] uneducated, whose utterance is slower, still make adverbs when they will by adding *like* to all manner of adjectives (as in 'he ran rapid-like')" (James Russell Lowell, *The Biglow Papers,* 1866) (2) See quote. "*Like* for *as* is never used in New England but is universal in the South and West. It has on its side the authority of two kings . . . Henry VIII and Charles I . . . without throwing into the scale the scholar and poet Daniel." (James Russell Lowell, *The Biglow Papers,* 1867) Lowell was writing, of course, of the usage in his time. (3) Almost. "She liked to drown."

like a cat in a strange garret Said of someone not at ease, wary, timorous. "She didn't know anyone there—acted like a cat in a strange garret."

like all get out Very fast, quickly. "He ran after them like all get out."

like all possessed To act wildly, violently, as if possessed by demons. "He began dancing like all possessed."

like a thousand of bricks Violently or vigorously. The term is first recorded in New England in 1836 and today is usually *like a ton of bricks.* "She came down on him like a thousand of bricks."

like Barney's brig In complete disorder. The expression probably has its origins in some terribly disorganized Maine sailor named Barney.

like diarrhea through a duck Same as LIKE SALTS THROUGH A GOOSE.

like eatin' pie Said of any untaxing enjoyable task. "It was like eatin' pie."

like haulin' a hog out'n a scaldin' tub Difficult work. Cited as a common expression in George Allen England, "Rural Locutions of Maine and Northern New Hampshire," *Dialect Notes,* Vol. IV (1914).

like salts through a goose Very fast; the salts here are a laxative, something geese hardly need. "She ran out of there like salts through a goose."

like the mill tail o' thunder In a quick, disorderly fashion. Cited as a common expression in George Allen England, "Rural Locutions of Maine and Northern New Hampshire," *Dialect Notes,* Vol. IV (1914).

lilac A flower (*Syringa vulgaris*) long associated with New England.

> Lilacs,
> False blue,
> White,
> Purple,
> Colour of lilac.

Heart-leaves of lilac all over New
England,
Roots of lilac under all the soil of
New England,
Lilac in me because I am New
England,
Because my roots are in it,
Because my leaves are in it,
Because my flowers are for it,
Because it is my country . . .
(Amy Lowell, "Lilacs," 1925)

limande A name given to the lemon sole (*Pseudopleuronectis americanus*) by French-speaking New Englanders; the fish is found off the New England coast in deep water.

limb In Victorian times, *limb* was a "mock-modest" term used in New England, and other places, instead of "leg." It was even used for the legs of animals and piano legs.

limb out To severely humiliate or dress down someone; in reference to the limbing or pruning of trees. "His father really limbed out John last night."

limpsy Lethargic, slow. "There comes Sam Lawson down the hill, limpsy as ever; now he'll have his doleful story to tell, and mother'll give him one of the turkeys.' " (Harriet Beecher Stowe, *Oldtown Folks,* 1869)

limp-to-quaddle An old-fashioned expression meaning to walk or hobble with a limping gait.

limsy An old word, rarely heard anymore, for *weak, flexible.*

line storm A term heard mainly in New England for a storm supposed to occur when the sun crosses the equator; therefore, *line storm* means any heavy storm occuring within a week to 10 days of the equinox, an equinoctial storm.

linguister An obsolete humorous word for a very talkative person.

Literary Emporium, the A nickname for Boston, Massachusetts, once the cultural center of America. "The literati of our Literary Emporium comprises but a small proportion of its inhabitants." (James Russell Lowell, *Lowell Offering,* 1840)

little lady Haley, a An old expression meaning a well-behaved little girl; origin unknown. "Now, isn't she a little lady Haley."

little million A lot, a great quantity. "He had a little million of them."

little mite A bit. " 'I felt a little mite better . . .', she said in her flat whine . . ." (Edith Wharton, *Ethan Frome,* 1911)

little off See HAS A SCREW LOOSE.

Little Rhody, or Rhody A nickname for Rhode Island, the smallest of the 50 states. An anonymous poet used it this way in an 1850 poem:

Old Newport, billow-cradled, sea,
On my Rhody's verdant shore;
'Tis there old Ocean shakes his
mane,
Resounding evermore.

little skeezicks A mischievous child. The word, altered slightly, became the name of a popular character in the comic strip *Gasoline Alley*. Also *skeezucks*.

live free or die See quote. "New Hampshire . . . *Live free or die* is our motto; low taxes our boast." (John Updike, *Memories of the Ford Administration*, 1992)

liver and lights Once a common term for the liver of a slaughtered animal and all the rest of its innards. Only the liver was of commercial value and normally used. See LIGHT PIE.

live short Live in poor circumstances, to live in an undesirable place. "Every once in a while somebody from Maine who is 'living short' in a far place will come home to visit . . ." (John Gould, *It Is Not Now*, 1993)

L.L. Bean A mail-order business, store and Maine institution that L.L. Bean of Freeport, Maine started with the famous Maine Hunting Shoe.

> . . . It was because his feet got tired and sore on hunting trips, in the period when he was managing a store, that he got the idea which founded his business. As an experiment, one day, he left off the heavy lumberman's boats which hunters customarily wore in the Maine woods, and went out hunting with only a pair of ordinary rubbers over three thicknesses of stockings. These kept his feet warm, dry and comfortable, but he felt the need of some support around the ankles, so he took the rubbers to Dennis Bibber, the local cobbler, and got him to sew some leather tops on them. This became The Maine Hunting Shoe with which Bean first went into the mail-order business. (Arthur Bartlett, "The Discovery of L.L. Bean," *Saturday Evening Post*, December 14, 1946)

load of cork-stopples An old-fashioned expression heard in coastal Massachusetts for a fishing boat that returns with little or no catch.

loaned See quote. "Only a parcel of spoons—'loaned,' as the inland folks say when they mean lent, by a neighbor." (Oliver Wendell Holmes, *Elsie Venner*, 1861)

lobbered milk Used for *clabber* in southwestern New England. Also called *loppered milk*.

lobscouse See quote. ". . . a prominent feature of the menu of a whaleship. It was a stew of soaked hard-tack, pork fat, or 'top o' the pot' (grease left after boiling 'salt horse'—salted beef) or any sort of 'slush' (sailor's term for grease), boiled with molasses and water." (William F. Macy, *The Nantucket Scrap Basket*, 1916)

Lobster Capital of the World, the A title claimed by Rockport, Maine, or at least by the town's chamber of commerce.

lobster glop A Maine dish of lobster pieces, bread crumbs, milk and butter.

Lobster Scoundrel A contemptuous name New England colonists gave the red-coated British soldiers before and during the Revolutionary War. See quote under BLOODY BACK.

lock horns This expression may have derived from New Englanders who witnessed moose fiercely battling over a female—their massive horns locked together—and invented this expression for a *violent clash*. There is no evidence of this derivation in the first American literary use of the phrase in 1839, however. When Swinburne used the phrase in 1865, he spoke of a heifer and her mate locking horns, which also could be the source of the expression.

lollygag One old source says "Lollygaggin'" was Grandmother's word for lovemaking." Maybe so, but I never knew Grandmother meant that by it. She always used the word *lollygag* to mean "fooling around," "wasting time," "talking idly." The word was first recorded in 1868, but its origin is unknown, though it may have something to do with the British dialect *lolly* (tongue). Given as a common expression in George Allen England, "Rural Locutions of Maine and Northern New Hampshire," *Dialect Notes*, Vol. IV (1914).

long drink of water A very tall person.

longer'n the moral law Very long or tall. Cited as a common expression in George Allen England, "Rural Locutions of Maine and Northern New Hampshire," *Dialect Notes*, Vol. IV (1914).

longer than a hard winter An excessively long time. "He's been talking longer than a hard winter."

longer than a wet week Said of something that takes an interminably long time, such as a week spent indoors in rainy, dreary weather.

longful while A long time. "It's been a longful while since I saw her."

long-jawed Prolonged and tiresome. "He sure made a long-jawed speech."

long lick An old term for *molasses*. "She added some long lick to it."

long of Because. "He did it long of her."

long ones Long underwear. "My grandfather wore his long ones until the day he died . . . [despite] subtle methods to modernize him . . ." (Hayden Pearson, *New England Flavor*, 1961)

long sauce A term old-timers had for *beets, carrots* and *parsnips*.

long sweetening Early New Englanders used this term for *molasses*. See LONG LICK.

longways Lengthwise. "Put it down there longways."

look-a-here Sometimes still heard in rural areas for *look here*. See CUTTER.

looked as if the devil kicked him (her) on end A simile heard in the region meaning he or she looked as if he or she had gone through hell.

looking for salt pork and sundown Said of a worker poor, hungry and tired. "He's lookin' for salt pork and sundown." Cited as a Vermont expression in Charles Edward Crane's *Let Me Show You Vermont* (1937). The expression also is used when a hired hand avoids work.

loppered milk An old Connecticut name for thick sour milk, which is called *clabbered milk* in Massachusetts and other parts of New England.

lot on Like, dote on. See quote under GORMING.

lot upon To count on; an old term deriving from *allot upon*. "He lotted upon going there."

love-car This may be a New Englandism for a car parked in a lonely place with a couple making love in the front or backseat, or it may have been invented by Robert Lowell in his poem "Skunk Hour" (1959): "I watched for love-cars. Lights turned down, / they lay together, hull to hull . . ." I've not seen or heard it used outside the poem. Either way, it's a nice description.

love-cracked Said of someone who acts foolishly or irrationally because he or she is deeply in love. "Christmas Jenny's kind of love-cracked." (Mary Wilkens Freeman, *A New England Nun,* 1891)

Lowell A cheap cotton cloth once manufactured in the Lowell, Massachusetts mills and used for many articles of clothing, including *Lowell pants.*

lower than whale shit As low as you can get; usually used to describe a person's character.

Lubberland An imaginary country in nautical mythology and once the name of a real village near Portsmouth, New Hampshire.

lucivee A "half-mythical" kind of wildcat also called the *loup-cervier* or *Injun devil.* Cited in George Allen England, "Rural Locutions of Maine and Northern New Hampshire," *Dialect Notes,* Vol. IV (1914). Pronounced *lucy-vee.*

lucky bugs See DOLLAR BUGS.

lug along To move at good speed. "They lugged along and made it with time to spare."

lull down Die down. "The wind is lulling down."

lumbago Rheumatism. " 'Old Farmer McCarty . . . He had the lumbago.' " (Thornton Wilder, *Our Town,* 1938)

Lumber State Another nickname for *Maine,* the Pine-Tree State, because of its important lumbering industry.

lumper's helper An unskilled laborer; a *lumper* is a dock worker.

lumpus Once heard in Massachusetts for *clumsy person.*

Lyme disease A serious disease transmitted to humans via deer ticks. "Then, worse yet, it developed that the deer population was crawling with the tiny tick *Ixodes dammini,* which in turn harbored the spirochetes of Lyme disease, named after the town in Connecticut where it was first recognized." (John Updike, "Wildlife," in *The Afterlife,* 1994)

M

mackerel gull See MACKEREL HAWK.

mackerel hawk A name for the gull *Larus ribibundus,* also called the *mackerel gull.* "The mackerel . . come in August with the mackerel hawks, marked with the same markings and moulded into the same projectile-like bodies, crying and screaming over the fish." (Robert Tristram Coffin, *Yankee Coast,* 1947)

mackerel sky A sky filled with small clouds suggesting a mackerel's markings.

mad Heard in Maine, meaning to anger. "She can really mad a person."

mad as a hopper Very angry. This simile rarely is heard anymore.

madder'n snakes in hayin! Extremely mad. Given as a common expression in George Allen England, "Rural Locutions of Maine and Northern New Hampshire," *Dialect Notes,* Vol. IV (1914).

madder than a wet hen Very mad. "She was madder than a wet hen and he knew enough to stay away from her."

Mahershallalhashbaz In early New England children commonly received long names from Scripture. This admirable, almost unpronounceable one is from the book of Isaiah and documented in Shebnah Rich's *Truro-Cape Cod* (1883).

mahn A pronunciation of *man.* "Bush was what the natives of the town called a 'hahnsome mahn.' " (Oliver Wendell Holmes, *Elsie Venner,* 1861)

Maine Maximillian Schele De Vere in *Americanisms* (1871) says that the name *Maine* may have been chosen for the New England state "in compliment to the Queen of England, who had inherited a province of the same name in France." According to George R. Stewart in *Names on the Land* (1945):

In a New England charter of 1620 the lawyers wrote "the country of the Maine Land," words which suggest a general description rather than a name. Two years later, however, a charter was granted to two old sea-dogs of the Royal Navy, Sir Ferdinando Georges and Captain John Mason, and in it the word had certainly ceased to be a description. Dated on August 10, 1622, the charter declared that "all that part of the mainland" the grantees "intend to name the Province of Maine." Some have thought that this name arose because of the greater number of islands off that northern coast, which made men have more reason to speak of "the main." Others have tried to connect it with the Province, or County, of Maine in France. But again, *main* as equaling *chief* or *important* would have been of good omen, if a little boastful. Moreover, about 1611 Captain Mason had served in the Orkneys, and must have known the name as used there.

Maine black fly A small dark biting fly of the family Simuliidae that is a terrible pest to Mainers and SUMMER-CATERS alike. "That mystic oriental goddess with sixteen arms is the only thing I've run into that can cope with the Maine Black Fly." (John Gould, *The Parables of Peter Partout,* 1964)

Maine hunting shoe See L.L. BEAN.

Mainiacs A humorous name given to residents of Maine, who are more properly called *Mainers*.

Maine molasses doughnuts An old Maine recipe, which concludes with this advice for men: "If you are looking for a wife, take one of the doughnuts, hold it up to the window and call in the first maiden lady who comes in sight and kiss her through the hole and she is yours."

Mainer A native or resident of Maine. "The traducers of the great Prohibition State assert that the Mainers get corned as often as they can." (*Courier Journal,* January 31,

1887) *Mainite* is an obsolete term meaning the same. See also MAINIACS.

Mainite An old obsolete nickname for an inhabitant or native of Maine. See MAINIACS, MAINER.

make a goose-run An expression used in Maine for any delay: "She would have been here earlier, but she had to make some kind of goose-run." Originally the term applied only to a hunting stop for a raft of ducks and the like that a coastal ship captain might make on a voyage.

make a great splather and splurge To put on a big show.

make a touse To make a great fuss, an uproar. "He's been making a great touse over his broken toe." Also *make a catouse*.

make long arms Help oneself at the table. "Make long arms, everybody!" Given as a common expression in George Allen England, "Rural Locutions of Maine and Northern New Hampshire," *Dialect Notes* (1914).

make me a child again just for tonight Not a regionalism but from the poem "Rock Me to Sleep" (1860) by Maine poet Elizabeth Chase Akers (1832–1911): "Backward turn backward, O Time, in your flight, / Make me a child again just for tonight."

make of An old Maine expression meaning to pet or fuss over. "The child was making of her cat when it scratched her.''

make out To make. ''I have to make out the butter.''

make things hum Since at least the early 18th century, *humming*, suggesting the blending of many human voices or the activity of busy bees and other insects, has been used to express a condition of busy activity. Two hundred years later, the expression *to make things hum* was invented in New England. Possibly the hum of machines in New England textile factories was the source for the phrase, in reference to the fabled Yankee mechanics who made things hum again when the machines broke down.

making land Clearing land of rocks, trees and brush for planting. '' 'Making land' is a term I no longer hear. But in 1910 when I was a boy, I can remember Father saying [it] . . .'' (Hayden Pearson, *New England Flavor*, 1961)

making up to Going to become, especially when used in regard to weather. ''It's making up to rain.''

malahack An old word noted in James Russell Lowell's *The Biglow Papers* (1866) meaning to cut up in haste, unskillfully. ''He malahacked it.''

man-cow A euphemism for a bull once commonly used; also called a cow-man.

mantilly A mantilla. ''[She wore] a black lace mantilly.'' (Mary Wilkens Freeman, *A New England Nun and Other Stories,* 1891)

man works from sun to sun but woman's work is never done An old New England proverb. ''Many of [the women mill workers] came from farms where 'man works from sun to sun but woman's work is never done . . .' '' (May Lamberton Becker, *Golden Tales of New England,* 1931)

maple honey Another name for *maple syrup* heard in New England and eastern Canada.

maple sugar, maple syrup ''There can't be a remedy better for fortifying the stomach'' than maple sugar, a pioneer wrote in 1705. *Maple sugar,* boiled from *maple syrup* and the only sugar the first settlers had, has a long history that dates from the time American pioneers learned how to make it from the Indians. The same, of course, applies to *maple syrup,* another maple-tree product Americans are still familiar with; other maple-derived products included *maple water, maple vinegar, maple wax, maple beer* and even *maple wine.*

> What's true of maple sugar
> May be true of you and me!
> The more we are fired and beaten
> The finer-grained we'll be.
> (Evelyn R. Cheney, 1845)

March meeting Once the annual town meeting in many New England towns. ''Town meeting was an important event in our community when I was growing up. We called it March meeting then, and would have continued to do so if some busybody hadn't succeeded in shifting the date back to February." (Edith A. Holton, *Yankees Were Like This,* 1944)

march of soldiers Sparks moving straight up the chimney from the back of a fireplace fire.

Martha's Vineyard Possibly discovered by Leif Erikson in the 11th century, *Martha's Vineyard,* an island about five miles off the southeast coast of Massachusetts, was once an important center for whaling and fishing. The Indians called the island *Noe-pe,* "Amid the Waters," while the Norsemen named it *Staumey,* "Isle of Currents." It was christened *Martin's Vineyard* by English navigator Bartholomew Gosnold in 1602, for no reason known to history. After a century it took the name *Martha's Vineyard,* probably because its name was confused with that of a little neighboring island to the southeast called Martha's Vineyard that Gosnold also had named. That little island is now called *No Man's Land,* after an Indian named Tequenoman. See NANTUCKET.

Martha's Vineyard eel stifle See EEL STIFLE.

Mary had a little lamb

Mary had a little lamb,
 Its fleece was white as snow
And everywhere that Mary went
 The lamb was sure to go;

He followed her to school one day,
 That was against the rule;
It made the children laugh and play
 To see a lamb in school . . .

There seems to be no doubt that the Mary and little lamb in the well-known nursery rhyme were real, but there is some uncertainty about who wrote the poem. Sara Josepha Hale first published the 24-line verse over her initials in the September 1830 issue of *Juvenile Miscellany.* Over the years it became known that it was based on the true experiences of 11-year-old Mary Sawyer, who had a pet lamb that followed her to the schoolhouse at Redstone Hill in Boston one day in 1817. In fact, half a century later Mary Sawyer confirmed the story during a campaign to save the famous Old South Church of Boston from being torn down.

Massachusettsian This tongue twister was once used as the name for an inhabitant of Massachusetts, employed by Cotton Mather and John Adams, among others. An anonymous 1650 broadside verse went: "You English Massachusettsians all / Forbear sometime from sleeping, / Let every one both great and small / Prepare themselves for weeping."

Massachusetts Roger Williams said that Massachusetts took its name from an American Indian word meaning Blue Hills. Writes George R. Stewart in *Names on the Land* (1945):

Captain John Smith wrote Massachuset as an Indian town. Though Smith may not have known it, the meaning is fairly clear, being the tribal name Mass-adchuseuck, "big-hill-people", which in English ears was blended with the name of the place, "Mass-adchu-ut, "at-big-hills". Smith made of the Indian word an English plural to indicate the tribe, and so came Massachusetts.

The Bay State was admitted to the Union in 1788 as our sixth state and had been called the Massachusetts Bay Colony before then. It is now officially called the Commonwealth of Massachusetts.

Massachusetts game, the A version of baseball, similar in some respects to the present game, whose rules were codified in about 1858 and is one of the forebears of baseball.

master A synonym for *excellent.* "He did a master job."

master chilly Very frightening. "The tale of Stafford's cabin, which was good, / Though 'master chilly' / after his own phrase . . ." (Edward Arlington Robinson, "Isaac and Archibald," *Captain Craig,* 1902)

Mast pine A tall straight eastern white pine (*Pinus strobus*), the kind once used for the masts of sailing ships.

matterating Festering or supperating. "His wound was matterating."

matto wacca An old name once heard in southern Connecticut, on Long Island Sound, for the saltwater herring (*Clupea harengus harengus*); from an Indian name meaning Long Island.

Matt Peasley, a A tricky sea lawyer; after a character in Mainer Peter B. Kyne's *Captain Rick's Stories* (ca. 1920). Also called *a Matt.*

May breakfast Traditional breakfasts held in Rhode Island in May in celebration of Rhode Island's declaration of independence from England on May 4, 1776; it was the first colony to do so. The most traditional of these breakfasts include clam fritters, ham and scrambled eggs, and appie pie—but there are many variations.

Mayflower American A term describing someone descended from the colonists who came to Plymouth, Massachusetts in 1620 on the ship named the *Mayflower.*

Mayflower Compact The former wine ship that transported the early settlers to America took its name from the mayflower, another name for the blossom of the hawthorn tree. The *Mayflower Compact* was signed aboard the ship by the 51 adult passengers. All agreed to stay together where they landed, choose their own leader and abide by majority rule; the compact marked the beginning of American democracy.

me See quote for one peculiar Maine usage. "Earle said he had been listening to this phonograph recording called 'Burt and I,' and he says if it was really Maine it would be called 'Me and Burt.'" (John Gould, *The Parables of Peter Partout,* 1964)

meadow dressing Manure.

mealin' An old Maine term for taking meals at a boarding house. "He's mealin' to Drewbie's." The mealer did not have to reside at the boarding house.

mean Poorly. "'I just felt so mean I couldn't sleep.'" (Edith Wharton, *Ethan Frome,* 1911)

mean enough to steal acorns from a blind hog Quoted as a contemporary saying in James Russell Lowell's *The Biglow Papers* (1867).

mean enough to take his wife's egg money Said of a very stingy man, one who would steal or forcibly take the pin money a woman had saved by selling eggs.

meaner'n tripe Lowdown, worthless. "'That so, Plupy, your old man's meaner'n tripe.'" (Henry A. Shute, *Plupy,* 1910)

meaner than goose grease Very mean and nasty. A simile once heard in New England.

mean woman An old Maine and New Hampshire term for a loose or disreputable woman.

meat pie Mince pie. "Mixed conversation chopped very small, like the contents of a mince-pie—or meat pie, as it is more forcibly called in the deep-rutted villages." (Oliver Wendell Holmes, *Elsie Venner,* 1861) Also *mince-meat pie.*

mebbe A common rural pronunciation of *maybe.* "Well then, it's Granny speaking: '. . . Mebbe I'm wrong to take it as I do . . .'" (Robert Frost, "The Generations of Men," 1914)

mechanical and artistic purposes Heard in Maine for *devious purposes.* Often shortened to *artistic purposes,* the expression originated with the old Maine prohibition law that permitted the use of alcohol when prescribed by a doctor for "mechanical and artistic purposes."

meddle and make Interfere. "I ain't one of them that meddles an' makes." (Alice Brown, "Mis' Wadleigh's Guest," 1895)

medrick A term used in New England for a small gull (also called a *swallow-tail*) or tern.

meech A many-purpose word that can mean sneak, cringe, be falsely humble, be sickly, lack backbone, procrastinate and the like. "She's so meeching butter wouldn't melt in her mouth." "But I ain't o' the meechin' kind, thet sets an' thinks fer weeks . . ." (James Russell Lowell, *The Biglow Papers,* 1867) "Told me all about her last days, how white and meechin' she looked, and how dreadful poor and skinny, and yet how she hung on, hung on till seem'ds if she never'd pass away." (Annie Trumbull Slosson, "A Local Colorist," 1912) Cited as a common

Nantucket expression by William F. Macy in *The Nantucket Scrap Basket* (1916).

meeting Church services. " 'Twas Sunday and Square Hole was dressed for meeting." (Robert Frost, "The Gold Hesperidee," 1936)

meeting house (1) A synonym for a church. (2) Another name for the flower usually called the columbine (*Aquilegia canadensis*).

meeting seed A name used for dried seeds such as anise, caraway, dill and fennel because they often were chewed during meeting or church services.

meet-up A close friend, buddy. "He's an old meet-up of mine."

meet with the rubbers To have bad luck, misfortune. Cited as a common Portsmouth, New Hampshire expression in Frederic Allen, "Contributions to the New England Vocabulary," *Dialect Notes*, Vol. I (1890).

mehbe The typical Maine pronunciation of "maybe."

mellered Made mellow. "I guess you mellered him some." (Alice Brown, " 'Mis' Wadleigh's Guest," 1895)

menhaden This abundant oily fish has a name related to its use. Caught in great numbers by American Indians and buried in their corn fields, it bears an Algonquian name meaning that which enrichens the soil, or fertilizer. It is also called *moss-bunker, bunker, marshbunker* and some 30 more popular names. (See the *American Naturalist* 12, 1878, pp. 735–739 for a listing.) In 1949 *Brevoortia tyrannus* was called "America's No. 1 fish . . . yielding some $10 million worth of oil, meal, and dry scrap last year."

men with beards See quote.

> Joseph Palmer [a member of Bronson Alcott's short-lived Fruitlands community] was jailed [in 1843] for wearing a beard . . . At eighty-four he died and was buried under a stone at North Leominster that gives his name and age, his portrait with the offending decoration, and the words "Persecuted for Wearing the Beard." Even Emerson, it seems, was not without a slight sense of superiority to the unshaved; he classified certain reformers as "men with beards." They were not tolerated in business or the professions in the [1840s]; curiously enough, by the seventies public sentiment had swung in precisely opposite directions." (May Lamberton Becker, *Golden Tales of New England*, 1931)

See also CHORING ROUND.

mercy no! An old-fashioned exclamation. " 'Mercy no! Not on such a night.' " (Edith Wharton, *Ethan Frome*, 1911)

merlan French-speaking New Englanders often use this name for the *whiting* (*Merluccius bilinearis*), a fish New Englanders also call the *hake*.

merluche A name given to the hake (*Merluccius bilinearis*), also called the New England hake or whiting, by French-speaking New Englanders.

Merrimac A popular cotton fabric once made in Lowell, Massachustts mills on the Merrimac River.

miching An old-fashioned word meaning skulking. "She went miching off, like a cat that had missed its mouse." See also MEECH.

middlesex Said in Maine of something ordinary, so-so. "It's a middlesex kind of day." Also the name of a Massachusetts county.

midnight ride of Paul Revere, the A literary reference to the ride of Paul Revere from Charlestown to Lexington and Concord, to warn Americans of the approach of British troops at the beginning of the Revolutionary War. It comes from Henry Wadsworth Longfellow's poem *Paul Revere's Ride* (1861).

mighty small potatoes and few in a hill An old New England saying meaning something or someone of little consequence. "That's mighty small potatoes and few of a hill."

miglet A word used in Massachusetts long ago for *marble*.

Milan Pronounced not like the Italian city but MY-lan; a town in New Hampshire.

milden Grown mild. "There was more wet in the air and it seemed likely to both men that the weather would 'milden' toward afternoon and make the going safer." (Edith Wharton, *Ethan Frome*, 1911)

milkshake In most of America a milkshake is a thick sweet drink made of milk, ice cream and syrup. An exception is Rhode Island and eastern Masschusetts, where such a drink is called a *cabinet,* after the wooden cabinet in which the mixer used to be encased; a *milkshake* in Rhode Island is just milk and syrup shaken up together. In northern New England the drink most Americans call a *milkshake* is called a *velvet* or a *frappé*.

Milk Street A Boston street so named because country slickers used to water their milk at a stream there before bringing it into market and selling it to city bumpkins.

millionist Maine parlance meaning millionaire. "The man was a millionist before he was 30."

mind Remember. "I mind the time he wasn't so proud."

mind your orts *Orts* here means odds and ends or scraps left on one's plate. Mothers exhorted youngsters to eat with the admonition *mind your orts,* that is, clean your plate. Recorded in Katherine M. Abbott, *Old Paths and Legends of New England* (1904).

minge A midge, a gnatlike biting insect of the family *Chironomidae* often found near ponds and lakes.

The word is generally heard in Maine and New Hampshire.

mingo A humorous obsolete term for a chamber pot; it derives from the Latin *mingo,* "I make water."

Minister's Rib Factory, the A name people jokingly gave to Mount Holyoke Seminary (which later became Mount Holyoke College) "because the South Hadley, Mass. school turned out so many wives for ministers and missionaries," according to Imogene Wolcott in *The New England Yankee Cookbook* (1939).

minnim An old word, perhaps obsolete now, for a minnow.

Minute Men See HAVEN'T SEEN YOU SINCE THE CONCORD FIGHT.

mite A little bit. ". . . it ain't a mite too fur back fer the fashion." (Mary E. Wilkins, "Life-Everlasting," 1891)

mite of a body, a A very small person. "A mite of a body she is, you know, lookin' as if you could blow her over with one breath, but tough and rugged." (Annie Trumbull Slosson, "A Local Colorist," 1912)

Moby Dick Mocha Dick, the stout gentleman of the latitudes, the prodigious terror whale of the Pacific, the redoubtable white sperm whale that fought and won over 100 sea battles against overwhelming odds—such was the reputation in the extravagant language of the time of the whale Herman Melville immortal-ized as *Moby Dick.* Melville probably first read about Mocha Dick in a piece by Jeremiah N. Reynolds in the May 1839 *Knickerbocker Magazine;* undoubtedly, though, he had heard of him long before in the forecastles of the New England whaling ships he had sailed on. The last mention in history of Mocha Dick is dated August 1859, when off the Brazilian banks he is said to have been taken by a Swedish whaler. He had already become legend when Herman Melville wrote *Moby Dick* in 1850—Melville changing his prenomen to *Moby* probably to suggest his amazing mobility and to avoid association with the color mocha for his white whale.

mockbird A mockingbird. "Singing she wrought, and her merry glee / The mock-bird echoed from his tree." (James Greenleaf Whittier, "Maud Muller," 1854)

mockernut Another New England name for the squarenut hickory (*Carya tomentosa*), also called the *walnut* and *white-heart.*

moger An old word once used in Maine for *logy* or *slow-moving.*

mohuh A common pronunciation of "more" in Boston.

mollyhawk To tease in an abusive way. "Stop mollyhawking that cat."

monadnock A hill on a plain worn by erosion; the word derives from New Hampshire's Mount Monadnock, whose name comes from the

Massachusetts Indian word meaning prominent mountain.

money cat A Maine term for a calico cat with three or more colors, perhaps because such cats were once thought to be worth a lot of money because they were so rare.

monkey wrench One would think the *monkey wrench* was so named because the wrench's sliding jaws reminded someone of a monkey's chewing apparatus. This may be the case, but there is some reason to believe that the tool was named after its inventor. While one source suggests that this mechanical wizard was London blacksmith Charles Moncke, the British use *adjustable spanner wrench* or just *spanner*, for what Americans call a *monkey wrench*, so this theory is suspect. A more likely explanation turned up several years ago in some clippings on word origins collected by a Boston doctor. One article from the *Boston Transcript*, appearing in the winter of 1932–33, attributed the wrench's invention to a Yankee mechanic by the name of Monk employed by Bemis & Call of Springfield, Massachusetts. Monk supposedly invented the movable jaw for a wrench in 1856, and although it was given another name at first, workers in his shop were soon calling it *monkey wrench*. The tale has not been confirmed, but the 1856 date coincides with the first use of the word in the *Oxford English Dictionary* (1858). None of the standard dictionaries make an attempt to trace the word's origin, not even to say that the wrench resembles a monkey's jaw, just as a crane resembles a crane's neck.

Montpelier Pronounced mon-PEEL-yur; the capital of Vermont.

Montpelier biscuits See COMMON CRACKERS.

mooncussers So called because these people cursed (cussed) the moon and the light that it brought, robbing them of their livelihood. During the early 19th century, these lowlifes lured merchant ships to shore on dark nights by waving lanterns that were mistaken for the lights of other vessels. When the ships were destroyed on rocks, their cargo was collected as salvage. American sailors called inhabitants of the "backshore" of Cape Cod *mooncussers*. Though these people were not often accused of luring ships to their destruction, they did salvage wrecks off the Cape. An old story tells of a man running up to a Cape church door one stormy Sunday morning and shouting "Wreck ashore!": "The minister called out authoritatively, 'Keep your seats until I have pronounced the benediction,' in the meantime making his way down the aisle as rapidly as his dignity permitted. Pausing at the door, he gave the blessing, adding, 'And now, my friends, let's all start fair.' " See WHITE GRAVEYARD OF THE ATLANTIC.

moonglade See quote. "Moonglade: a beautiful word for the track of moonlight on the water." (James Russell Lowell, *The Biglow Papers*, 1867)

more airs than a country stud horse
Very conceited. A simile heard in old
New England.

more grog shops than water pumps
An East and South Boston boast in
the mid-19th century. A grog shop
was a bar or a liquor store.

more'n common stupid Very stupid.
" 'Lobsters climb int' the pot
through the hole in the nettin' 't the
end,' explained one Down-East lobster fisherman . . . 'Eat the bait, 'n
then, being more'n common stupid,
can't find the hole t' git out agin.' "
(Bruce Ballinger, *The Lobster Almanac,* 1988)

morey To a Mainer something
morey is something one wants more
of, something excellent. "We had a
real morey chowder."

Morgan horse Justin Morgan is the
only American horse ever to sire a
distinctive breed. A bay stallion
foaled in about 1793, he was probably a blend of Thoroughbred and
Arabian with other elements and
fairly small at 14 hands high and 800
pounds. Justin Morgan (1747–
1798), a Vermont schoolteacher and
an aspiring musician, bought his colt
in Massachusetts, naming him Figure
and training him so well that he won
trotting races against much larger
Thoroughbreds. Eventually Figure
came to be called after his master.
When his owner died, Justin Morgan
was bought and sold many times in
the 28 years of his life. One of those
unusual horses whose dominant
traits persist despite centuries of in-
breeding, his individual characteris-
tics remain essentially unchanged in
the *Morgan* breed of horses he sired.
Morgans are still compact, virile
horses noted for their intelligence,
docility and longevity, many of them
active at 30 or more years of age.
Heavy-shouldered, with a short neck
but delicate head, they are noted for
their airy carriage and naturally pure
gait and speed. Morgans were long
the favorite breed for American trot-
ters until the Hambletonian strain
replaced them.

Morocco shop The name for Yankee
tanneries that processed goatskins, as
the process they used had been developed in Morocco.

mortal Very, extremely. "It's cause
they're so mortal homely themselves." (Mary Wilkins Freeman, *A
New England Nun and Other Stories,*
1891)

mortal sight o' A great deal of. "My
old woman soon got well of her
fit . . . and she says the stuff [medi-
cine] did her a mortal sight o' good."
(Nathaniel Hawthorne, "The
Haunted Quack," 1831)

most Almost. "Most everybody's
asleep." (Thornton Wilder, *Our
Town,* 1938)

Mother Hubbard sling A humorous
old name for SWITCHEL.

Mother of States Usually applied to
Virginia, because it was the first state
settled by the English, this nickname
also has occasionally been given to
Connecticut.

moules A name French-speaking New Englanders use for *mussels,* along with *bouchots.*

Mount Desert An island off the Maine coast south of Bangor. ". . . Mount Desert—indeed, one's affection for the island even shares the local accent. As decreed by the natives, one spells it Mount Desert, but the pronunciation is Mount Dessert. The view is as fine as sugar frosting to a New Englander's eye." (Norman Mailer, *Harlot's Ghost,* 1991)

Mount Katahdin Pronounced Mount kuh-TAH-dun; a peak in Maine.

move like a toad in a tar bucket Said of someone who works very slowly. "He'll never get finished—moves no better'n a toad in a tar bucket."

mow Usually used with *away* in New England speech; "We mowed the hay away last week."

Moxie Wrote the late E.B. White of this soft drink: "I can still buy Moxie in a tiny supermarket six miles away. Moxie contains gentian root, which is the path to the good life. This was known in the second century before Christ and is a boon to me today." The rather tart flavor of Moxie, a popular New England tonic (as soda pop is often called in the area), may be the reason it yielded the slang word *moxie* for courage, nerve, or guts. Or maybe Moxie braced up a lot of people, giving them courage. These are only guesses, but the tonic, a favorite since at least 1927, is definitely responsible for *a lot of moxie* and other phrases, which, however, aren't recorded until about 1939. I've read that Moxie was originally a nerve tonic, dating back to the 1880s. This would go far in explaining *moxie* (nerve or courage), if earlier uses for the term could be found.

Mr. Man Often used as a hostile form of address: "Watch your step, Mr. Man." Also *mister.*

much of a man An old expression meaning a man of good qualities. "He's very much of a man."

muckle (1) Heard in Nantucket for to bother, fret. " 'Twould muckle me dredful to go to the bottom in an old tub like this." (2) To putter. "He muckled with it all day."

mud season Used jokingly for the time between winter and spring when the roads are exceedingly muddy.

mud time See quote. "It is not many years since the schools let out for three weeks in March because 'the bottoms of the roads had fell out.' The children were always jubilant at mud time, shrilling their yearly cry of 'Mud time! Six weeks to bare feet!' " (Marion Nicholl Rawson, *New Hampshire Borns a Town,* 1942)

mudworm An old term for *earthworm.*

muggid An old-fashioned word heard in Maine for *muggy*. "It's a muggid day out."

muggs A word, origin unknown, once used for a root cellar where vegetables were stored. "They had lots of potatoes in the muggs."

mug up A Maine fisherman's coffee break.

mulberry mania A craze for planting the white mulberry variety *Morus multicaulis* in expectation of making great profits in the silk industry. The leaves of these trees were said to be superior to all others for silkworm feeding, and millions of them were planted in the *multicaulis fever* that ensued. The fever began in Connecticut, where the seven Cheney brothers founded America's first silk mill at South Manchester in 1838. It ended a few years later when mulberry trees glutted the market.

mummichog, mummachog A name used in Connecticut and other areas of New England for the barred killifish and killifish. It derives from the Narragansett Indians' *Moamitteaug*, "a little sort of fish," and is first recorded in 1787 as "Mummy Chog."

musical An obsolete synonym for *amusing* that had its day in the mid-19th century. "He's a very musical fellow."

muslin toast A rye shortcake. "Muslin toast was a favorite New England supper dish, prepared with nicety and precision." (Alice J. Jones, *In Dover on the Charles,* 1906)

mussel chowder A milk-based chowder made with mussels instead of clams that is commonly served on Nantucket.

mustarded coffee A historical term for a crude coffee flavored with powdered mustard that 18th-century settlers in Maine drank; they later used the "mustarded coffee" to spice meat gravy.

mutual admiration society Two or more people form a *mutual admiration society* when they continually praise each other. Oliver Wendell Holmes did not coin the expression in his *Autocrat of the Breakfast Table* (1858), as is generally believed. For its true inventor, see FROZEN YANKEE DOODLE.

mux Muss; an old variation not heard anymore. "Don't mux my hair."

my care! A once-common old-fashioned exclamation, of which there are many beginning with "my," including *my goodness alive!* " 'Oh my goodness alive!' exclaimed Mrs. Flagg . . ." (Sara Orne Jewett, "The Guests of Mrs. Timms," 1895); *my gracious! my land! my land o' livin'! my sakes!* (" 'My sakes, you must be her great-grandaughter!' " [Dorothy Canfield, "Almera Hawley Canfield," 1925]; *my sakes alive! my soul and senses! my soul and deliverances! my soul and body!* and *my stars and body!* an archaic but rather nice exclamation my dear old grandmother (a New Englander) used to exclaim.

N _____

Nahant Pronounced na-HAHNT; a Massachusetts resort village.

nail to the counter Here the allusion is to a storekeeper nailing a counterfeit coin to the counter, where clerks could easily compare it with others of its kind. Figuratively, the expression came to mean "to declare publicly that a lying statement is just that." Oliver Wendell Holmes is the first recorded user of the expression, in *Homeopathy and Kindred Delusions* (1842), where he writes of alleged facts that "have been suffered to pass current so long that it is time they should be nailed to the counter."

nanny-plum tea An old-fashioned, thankfully or hopefully obsolete, home remedy for the measles and other ailments; it was made of sheep droppings soaked for a few minutes in rainwater.

Nantucket There is a hoary tale, probably untrue, that an old seaman owned an island group off Massachusetts. To his oldest daughter he gave his most productive island, which he named Martha's Vineyard; to his next, he gave the island closest to home, Elizabeth's Island; and to his last daughter, Nan, he just offered what remained and *Nan-tuck-it*. No one is sure of *Nantucket's* real derivation. See MARTHA'S VINEYARD.

Nantucketer A Nantucket inhabitant. Also *Nantucketeer*.

Nantucketism A word or expression heard exclusively or mainly on the island of Nantucket, Massachusetts.

Nantucket owls A humorous old term for a meal of codfish.

Nantucket sleigh-ride This expression refers to a whaleboat fastened to a whale, which runs off furiously towing the boat behind it. Such Nantucket sleigh-rides, often lasting for miles, are described in Melville's *Moby Dick* (1850) and other great books of the sea.

naow A common pronunciation of *now* in Maine and elsewhere. "Let go o' that are coat, naow." (Oliver Wendell Holmes, *Elsie Venner,* 1861)

Narragansett (1) An Algonquian Indian tribe of New England, especially Rhode Island; their name is from an Algonquian word meaning small point of land, in reference to their original dwelling place. (2) A small horse developed in Rhode Island near Narragansett Bay in the 17th century; the breed was later used as pacers. Also *Narragansett Pacer*.

Narragansett draft A popular beer in Rhode Island. " 'I'll have the chowder, onion rings, a burger medium-well, and a Narragansett draft. You want a beer?" (Susan Dodd, "Rue," 1984)

narrow-contracted Stingy, tightfisted. "He's a narrow-contracted man." Also *narrow-gutted*.

narsty A pronunciation of "nasty." "That's narsty weather up there."

nary Not any, not even, no; an old-fashioned usage. "I ain't got nary one."

nash Used chiefly in Maine to describe someone very sensitive to nature; sometimes used in a derogatory way for a man with a sensitive disposition.

nasty Bad, disagreeable. " 'Nasty place. Even in 1917 it was a nasty place.' " (Stephen King, *Pet Sematary*, 1983)

nasty-neat Fanatically clean and orderly. "She's nasty-neat, you're afraid to sit on a chair in her house."

nation! New Englanders once used this exclamation as a euphemism for *Damnation!* Not in currency anymore.

native beef Deer and other game shot out of season.

native corn Locally grown eating corn in Connecticut. Across Long Island Sound in New York it is called *local corn*.

nat'ral how d'ye do Charisma. "Though the pastor had never been altogether liked by the out-districs— not having enough 'nat'ral how d'ye do' about him, it was thought . . ." (Bliss Perry, *"By the Committee,"* 1899)

natural turn Natural ability. "Mattie had no natural turn fer housekeeping." (Edith Wharton, *Ethan Frome*, 1911)

nature See U.

nawthin A common pronunciation of *nothing*.

near Cheap, miserly. "Alvah Bayley is 'near'; he has made money and it will no doubt continue to squeal under his clutch . . ." (May Lamberton Becker, *Golden Tales of New England*, 1931)

necessary An old term in eastern New England for *outhouse*; also called a *necessary house*.

necessity mess See VERY POOR MAN'S DINNER.

neck twister A potent Yankee drink, the recipe for which is apparently lost to history.

neighborin', go To make an informal visit; used chiefly in rural Maine.

nekkid A common rural pronunciation of "naked."

nervous as a rat Very nervous, jittery. " 'Ruth Varnum was always as nervous as a rat . . .' " (Edith Wharton, *Ethan Frome,* 1911)

netop An Algonquian Indian word meaning close friend, crony, or loved one that was adopted by early colonists. *Neatrup, meet-up* and *eat-up* were among the ways the colonists pronounced the Indian word.

never grab with both hands, just grab with one A New England maxim instructing a person not to be greedy and grasping but not to be too altruistic either, especially in business dealings.

New Connecticut A 4-million-acre tract in northwestern Ohio claimed by the state of Connecticut in the early 19th century.

New England Captain John Smith thought that the area now called New England in North America greatly resembled England. He was the first to record the name, on a map he made in 1616: "That part we call New England . . . betwixt the degree 41. and 45."

New England aster A perennial purple aster common in New England.

New England boiled dinner Meat, often corned beef, boiled with vegetables such as potatoes, carrots, turnips and onions. "Such a dish was a meal of itself, neither dessert nor bread being regarded as necessary to its completeness." (Mary Caroline Crawford, *Social Life in Old New England,* 1914)

New England boxwood A regional name for the common flowering dogwood tree (*Cornus florida*).

New England Brahmin See BOSTON BRAHMIN.

New England Clam Chowder See CHOWDER.

New England conscience A stern, unrelenting conscience. This phrase is often illustrated by a story about William Ellery of Rhode Island, a signer of the Declaration of Independence. When Ellery was a collector of customs in 1790, his grandson dropped into the office. Casually taking a sheet of paper off his grandfather's desk to write a letter, he felt Ellery's hand restraining him. "My boy," the old man said, "if you want paper, I'll give you some, but this is Government paper."

New England dialect The first dialect in the United States to be given a name. *New England dialect* was recorded in 1788 in the diary of a visitor to the region.

New England diamonds Gravel. "Sometimes a poor farmer finds that his hills are heaps of 'New England diamonds' and sells whole hills to the road maker." (Robert P. Tristram Coffin, *New England,* 1951)

New England hardscrabble A pudding made from hard crusts of brown bread, milk and water and served with syrup. See also BREWIS.

New Englandish Resembling or pertaining to New England. "A respectable-looking woman . . . decidedly New Englandish in figure and manner, came to my office." (Nathanial Hawthorne, *Our Old Home,* 1863)

New Englandism A term first recorded in 1831 for a word or expression typical of New England.

New England mansion house A stately 19th-century style of New England architecture. "It was one of those old buildings which aped the New England mansion houses without once approaching their solid state." (Mary E. Wilkins, "Life-Everlastin'," 1891)

New England Mayflower Another name for the trailing arbutus or ground laurel (*Epigaea repens*).

New England of the West An old nickname for *Minnesota,* after the many New Englanders who settled there.

New England pine The valuable timber tree white pine (*Pinus strobus*).

New England Psalmody A collection of hymns popular in New England. "They roll onward . . . shuffling their heavy heels into an instinctive dance and roaring out some holy verse from the New England Psalmody." (Nathaniel Hawthorne, "Sir William Pepperell," 1833)

New England short o A vowel sound closely resembling the short *u* that many New Englanders use in such words as *home* and *stone*.

New England twang See quote. "There would be a tone in the [New England] voices, a blend of *timbre* and *tempo* that we call a "twang" because, like a plucked string the last note lingers . . ." (May Lamberton Becker, *Golden Tales of New England,* 1931)

New England weather An old term for very varied, unpredictable weather. Mark Twain had this to say about it at a dinner of the New England Society in 1876:

> There is a sumptuous variety about the New England weather that compels the stranger's admiration—and regret. The weather is always doing something there; always attending strictly to business; always getting up new designs and trying them out on people to see how they will go. But it gets through more business in Spring than in any other season. In the Spring I have counted one hundred and thirty-six different kinds of weather inside of twenty-four hours.

New England whiting The silver hake (*Merluccius bilinearis*), a common New England fish.

New English (1) An obsolete term for *New England inhabitants*. (2) Anything of or pertaining to New England. "All their unconscious training by eye and ear, were New English wholly." (James Russell Lowell, *Among My Books,* 1870)

New Hampshire When John Mason was granted the land including this state in 1622, he named it after his homeland—England's Hampshire County. The Granite State was admitted to the Union as the ninth state in 1788.

New Hampshire screwdriver A humorous term heard in Maine for a hammer; the expression suggests that Maine carpenters are superior to their New Hampshire brethren.

nigh Used in times past for *near, nearby, close.* "I'm pretty nigh beat out . . .". (Oliver Wendell Holmes, *Elsie Venner,* 1866)

night mail A name given to a night express train that speeds through New England.

niminy piminy Spoiled, precious, conceited. " 'I detest rude, unladylike girls.' 'I hate affected, niminy piminy chits.' " (Louisa May Alcott, *Little Women,* 1868)

nimshy An admiring old-fashioned name for a person, especially a young woman; from the biblical character Nimshi. "She was a right smart young nimshy." Also *nimshi.* Cited as a common expression in George Allen England, "Rural Locutions of Maine and Northern New Hampshire," *Dialect Notes,* Vol. IV (1914).

nine months winter and three months late in the fall An old saying about New England weather quoted in Arthur G. Crandall, *New England Joke Lore* (1922).

ninepence A historical term for a coin worth 12½ cents.

nippers Large woolen mittens fishermen wear, to keep the cold from nippin' their hands.

no bigger'n a pint o' cider Very small. Given as a common expression in George Allen England, "Rural Locutions of Maine and Northern New Hampshire," *Dialect Notes,* Vol. IV (1914).

no breakfast; no supper Old derisive terms used in New England for vessels hailing from New Brunswick and Nova Scotia; the names derive from the initials N.B. or N.S. on their sides.

nocake A meal made of parched Indian corn; from the Narragansett Indian *nokehick,* "it is soft."

no earthly good An old-fashioned expression meaning no good at all. "He's up to no earthly good, that's for sure."

noggin A lightweight milk bucket. "No home in central New Hampshire in the old days was considered completely equipped if it had not a noggin for milk and a PIGGEN for sap . . . Its lightness is part of the noggin's efficiency. One of its uses . . . was to carry out to barn or pasture . . . when milk fell short in the house." (Cornelius Weygandt, *New Hampshire Neighbors,* 1937)

no great kill or cure Of no great importance. "It ain't no great killer-cure whether they come or don't.'' Given as a common expression in George Allen England, "Rural Locutions of Maine and Northern New Hampshire," *Dialect Notes,* Vol. IV (1914).

no great of An old-fashioned expression meaning no excellent example of. "She is no great of a cook."

noise See quote. "The elegant Gray said *naise* for *noise* just as our westies do." (James Russell Lowell, *The Biglow Papers,* 1866)

No Man's Land The name of a small island close to MARTHA'S VINEYARD, Massachusetts. It is named after an Indian named Tequenoman, who once lived there.

no more heat in the sun than a yellow dog Used to describe a cold winter day in Maine.

no-nation An old-fashioned term meaning no good, worthless. "You're a no-nation S.O.B.!''

nooning A noon rest period or lunchtime in Maine. "So, as you harvesters / Make glad their nooning underneath the elms / With tale and riddle and old snatch of song / I lay aside grave themes." (James Greenleaf Whittier, "Among the Hills," 1867)

nor-easter A northeaster, a wind or gale from the northeast. "Weather would hit oddly hard, so that power would be lost for the week after a nor-easter that had hardly touched the rest of the coast . . ." (John Updike, "Wildlife," in *The Afterlife,* 1994)

nor more use for them than Meader had for his teeth A saying that derives from the old story about a man named Nick Meader who at about the time of the War of 1812 borrowed a hammer to knock out all his teeth, claiming "I have no need of them, for I can get nothing to eat." Quoted in William F. Macy, *The Nantucket Scrap Basket* (1916).

northern fox grape A wild grape ranging from New England to Illinois and south to Georgia that is so named because it supposedly "smelleth and tasteth like unto a foxe." It is the source of the Concord and other cultivated grape varieties.

Norwegian steam A humorous, mildly derogative term used by old salts for *human muscle power.*

norwester A northwester, a northwest wind.

Norwich The Connecticut city's name is pronounced *Nor-itch.*

no-see-um The name for the small stinging flies Henry David Thoreau mentioned in his *Maine Woods* (1848); the name is possibly Penobscot Indian in origin or is simply a humorous name for the small flies.

not as much light as a yellow-eyed bean Used by Mainers to describe very poor lighting; the *yellow-eye* is a favorite bean in the state.

not backward in going forward Used to describe a very pushy person. Cited in Annie E. Perkins, "Vanishing Expressions of the Maine Coast," *American Speech* (December 1927).

not by a jugful! No way! An old-fashioned exclamation.

notch (1) A mountain pass. Used in place-names such as Franconia Notch. (2) Franconia Notch. "They had found the herb, 'heart's ease,' in the bleakest spot of all New England. This family were situated in the Notch of the White Hills [White Mountains] where the wind was sharp throughout the year, and pitilessly cold in the winter . . ." (Nathaniel Hawthorne, "The Ambitious Guest," 1835) For the best lengthy description I know of the notch, see Hawthorne's story "Sketches From Memory" (1835). See also FLUME.

notches See CORNER.

nothard Northward. "It blowed fresh from the nothard."

nothing marrying nothing Used to describe a poor marriage. Cited in Annie E. Perkins, "Vanishing Expressions of the Maine Coast," *American Speech* (December 1927).

notional Once a common synonym for *fanciful, whimsical*. "He's a very notional fellow."

notions An old word that still has some currency as a term for *small wares* or *goods*.

not right Mentally unfit, crazy. "My father's brother wasn't right. They kept him / Locked up for years back there at the old farm." (Robert Frost, "A Servant to Servants," *North of Boston*, 1914)

not to know beans The nationally used *not to know beans* may initially have been a Boston expression, suggesting that anyone who didn't know how to make baked beans in Boston, "the home of the bean and the cod," would have to be incredibly ignorant.

not worth a chaw of tobacco See quote. "[Among New England whalers] a thing which is nearly worthless is 'not worth a chaw of tobacco.' " (William Hussey Macy, *There She Blow!* 1877)

not worth a Hannah Cook Worthless, of no account, insignificant. "He's not worth a Hannah Cook." The expression originally was nautical, but no one has identified a real no-account Hannah Cook behind the phrase. It may be folk etymology for a *hand* or *cook* aboard a ship, hands and cooks making less money than other seaman and thus having lower status.

not worth a hole in the snow Worthless.

now See quote. " 'Now,' he said, pronouncing it *naiow*, 'it's not as though a man looked real close up at my district . . .' " (George V. Higgins, *Victories*, 1990)

nowadays At the present time, currently. "I never twist a spigot [on a hard cider barrel] nowadays . . . But I thank God for orchards . . ." (Edward Arlington Robinson, "Isaac and Archibald," *Captain Craig*, 1902)

nubblin A poor ear of corn, small or with kernels missing; often called a *nubbin* in other places.

nubbut A pronunciation of "nothing but" heard in New Hampshire and Maine. "He's nubbut a lot of trouble."

numb A polite way to say "dumb" in Maine. "Let's not be numb about this, Bill."

numb as a hake Very stupid, as dumb as a dead fish.

nummy Food or a meal, especially lunch. The term once was common in Massachusetts and New Hampshire.

Nutmeg State Connecticut. See also YANKEE PEDDLER.

Nutmeg Stater A resident of Connecticut, the Nutmeg State. "Driving down Route 86 into the blinding splinters of a sunset, he heard the disc jockey crow, 'Get your long johns out of the mothballs, Nutmeg Staters, w're going to flirt with zero tonight!' " (John Updike, "Grandparenting," in *The Afterlife*, 1994)

Nutmeg Yankee A nickname for a Connecticut inhabitant. "He had expected him, also, to be taciturn, as befitted a Nutmeg Yankee." (Eric Hodgins, *Mr. Blandings Builds His Dream House*, 1946)

nyu A pronunciation of *now* frequently heard in New England.

O

oak-acorn A redundancy heard in Maine. "He gathered a bagful of oak-acorns."

o-be-joyful Any potent liquor. "He was full of o-be-joyful." Given as a common expression in George Allen England, "Rural Locutions of Maine and Northern New Hampshire," *Dialect Notes,* Vol. IV (1914). See quote under BLACK BETTS. Also heard as OBJ.

obleeged An old pronunciation of "obliged." "Much obleeged to you." (Oliver Wendell Holmes, *Elsie Venner,* 1861)

obstropulous An old-fashioned humorous word meaning obstreperous.

ocean pout A name used mostly in Boston for the eellike fish generally called *lote* or *eel-pout* (*Zoarces viviparus*).

Off An abbreviation of "off-island" used on Nantucket, as in "Haven't seen you lately—have you been Off?" or "When did you come On from Off?" Cited by William F. Macy in *The Nantucket Scrap Basket* (1916).

Off-Caper A name Cape Cod residents give to anyone who doesn't live on Cape Cod.

off islander (1) A name given by Nantucketers to people who do not live on their island. (2) Someone who lives on the mainland rather than on any of the islands off New England.

off soundings Far out at sea, in deep water where soundings of depth can't be made with the lead line; by extension, the term can describe anyone having a hard time getting his or her bearings.

o fush! An old-fashioned interjection similar to *o fudge!* or nonsense. "O fush! What a lot of foolishness that is!"

o-grab-me The Embargo Act of 1807, and acts of following years, restricted the number of American ships departing from ports, to prevent hostilities on the seas. But since it harmed our British and French enemies less than it harmed Americans, New England shipowners began spelling *embargo* backward and called the acts the *o-grab-me acts.*

oh dear me, suz! An expressive Yankee exclamation that translates as "Oh dear me, sorrow!" Recorded in Katherine M. Abbott, *Old Paths and Legends of New England* (1904).

oh fiddlesticks! A common old-fashioned expression of annoyance,

172

impatience, disbelief and disapproval.

oh Rinehart See quote. ". . . 'Oh, Rineheart!' began . . . after a student of the name had repeatedly been shouted to by noisy friends. In the course of time it has become a sort of Harvard battle-cry, and the word is now used to describe any yard uproar, in which the calling of Mr. Rineheart's undying name is an inevitable feature." (Samuel Eliot Morison, *Three Centuries of Harvard,* 1936) It has been established that the man the historical expression honors was James Brice Gordon Rinehart, Harvard class of 1900.

oh the devil! An old-fashioned exclamation. ". . . [there] appeared a story [in a mid-19th century Lowell, Massachusetts magazine] about the doom of a girl not so careful about her language as she should have been—indeed, on one fatal occasion, while entertaining a young man believed to be on the edge of proposing, she pricked her finger on the embroidery needle and cried out, 'Oh the devil!' The young man immediately left for South America and has never yet returned." (May Lamberton Becker, *Golden Tales of New England,* 1931)

oh, we jist fumigate A humorous reply of Mainers to summer people who ask, "What on earth do you do here after the summer people leave?" Quoted in Arthur Bartlett, "Maine," *Holiday* (August 1947).

oilnuts Another name for butternuts.

old baster (1) An affectionate name for *male friend.* "Haven't seen you for ages, you old baster." (2) Said of anything large in size. "He sure caught himself an old baster."

Old Bay State A nickname for *Massachusetts.*

"Old Cape Cod" A popular romantic song of the 1950s about love on Cape Cod.

Old Clock on the Stairs, the A landmark in the city of Pittsfield, Massachusetts.

Old Colony A historical term for the Plymouth Colony in Massachusetts.

Old Driver See quote. "Old Driver, Old Splitfoot": the devil." (James Russell Lowell, *The Biglow Papers,* 1867)

older than Methuselah's billy goat An old-fashioned saying meaning very old.

old fuddy dud Someone very fussy or finicky; used especially in Maine rather than *fuddy duddy,* which may be more common nationwide. Also *an old fubdub.*

Old Glory This popular name for the American flag was coined by Captain William Driver, who was presented with a U.S. flag before sailing from Salem on his brig *Charles Doggett* on August 10, 1831. Captain Driver so christened the flag on that day or shortly thereafter.

Old Ironsides The famous nickname of the U.S. frigate *Constitution,* built in 1797 and now moored in the Boston Navy Yard, America's oldest warship still afloat. The high point of her illustrious career came on August 19, 1812, when she engaged and defeated the British frigate *Guerriere* off Nova Scotia. During the battle an American sailor, watching British shots fall into the sea, cried: "Huzza! Her sides are made of iron!" And *Old Ironsides* she has been since that day. In 1830 Oliver Wendell Holmes, hearing that she was to be sold by the navy, wrote his famous poem "Old Ironsides" in protest and she was saved.

old jeezer A term used in Maine for *old fellow, old guy.* "The old jeezer still does his share of the work." Perhaps suggested by *geezer* and *old geezer.*

Old Man of the Mountain A natural formation on a mountainside in New Hampshire's White Mountains that resembles the face of an old man.

Old Manse, the The name of Emerson's and later Hawthorne's house in Concord, Massachusetts.

old man, the/the old woman When any old man or old woman is mentioned, the expression usually is prefaced with *the.* "How's the old woman Carson today?"

old Medford rum A potent rum made in Medford, New Hampshire. "I saw an inchworm take a drop of this [old Medford rum] one day and he stood right up on his heels and bit

a bee." (Stephen Vincent Benét, "The Devil and Daniel Webster," 1937)

Old Nick The devil. "Such pounding and expounding . . such slapping with his open palm, thumping with his closed fist, and banging with the whole weight of the great Bible, convinced me that he held, in imagination, either the Old Nick, or some Unitarian infidel at bay . . ." (Nathaniel Hawthorne, "Passages from a Relinquished Work," 1834)

old niddy-noddy, an Once a common expression for someone very erratic and unsettled. The niddy-noddy is a device for winding yarn; persons using one had to move their hands in a seemingly erratic fashion.

Old Scholar, the A term for *God* once common among mariners.

old seed folks Ancestors; old residents born in New England

Old Splitfoot See OLD DRIVER.

old stock People whose ancestors have been in New Hampshire or other parts of New England for generations. " 'But don't you think we sometimes make too much / Of the old stock? What counts is the ideals . . ." (Robert Frost, "The Generations of Men," 1914)

Old Town Turkey A nickname among Nantucketers for any resident of Martha's Vineyard; Edgarstown on Martha's Vineyard once was known as Old Town. Cited in William F. Macy, *The Nantucket Scrap Basket* (1916).

old whale A term once applied to sailors by New Englanders.

on (1) Frequently used in past years for *of*. "... if y' a'n't afeared on him!" (Oliver Wendell Holmes, *Elsie Venner,* 1861) (2) Used in such expressions as "Seein' on 'em home," "Doin' on it."

one and another One after another. "Minty . . . milked the cows, one and another." (Mary Wilkens Freeman, *A New England Nun and Other Stories,* 1891)

one fishball The popular song "One Meatball," with its well-known line "you get no bread with one meatball," was adapted from a New England song called "The Lay of One Fishball," apparently written by Harvard professor George Martin Lane in 1857 or thereabouts. Lane's line was: "We don't give bread with one fishball!"

one holer See BACKHOUSE.

one perry and one porter were too much for John Bull to swallow! A popular Yankee slogan after the War of 1812, this punning expression refers to American naval heroes Oliver Perry, whose last name means a hard cider made of pears, and David Porter, whose last name means a strong, dark beer. John Bull, of course, is the national nickname for *England*.

on the coast A Nantucketism meaning nearby, close at hand. "A gallant lover will assure his lady-love that if she will only fix the day, 'he'll be sure to be on the coast with the parson.' " (Maximilian Schele De Vere, *Americanisms,* 1871)

on the flakes Dead, laid out, as fish are on a flake (a drying platform). "Old Billy's on the flakes down at Hannigan's Funeral Parlor."

on the gain Recuperating, getting better, on the mend. "She's been very sick but is on the gain."

on the hind tit (or teat) Used to mean someone "isn't getting as much as everyone else": "I'm always on the hind teat when it comes to overtime." The analogy is to a last pig feeding on a sow, though there is no proof that a mother pig's last teat offers any less milk than any other.

on the mending hand Said of someone convalescing. Cited as "a common New England phrase" in Frederic D. Allen, "Contributions to the New England Vocabulary," *Dialect Notes,* Vol. I (1890).

on the town Someone on welfare or public assistance, someone who receives financial help. "He's been on the town three years now."

on your own hook On your own. This expression comes to us from New England fishermen working the Grand Banks on big boats in the 19th century. They were paid according to what they caught individually on their own hooks and lines.

open and shet's a sign of wet See LIGHT AND SHUT.

open and shut day A day when the sun pokes in and out of the clouds.

open day A sunny day, when the sun isn't behind clouds.

open weather Clear weather; no clouds.

opodildocs A humorous term once used to describe a very spirited horse. "He's on his opodildocs." An *opodildoc* was apparently a strong liniment.

oquassa A tasty freshwater trout (*Salvelinus oquassa*) found in western Maine's Lake Oquassa and others of the Rangeley Lakes.

Orleans Pronounced orr-LEENS; Vermont and Cape Cod towns.

orpicues A term used on the Maine coast meaning flourishes in handwriting, curlicues, and the like.

orts Leavings or refuse, from table scraps and inedible hay to cattle droppings and fish entrails. This Old English word meaning spoiled hay survives in New England speech, chiefly in Maine.

otter A pronunciation commonly heard in Boston for "order."

ought Sometimes used for the zeroes in dates, as in *19 ought three* (1903).

our country's bird The bald eagle. "Our country's bird alookin' on an' singin' out hosanner." (James Russell Lowell, *The Biglow Papers*, 1846)

our folks Local people, people who belong to one's community. "Miss Ophelia took Topsy home to Vermont with her, much to the surprise of that grave deliberative body whom a New Englander recognizes under the term 'Our folks.' " (Harriet Beecher Stowe, *Uncle Tom's Cabin*, 1852)

oursins A name used by French-speaking New Englanders for *sea urchins* (*Arbacia punctulata*).

out See quote. "Along the [New England] seaboard, the wind is 'out' or 'has got out' when it blows from the sea. The expression is known in Portsmouth, Salem, and Plymouth. I do not think it is common in Boston." (Frederic D. Allen, "Contributions to New England Vocabulary," *Dialect Notes*, Vol. I, 1890)

outlandisher Someone from out of state, a "foreigner"; an expression once commonly used in Massachusetts.

out of kin Mainers use this expression to mean "no relation." "He's out of kin to me."

out of pure cussedness To do something solely because one is mad and spiteful. " 'He done it o' pure cussedness,' and 'He is a nateral cuss,' have been commonly thought Yankeeisms . . . But neither is our own [going back centuries]." (James Russell Lowell, *The Biglow Papers,* 1867)

out-of-the-wayest Strangest, most unusual. "She had out-o'-the-wayest words for everything." (Annie Trumbull Slosson, "A Local Colorist," 1912)

outspoken as a norwester Very outspoken. "He wuz as outspoken as a norwester, he wuz . . ." (James Russell Lowell, *The Biglow Papers,* 1867)

out Yankee To outwit or get the better of, especially in trading. "He out Yankeed him at every turn."

over in one's book Getting old, near the last chapter or page of one's life. "I'm getting over in my book and want to thank everyone now—wouldn't have lasted this long without a lot of understanding folk."

over street In town, downtown. "He's over street to the doctors." Also *down street.*

over the bay Drunk; perhaps patterned on the expression *half-seas over.*

over to Over at. " 'Howie Newsome says it's ten below over to his bar.' " (Thornton Wilder, *Our Town,* 1938)

over to the continent An expression used by natives of Nantucket when they leave the island to visit the mainland: "I'm going over to the continent."

owah A pronunciation commonly heard in Boston for *hour.*

owlin' around Said of someone up late at night, from a reveler to an insomniac.

owning to it Admitting something. " 'I'm a Yankee,' said Slick, 'and I ain't above ownin' to it . . .' " (Thomas C. Haliburton, *The Clockmaker,* 1837)

P

package store   A store that sells bottles of liquor and wine. "Outside the Midway's package store, he paused with his hand on the doorknob." (Robert Stone, "Helping," 1987)

Padanaram   Pronounced PAD-uh-neer-um; a Massachusetts town.

paddy wagon   Heard in Boston for *police car*.

pahk the cah in Hahvahd yahd   Park the car in Harvard Yard. Often cited as a humorous example of the Boston broad *a*. See the Introduction.

painted Jezebel   A prostitute; the words rarely are heard anymore. " 'I have told him that you are a radical, and you may tell him, if you like, that I am a painted Jezebel." (Henry James, *The Bostonians,* 1886)

paint up   An old-fashioned way to say "to paint." " 'We did pretty well with the hotel, and my wife was always at me to paint up . . . Well, I put it off . . . till one day I gave in, and says I, 'Well, *let's* paint up." (William Dean Howells, *The Rise of Silas Lapham,* 1885)

pale as dishwater   Very pale. Given as a common expression in George Allen England, "Rural Locutions of Maine and Northern New Hampshire," *Dialect Notes,* Vol. IV (1914).

pally   Often heard in Boston for *pal, friend, buddy*. " 'Keep yah shirt on, pally,' Brennan said complacently in the driver's seat.' " (George V. Higgins, *Bomber's Law,* 1993)

pan fried potatoes   Home fries.

pantod   Frequently used in Massachusetts and Connecticut in former times to describe anything from a violent pain to a mild discomfort. "You act like you had the pantod."

paper birch   A common New England tree (*Betula papyrifera*) once much used to make canoes, canoe paddles and snowshoes.

paper the wall   To talk excessively. "He went on and on, papered the wall with it." Used chiefly in Maine.

parin' bee   See APPLE CUT.

park   Often pronounced *pack*. "The inhabitants [of Ayer, Massachusetts] pronounced 'park' as if it were 'pack'." (Frank Sullivan, *The New Yorker,* February 22, 1945)

parkway   A divided highway with plantings on each side and in the middle.

parlor stove The woodburning stove kept in the parlor in days past; basically no different from any other such stove but handsomer, often nickel plated.

Parmachenee Belle An artificial trout fly named after Parmachenee Lake in Maine.

parson's nose The walnut-size protuberance on the end of a turkey or other fowl that is actually the bird's tail (minus the feathers) and is also jocularly called *the part that went over the fence last*. "Thanksgivings Aunt Edwina always asked for the 'parson's nose.' "

parted her fasts A nautical term that means a ship that strayed from its mooring. Often applied figuratively.

partridge Used in Maine, which has no native partridges, for *grouse*. Pronounced *pa'tridge*.

part that went over the fence last See PARSON'S NOSE.

passel This pronunciation of *parcel* is found in New England, Southern and New York City speech. The form dates back to the 15th century, though the use of *passel* as a collective noun indicating an indefinite number dates back to 19th-century America.

patched like a whaleman's shirt An old nautical term used for anything in poor repair, barely held together.

Patriots Day A legal holiday marking the anniversary of the battle of Lexington on April 16, 1775; celebrated in Massachusetts and Maine since 1894.

payback Revenge. " 'Oh, bitch, ain't you gonna get a payback,' he says." (Stephen King, *Dolores Claiborne,* 1993)

pea beans Small white beans used in many New England dishes.

Peabody Bird See SAM PEABODY.

Peacham Pronounced PEE-chum; a Vermont town.

peaked Often pronounced PEE-kid in Maine.

Peaked Hill Bars A dangerous reef off Cape Cod. The *Peaked* in the name is pronounced *pick-ed* or *picket*.

pea soup fog A very thick fog through which a fisherman can barely see the end of his outstretched arm on the water. This expression is used in other regions as well.

peavey A short pole with a hook used in logging; invented in 1858 by Maine blacksmith Joseph Peavey.

pecker-fretted Riddled with holes made by a woodpecker. "A few old pecker-fretted apple trees." (Robert Frost, "Directive," 1947)

peep A nickname for any sandpiper (*Actitis macularia*), especially the least sandpiper; after the sound this shore bird makes.

peep of day Dawn. " 'Home, or we'll set you in the stocks by peep of day.' " (Nathaniel Hawthorne, "My Kinsman, Major Molineux," 1832)

peg out To die. "He'll peg out before winter ends." Given as a common expression in George Allen England, "Rural Locutions in Maine and Northern New Hampshire," *Dialect Notes,* Vol. IV (1914).

pell-mell for a cat-race! Very fast. A common expression a century ago.

pelter An old, worn-out horse; the term was heard mostly in Massachusetts in the early 1900s.

Penobscot An Indian tribe of the Maine Penobscot River and Bay area. "When the first Europeans came blowing by, the Maine coast was the home of the Abenakis, a tall Algonkian Indian race—Sokokis, Anasaqunticooks or Androscoggins, Canibas or Kennebecs, Wawennacks or Penobscots." (Robert P. Tristram Coffin, *Yankee Coast,* 1947)

Penn Yan, New York This old New York town, settled by New Englanders, is said to have been named from the first four letters of *Penn*sylvania plus the first three of *Yan*kee.

Pequot An Algonquian Indian tribe once dominant in southern New England. "The Pequots were probably the bravest and most ferocious of all the New England tribes." (Clarence Webster, *Town Mutiny County,* 1945)

perambulate the bounds To inspect the boundaries between towns, a practice required by law since colonial times in New England. Selectmen from the towns periodically meet to do this to make sure their boundaries have not been relocated.

perceivance An old term meaning notice. "He took no perceivance of it."

perch A measurement of 16½ feet once commonly used in New England. Better known as a *rod,* a perch was usually measured off with a perch pole of that length.

Perkins' tractors A historical term for a set of three-inch-long rods, one brass and one steel, that were said to relieve aches and pains by magnetism when they were drawn over affected areas of the body. Named for their inventor, Dr. Elisha Perkins (1741–1799) of Norwich, Connecticut, they were very popular in their day.

persneckity Overly concerned about small details, fastidious, fussy. The origin of the word is unknown.

pesky A nationally used term meaning troublesome or annoying that originated in New England, where it possibly was introduced directly from England's Essex dialect.

pestle around A Vermont term dating back to the days of mortar-and-pestle describing any hasty, puttering actively. "He's been pestlin' around all day."

petoncles, pelerines Names French-speaking New Englanders use for *scallops.*

petticoat government A household ruled by the women or woman of the house. " 'I am a poor good-for-nothing critter . . . I am under petticoat government here.' " (Henry David Thoreau, *Cape Cod,* 1865)

peverly bird A name in New England for what is more commonly called the peabody bird and white-throated sparrow elsewhere. The little sparrow is said to sound like it's singing, "Old Sam Peabody, Peabody, Peabody," hence *peabody bird.* As for *peverly bird,* an old story has it that a Mr. Peverly, a New England farmer, was walking in his fields one early spring day trying to decide whether he should plant his wheat yet. A little sparrow in the adjacent woods seemed to sing, "Sow wheat, Peverly, Peverly, Peverly!" so Mr. Peverly went ahead and did so, reaping an abundant harvest that fall. Ever after the little sparrow was called the *peverly bird* in New England.

P.I. See quote. "Strictly speaking a P.I. is one who hails originally from Prince Edward's Island; but around here [Maine] it has come to mean any Canadian who isn't a Frenchman. A Canadian Frenchman is just a Frenchman. If you mean a man from France—and you very seldom do—you say a French Frenchman." (Louise Dickinson Rich, *Happy the Land,* 1946)

piazza A porch. " 'That's right. Mrs. Lothrop said they'd have the Herreshoff teas on that porch.' 'The correct term,' said Ma, 'is piazza.' " (Susan Minot, "Thanksgiving Day," 1986)

pick In most places potatoes are *dug,* but in Maine they are *picked.*

pick-ed Pointed. "He stepped on the pick-ed end of the eel spear."

pickled oyster See SHELL-OYSTER.

pictur Picture. "The Yankee always shortens the *u* in the ending *ture,* making *ventur, natur, pictur* and so on." (James Russell Lowell, *The Biglow Papers,* 1866)

picture See U.

pie See quote.

> The pie is an English institution, which, planted on American soil, forthwith ran rampant and burst forth onto an untold variety of genera and species. Not merely the old traditional mince pie, but a thousand strictly American seedlings from the main stock, evinced the power of American housewives to adapt old institutions to new uses. Pumpkin pies, cranberry pies, huckleberry pies, peach, pear and plum pies, custard pies, apple pies, Marlborough-pudding pies—pies with top crusts and without—pies adorned with all sorts of fanciful flutings and architectural strips laid across and around, and otherwise varied, attested the boundless fertility of the feminine

mind, when let loose in a given direction. (Harriet Beecher Stowe, *Old Town Folks,* 1869)

piece out Last, make do. "We've got enough wood to piece out the winter."

pieplant Another name for *rhubarb* (*Rheum rhabarbarum*), because it often is used in pie fillings.

pierce See FIERCE.

pigeon roost A large area, often up to 100,000 acres, where passenger pigeons once roosted, so many of them that the sun never reached the ground.

piggin A small bucket used to collect sap from maple trees. See NOGGIN.

pilch A quilted mattress cover.

pile on the agony To act theatrically or very emotionally. "Don't you think you're piling on the agony a bit too thick?"

Pilgrim See quote.

"Pilgrims" is little more than a century old, having come into common usage since 1840 . . . The Pilgrims had no name for themselves as a group. For generations they were known to their descendants merely as the Forefathers, a name preserved in the only holiday officially dedicated to their memory, Forefathers' Day, tardily instituted in Massachusetts in 1895 . . . (George F. Willison, *Saints and Strangers,* 1945)

Willison adds that the name "Pilgrims" for the "Forefathers" or "First Comers" was used first by Governor William Bradford in 1630 in the phrase "they knew they were pilgrims" in his manuscript chronicle of *Plimoth Plantation,* a manuscript that wasn't widely available for over two centuries. The story of the 102 Pilgrims who founded Plymouth Colony is too well known to bear repeating here, except to say that these Pilgrim Fathers landed on Plymouth Rock instead of in Virginia, as planned, because bad weather had kept them too long at sea and they had run out of beer, among other supplies. Plimoth Plantation in Plymouth, Massachusetts is a re-creation of the second permanent settlement in America as it appeared in 1627, seven years after the Pilgrims landed. The word *pilgrim* means wanderer, traveler, person who journeys a long distance to a sacred place. It has an interesting history, coming from the Latin *peregrinus,* "stranger." It came into English as *pelegrin* in about 1200, but dissimilation and slothful pronunciation over the years eventually made *pilgrim* out of *pelegrin.* Thus, the Pilgrim Fathers, a proverbially industrious group, take their name from a lazy man's word.

Pilgrim City An old nickname for *Boston.*

Pilgrim mothers One of the women founders of the Plymouth Colony in 1620.

Pilgrim people A nickname for inhabitants of Massachusetts.

Pilgrim shell An old name for what is now generally called the scallop shell.

Pilgrim society An organization founded in 1820 to honor the Pilgrims who founded Plymouth, Massachusetts.

pillow bier An old-fashioned word, rarely used today, for *pillow case*.

pimping This obsolete term is far removed in meaning from the modern definition of the word. *Pimping* was used in the 19th century to mean "little, petty": "It's such a pimping thing to fight about."

pindling A child, adult or even an animal who is pale, small, undernourished.

pine cone and tassel The state symbol of Maine.

pine knot A knot of wood from the pine tree used for firewood.

pine-tree cod A name for *cod (Gadus callarius)* in southeast Maine.

pine-tree flag An early New England flag with a pine tree as an emblem.

pine-tree shilling A coin with a pine tree as an emblem issued by the Massachusetts colony in 1652.

> His enemies had a ridiculous story that Master ("Ichabod") Pigsnort ("a weighty merchant and selectman of Boston") was accustomed to spend a whole hour, after prayer time, every morning and evening, in wallowing naked among an immense quantity of pine-tree shillings, which were the earliest coinage of Massachusetts. (Nathaniel Hawthorne, "The Great Carbuncle," 1837)

Pine Tree State A nickname for *Maine*.

Pine-tree stater A Mainer.

pinkletink An old term for a young frog of the genus *Hyla* heard on Martha's Vineyard and in southwestern Massachusetts.

pinkwink A Cape Cod term for a tadpole, based on the sound tadpoles make.

pinky This old type of sharp-sterned New England fishing schooner probably took its name from the dutch *pinche*, "narrow," in reference to its long, narrow counter (the part of the stern that hangs over and protects the sternpost).

pint! An order to behave quietly; heard on Isleboro, off the Maine coast.

piny An unusual New England pronunciation of "peony," which is bested only by the old Washington State rendering of the name peony: *piano plant.*

pious as a barn rat A sarcastic old expression used to describe a sanctimonious person.

pismire Used in New Hampshire for *ant,* usually a red one.

piss-cutter A show-off, often said to a man who is all dressed up; heard mostly in Maine.

pissybed A dandelion, because folklore holds that eating it causes nocturnal wetting of the bed.

pistol The word for a Maine lobster with only one claw or none.

pixilated Dazed, bewildered, daffy. Used frequently in the screenplay *Mr. Deeds Goes to Town* (1936).

pizen neat An old often complimentary term heard in Maine and elsewhere for very neat. *Pizen* here is a pronunciation of *person*.

plagued Cussed, ornery. Often pronounced *pleg-ged*. "I wish those plegged tourists would go home."

plaguey sight, a A great deal. "I'd a plaguey sight rather see Ascot than anything else in England." (Thomas C. Haliburton, *The Attaché or Sam Slick in England*, 1843–44)

plaguing Annoying, teasing. "He's been plaguing the little ones all day." Often pronounced *pleging*.

plaguing at Insisting in an annoying way. "And there he stuck year after year, with the whole town plaguing at him to quit." (Dorothy Canfield, "Old Man Warner," in *Raw Material*, 1925)

plain speaking Speaking directly to the point, bluntly, without any euphemism or adornment. " 'Folks in her day were given to plain speaking.' " (Robert Frost, "The Generations of Men," 1914)

plantations A humorous old term for *human feet*.

plaster A name used in Massachusetts for the surf scoter duck (*Melanitta perspicillita*), because of the large plasterlike splotch on the adult male's bill.

plate full up with Filled with. " 'Sickness and trouble: that's what Ethan's had his plate full up with, ever since the very first helping.' " (Edith Wharton, *Ethan Frome*, 1911)

playing possum Making believe one is dead. "Winter only was playing possum." (Robert Frost, "Two Tramps in Mud Time," 1936)

play Yankee with An obsolete term meaning to cheat.

please one about to death Please someone greatly. ". . . we'll go right over an' see poor old Miss Nancy Fell; 't will please her about to death." (Sarah Orne Jewett, "The Guests of Mrs. Timms," 1895)

please up Please. "I'm sure that we'll please him up."

pleasuring Holidaying, vacationing, anything done for pleasure as opposed to work; often said of sailing for pleasure. "Let's go pleasurin' this weekend."

plucky Courageous, full of spirit. "We grew plucky women in New Hampshire." (Stephen Vincent Benét, "The Devil and Daniel Webster," 1937)

plum Blueberries are not picked in Maine but *plum-ed*. They are also *raked*, after the implement used to harvest lowbush berries. The berries certainly are not anywhere near plum size, so the origin of expressions such as "Let's go plumming tomorrow" are something of a mystery.

plumb smackety-dab Squarely. "He stepped plumb smackety-dab into it."

plum crazy Completely crazy, an expression once common in New England speech.

Plymothean An inhabitant of Plymouth, Massachusetts; the term was first recorded in 1631.

Plymouth Pilgrim A term Southerners used derisively for *Union soldier* during the Civil War.

Plymouth Rock (1) A large granite boulder in Plymouth Harbor where the first European settlers landed in 1620. (2) A variety of chickens first bred in Plymouth, Massachusetts in the mid-19th century.

poach Used a century ago to mean "tread soft ground and leave deep tracks" as cattle do.

podge To move slowly. "There he goes podgin' along."

Podunk Small backward towns have been called *Podunks* since before 1841, when the term is first recorded. The first Podunk was an Indian place-name between what is now Hartford and Windsor, Connecticut, the name deriving from the Mohegan Algonquian word for *neck or corner of land*. The humorous sound of *Podunk* led Americans to use it derisively for *little, insignificant place*.

pogy Often used in New England for *menhaden* (*Brevoortia tyrannus*), a fish caught mainly for its oil in days past. Apparently a corruption of *porgy*, which is another fish entirely.

poisson blanc A name for whitefish (of the family Coregonidae) used in parts of New England where there is French influence; it is French for *white fish*.

poke (1) A synonym for *stomach*. "My poke's all filled up." (2) *Poke* means a paper bag in other regions.

pokeloken A word used by lumbermen for a marshy bay area.

Polack fiddle A lumbering term for *bucksaw*, which Polish lumberjacks in Maine used so expertly that they made it sing.

pole cat See POLE CAT TRAIL.

pole cat trail A *pole cat* is another name for skunk, and a *pole cat trail* is an easy skiing trail for poor skiers or beginners without sharp turns or pitches. See WILD CAT TRAIL.

polpisy Heard in Nantucket for *awkward, countrified*. "He acts polpisy."

pom-pom-pete-away A once-popular game of tag. Also *pump-pump-pullaway*.

pond Often applied to any inland waters, no matter how large or small. Indeed, the Atlantic and Pacific oceans have been described humorously as ponds.

poochin' out Sticking out. " ' . . . his lower lip poochin' out in that ugly way it had.' " (Stephen King, *Dolores Claiborne*, 1993)

pooquaw Ask for a pooquaw in New England today and all you'll get is a "What?" But the term was once common for the quahog clam, especially in Nantucket. It derives from a Narraganset Indian word.

poor as poverty in a gale o' wind Very poor. Given as a common expression in George Allen England, "Rural Locutions in Maine and Northern New Hampshire," *Dialect Notes*, Vol. IV (1914).

poored away Grown thin, wasted away. "He has poored away."

poorly In bad health. "I been poorly all this year, but I think I'm feeling better now."

poor man's manure Snow that falls in early spring; it is thought to provide the soil with nutrients and to provide a better source of moisture because it doesn't run off and cause erosion. The term is also used in other regions.

poor old country railroad A nickname given to Maine's Portland & Oxford Central Railroad, the appellation based on its initials and the many mishaps on the line.

popple A rural pronunciation of "poplar." "It's under the popple tree."

popular In the 1867 *Biglow Papers*, James Russell Lowell gave *popular* as a New England synonym for *conceited*.

porch An ell kitchen.

> The word porch is dictionary-defined as a "covered way or entrance whether enclosed or unenclosed." In ecclesiastical architecture, where it presumably originated, it describes the covered and usually enclosed entrance built on to a church or cathedral—for all the world, in general outline and appearance, like the ell kitchen of a typical old Nantucket house . . . The use of the word porch as applied to a veranda is modern U.S. and more or less local at that. (William F. Macy, *The Nantucket Scrap Basket*, 1916)

Porchmuth A New Hampshire pronunciation of "Portsmouth," a seaport in southeast New Hampshire.

porcupine See HEDGEHOG.

porkpick Another word for *porcupine* heard in Maine and vicinity; a corruption of the French *porcpeque* for the animal. See also HEDGEHOG, QUILL-PIG.

porridge Frequently pronounced *por-ritch*, as in the old rhyme "There was a young man from Noritch / Who burnt his mouth on Bean Por-ritch."

Portagee Portuguese. "What'n thunder'r'y abaout, y' darned Portagee?" (Oliver Wendell Holmes, *Elsie Venner*, 1861)

Port Clyde sardines A sardine caught in Port Clyde, Maine, said to be the equal in taste to any in the world.

Portlander A native of Portland, Maine or Portland, Oregon.

Portsmouth Pronounced PORTS-muth; a New Hampshire city and Rhode Island town.

potato Often pronounced *pertetter* in Maine.

potato bargain An inexpensive traditional New England dish made of salt pork, potatoes, onions and bread.

pot cheese See COTTAGE CHEESE.

pot head In Maine this term has nothing to do with habitual users of marijuana, meaning instead someone of very limited intelligence.

pot luck See quote. "From the town of East Lee [Massachusetts] is said to come the phrase 'pot luck' as applied to a delectable New England boiled dinner . . . 'Pot luck' was well-known in 1791, in the town of Lee which was settled by Cape Cod people mostly." (Federal Writers' Project, *The Berkshire Hills,* 1939) See

NEW ENGLAND BOILED DINNER. *Pot luck* has come to mean eating anything your host is having for dinner when you drop in unexpectedly ("You're welcome to have pot luck with us"), or any dinner to which the participants bring a dish of their own making.

potty A pronunciation commonly heard in Boston for *party.*

pound up Beat up. "He pounded him up so bad his own mother didn't know him."

poverty grass *Hudsonia tomentosa,* a beach grass found on Cape Cod and elsewhere. "All winter long [the carpet of] this grass has been a kind of rag gray . . . but now it wears one of the rarest and loveliest greens in nature. I shall have to use the term 'sage green' in telling of it . . ." (Henry Beston, *The Outermost House,* 1928)

powerful Very. " 'It *is* powerful cold down here.' Ethan assented . . ." (Edith Wharton, *Ethan Frome,* 1911)

prayer-handles A humorous word for *knees.* "He got down on his prayer-handles." Given as a common term in George Allen England, "Rural Locutions of Maine and Northern New Hampshire," *Dialect Notes,* Vol. IV (1914).

Praying Indian A term used in early New England for an Indian converted to Christianity.

presume likely The Nantucket equivalent of the Southern "reckon" or the "guess" other Yankees might use. "I presume likely they're coming."

pretty nigh fin out An old Nantucket way to say one is seriously ill, the reference to the way a dying whale rolls over on its side, showing a fin above water. Cited in William F. Macy, *The Nantucket Scrap Basket* (1916).

privileged A nautical term for a vessel with the right of way that is sometimes applied to traffic on the road. Someone who had the right of way on the highway might say "I was privileged."

prized up Pried up. "He prized up the nails."

professor An obsolete word for a fervent church member.

prolly A common Boston pronunciation of "probably," though both can be used in the same sentence depending on the emphasis, as in this quote: " 'I guess prolly though his can't be as good, probably, the first one that he got, I mean.' " (George V. Higgins, *Bomber's Law*, 1993) Also common in Maine.

prop'ty An old-fashioned pronunciation of "property." "A real lovely friendship with a young woman who had, as Mrs. Tarrant expressed it, 'prop'ty' . . ." (Henry James, *The Bostonians*, 1886)

prudent Sometimes used for *prudently*. "Spend it prudent!" (Alice Brown, "Mis' Wadleigh's Guest," 1895)

pshaw! An exclamation of disbelief very common a generation ago.

P-town A nickname for *Provincetown* used on Cape Cod. "P-town was a strange two-faced kind of place, he thought. And it had been that way even in his youth, a hard-working town where a lot of people seemed to be playing all the time." (William Martin, *Cape Cod*, 1991)

public school Grammar school. " 'Public School's over yonder. High School's still farther over.' " (Thornton Wilder, *Our Town*, 1938)

puckerbrush A word used in Maine and New Hampshire for the woods or wilderness. 'He went up into the puckerbrush and ain't been seen since."

puckersnatch The term proud seamstresses of old used to mean "hasty and poor sewing," often all bunched up.

Pudding Town An old nickname for *Northhampton, Connecticut*; from the widespread custom in the town of having hasty pudding and milk for Saturday supper. Recorded by Clifton Johnson, *Historic Hampshire in the Connecticut Valley* (1932). Residents of Pudding Town were called *Puddingers*.

pudgetty Sullen, grouchy. "He's a pudgetty old man."

pudge up An old-fashioned expression meaning to prod or stimulate. "She tried to pudge him up."

puffing like a grampus (whale) Breathing hard. A simile once heard commonly in New England.

pug A synonym for *hair bun*.

Pumpkin-Heads See quote.

New Haven is celebrated for having given the name of "pumpkin-heads" to all New Englanders. It originated with the "Blue Laws," which informed every male to have his hair cut round by a cap. When caps were not to be had, they substituted the hard shell of a pumpkin, which being put on the head every Saturday, the hair is cut by the shell all round the head." (Rev. Samuel Peters, LL.D, *General History of Connecticut*, 1877)

pumpkin pie See quote. "Punkin pi iz the sass ov New England . . . Enny man who don't luv punkin pi, wants watching cluse . . ." (Josh Billings, *Old Probability—Perhaps Rain, Perhaps Not*, 1875)

pumple-footed Club-footed. Given as a common term in George Allen England, "Rural Locutions of Maine and Northern New Hampshire," *Dialect Notes*, Vol. IV (1914).

pumple stones Round beach stones used for flower gardens, borders and the like.

pung A shortening of the old-folk term *tompung* for *toboggan*.

pungy A small boat or schooner once used in Massachusetts. Also called a *pungo*.

punk A name old-timers gave to any rotten wood.

punkin A common pronunciation of *pumpkin*.

purgatory See quote. "Along the coast of New England, and in the interior, narrow ravines with nearly perpendicular walls are called purgatories." (Alexander Whitney, *Names and Places*, 1888)

Puritan Fathers Same as PILGRIM FATHERS.

Puritan Provinces New England. "Within the boundaries of the Puritan Provinces . . . no depth of solitude of the wilderness could exclude youth from all the common opportunities of moral, and far more than the common ones of religious education." (Nathaniel Hawthorne, "Sir William Phips," 1830)

purse A New Hampshire pronunciation of "pierce," as in Franklin Pierce (1804–1869), the New Hampshire-born 14th President of the United States. "She [New Hampshire] had one President. (Pronounce him Purse, / And make the most of it for better or worse. / He's your one chance to score against the state.)" (Robert Frost, "New Hampshire," 1923)

push rowing A fisherman's term meaning rowing a boat while facing forward.

pussley See quote. "Purslane, whose lovely, Elizabethan-sounding name farmers from New England to Georgia corrupt into "pussley.' " (*The New Yorker,* March 10, 1943)

pussy An old term heard in New Hampshire and Maine for a fat man; a corruption of "pursy." "He was considerable pussy."

pussyflage Nonsense, foolishness. " 'I was reading the pussyflage you wrote about plantin' gardens . . ." (John Gould, *It Is Not Now,* 1993)

put a flea in one's ear Giving someone a hint, warning or suspicion of something; to put an idea in someone's head.

put for To hurry. "She put for the house."

put on a corn sweat Make a great effort: "He put on a corn sweat to get the job finished." The expression, heard chiefly in Maine, has its roots in an old cure that used ears of corn to help a sick person sweat out a cold or fever.

putter An old term heard on Cape Cod meaning to walk faster, hurry. "He was really puttering along."

put the John D. to her John D. Rockefeller, of course, made his great fortune in oil. Therefore, loggers used his name to mean kerosene, especially in the expression *put the John D. to her!,* that is, kindle or start a fire.

put the oakum to To shut someone up with sharp or clever words; oakum is used to caulk or close up boat seams.

put to one's stumps Made to put forth one's best efforts. "[I urged] them to show these Britishers what the Yankee could do when put to his stumps." (Ward McAllister, *Society As I Knew It,* 1890)

putty To putter around. "He putted with the car all day."

Q

quahaug *Venus mercenaria,* the edible hardshell clam. Indians introduced this name and the clams themselves to the first European settlers in New England. Quahaugs usually are divided into *chowders,* as large as four inches at the widest point; *cherrystones,* half-grown quahaugs; and *littlenecks,* the most tender and smallest of quahaugs at two inches or so. "Certain words trap the stranger. *Quahaug* is the worst offender. Let us at once solve the mystery of its pronunciation by saying that if you call it 'co-hog' you will be talking the language of the native fishermen." (Arthur Wilson Tarbell, *Cape Cod Ahoy!* 1932) See HARDSHELL CLAM.

Queen's-arm An old term for *musket* mentioned in James Russell Lowell's *The Biglow Papers* (1866).

quee-uh See QUEER.

queer Strange, odd. " 'Queer the barn ain't open,' she thought to herself." (Mary E. Wilkins, "Life-Everlastin'," 1891). Commonly pronounced *quee-uh.*

quick To boil something rapidly, just until it is tender. "Just quick it, don't have it on the stove too long."

quill-pig A synonym for *porcupine.* See PORKPICK.

quilting bee A gathering in which women assembled to sew together the squares that were to be the outside covering of the quilt.

Quincy The Massachusetts city's name is properly pronounced KWIN-zi.

quint An old-fashioned word for a fussy old maid heard in Massachusetts.

quishion A probably obsolete pronunciation and spelling of "cushion" once commonly heard in Massachusetts and other parts of New England.

quitter Used to describe the sound a turkey makes. "The old tom-turkey a struttin' and a-sidlin and a-quitterin' sayin', 'Talk! talk! and quitter! quitter!'" (Harriet Beecher Stowe, "The Minister's Housekeeper," 1871)

quoddy A fast sloop-rigged boat used by fisherman and lobstermen in New England; named after Passamaquoddy Bay, where it was developed. *Passamaquoddy* is an Indian word meaning plenty of pollock.

Quonset hut The *Quonset* or *Quonset hut* is a prefabricated corrugated metal building shaped like a tunnel that is named for its first place of manufacture, Quonset Point, Rhode Island, during World War II. Virtually the same thing by another name is the Nissen hut, designed by British engineer Lt. Col. Peter Nissen in 1930.

R _____

R See quote.

> The . . . Eastern American habit of adding superfluous (r), as in *the idear of it,* is frequently misunderstood. This is subject to the same law—the superfluous (r) is added only when a vowel quickly follows. The Bostonian . . . is apt to say *Americar and France,* though he says *France and America* as Westerners do. I recently heard from a native of Boston, 'No, this is not the piazza; the piazzar is here." (John S. Kenyon, "Some Notes on American R," *American Speech,* March 1926)

See also the Introduction.

race A strong or swift channel of water. "The other evening my friend Bill Eldridge, of Nauset, told me that there had been a disaster that same morning off the Race." (Henry Beston, *The Outermost House,* 1928)

racing Said of an animal in season or heat. The term is not commonly heard today.

rackergaited Loose-jointed. Given as a common term in George Allen England, "Rural Locutions of Maine and Northern New Hampshire," *Dialect Notes,* Vol. IV (1914).

rag out To outfit with clothes; probably from the old nautical practice of sailors outfitting themselves from the "slop chest" kept on board for that purpose.

raie See STING or STING RAY.

raise a ruction To make a big fuss out of something that may not be worth the effort. "No sense raisin' a ruction about death or taxes." *Ruction* may be a corruption of *insurrection.*

raise Ned To make a great disturbance, to raise Cain or the devil.

raising hightantrabogus Raising hell, having a noisy good time.

raked See PLUM.

raking down Reprimanding, dressing down someone severely. "She gave him some raking down for being so late to school again."

ramming Having a wild time out on the town. "He was ramming around the whole night."

rantum scoot See quote.

> A term, we believe, peculiar to Nantucket, and very old. It means a day's "cruise" or picnic about the island, usually a drive, but it might be on foot. The distinctive

feature of such an excursion is that the party has no definite destination . . . in which respect such a trip differs from a SQUANTUM. "Rantum" is probably a corruption of random. (William F. Macy, *The Nantucket Scrap Basket,* 1916)

rap full Full to capacity. "He stuffed himself till he was rap full." Originally a nautical phrase for *sails filled with wind.*

raspberry Often pronounced *raspberry,* with the *p* sounded.

rat A Maine cheese. " 'I got a wedge of rat that's just about ripe.' " (Stephen King, *Pet Sematary,* 1983)

rather be shaved by a sharp razor than by a dull one Rather a clean fast cut, which hurts less than a dull slow one. "The peddler . . . was . . . keen at a bargain, but none the worse liked by the Yankees; who, as I have heard them say, would rather be shaved by a sharp razor than a dull one." (Nathaniel Hawthorne, "Mr. Higginbotham's Catastrophe," 1834)

rauncher (1) A large male deer. (2) Any large oversize thing, from a wave to a tree. *Rauncher* may derive from *raunchy* in reference to male deer during the rutting season.

razoo An old term used in Maine for *to treat roughly, manhandle.*

r-dropping See the Introduction.

Reach See quote. "A Reach is a body of water between two bodies of land, a body of water which is open at either end. The old lobstermen's joke went like this: know how to read y'compass when the fog comes, boys; between Jamesport and London there's a mightly long Reach." (Stephen King, "The Reach," 1981)

real blinger, a Heard in Massachusetts for a good joke, a thigh-slapper. "That's a real blinger!"

receipt A recipe. "Give me your receipt for those beans."

reddance A pronunciation of "riddance," as in "Good reddance to you!"

red flannel hash A traditional New England hash made with corned beef, potatoes, turnips, spices and a few chopped red beets for color. *White flannel hash* eschews the beets.

redhead Another word for *coral,* a lobster's orange roe.

Red Paint Men An extinct Indian tribe once resident in Maine. "Before the dawn and the Dawn People, there were the Red Paint Men . . . They have been gone so long now that not even the teeth of them are left [in their graves], only the red paint, color of life, they smeared their bodies with." (Robert P. Tristam Coffin, *Yankee Coast,* 1947) Also called *Red Paint Indians, Red Paint People.*

red shrimp See BAY SHRIMP.

Red spruce *Picea rubens,* a common New England tree whose wood is used to make pulp.

reelin' An expression used in Maine for *unrelenting noise, a din or racket*; after the hammers called *reels* once used by workers in granite quarries. "You kids better stop that reelin'."

regular coffee Throughout the United States this is generally coffee served with cream and sugar on the side but not added to it. In Boston and other New England areas it is coffee with cream added to it and just sugar served on the side. In Rhode Island it means with milk and sugar.

regular hurrah's nest, a A mess. "That house is a regular hurrah's nest." Given as a Vermont expression in Charles Edward Crane's *Let Me Show You Vermont,* 1937. But the term has had wide currency throughout New England and elsewhere.

Rehoboth The city's name is properly pronounced RE-ho-both.

rent Heard in Maine for an apartment or any rented quarters. "We have a nice rent near the water."

reverse nod True Yankees don't even wave, it's said; they simply nod lifting the chin up, a "reverse nod."

rheumatiz Rheumatism. "He's all crippled up with rheumatiz."

Rhode Island One story has Verrazzano, in 1524, observing the island now called Aquidneck in Narragansett Bay and naming it Rhodes Island because it reminded him of the island of Rhodes in the Mediterranean. Later, the island gave its name to the state. Most scholars contend that *Rhode Island* takes its name from the Dutch *Roodt Eylandt,* "red island," for its red clay. See COMMONWEALTH; ROGUES ISLAND.

Rhode Island clambake Perhaps the most famous of New England clambakes, though all the other states might strongly dispute this. Exclaimed Christopher La Farge in his poem "Rhode Island Clambake":

> O clams that are still fresh from mud!
> O lobsters slowly turning red!
> O delicate young Irish spread!
> O corn whose husk has not been shed!

Rhode Island Red A breed of fowl with brownish-red feathers that was developed in Rhode Island by crossing a Brown leghorn with a Malay hen. The Rhode Island Red is a prolific layer of brown eggs.

Rhode Island White A white-feathered variety of the RHODE ISLAND RED.

rid See INSTEAD.

ride-out Messy, disorderly. "The house looks like ride-out." Cited as a common expression in Portsmouth, New Hampshire and on Cape Cod in

Frederic D. Allen, "Contributions to New England Vocabulary," *Dialect Notes* (Vol. I, 1890).

right around Early. "He's right around this morning."

right as bean water A simile not heard much anymore. See RIGHT AS RAIN.

right as rain The best of anything, something unsurpassable, that couldn't be better.

righten up Tidy up. "Why don't you righten up your room."

right off An expression coined in 19th-century New England that means directly, right away. "I'll be with you right off."

right quick Quickly. "She learned it right quick."

right smart (1) Considerable. ". . . it must have been a right smart walk / That we had that day from Tillbury Town . . ." (Edward Arlington Robinson, "Isaac and Achibald," *Captain Craig*, 1902) (2) Accomplished, talented. "He's a right-smart ballplayer." Used in the South as well as New England.

rim Ream. "Rim out the hole so the peg will fit."

rinktum Once commonly used for a party or dance; a contrivance, design. Also spelled *rinctum*. "That rinktum didn't end till early in the morning."

rinse See INSTEAD.

rise Raise. "He's going to rise chickens."

risse Used for the past tense of *rise*. "Of Yankee preterites I find *risse* and *rize* for *rose* in [the English writers] Middleton and Dryden." (James Russell Lowell, *The Biglow Papers*, 1867)

ritiracy A word once used as a synonym for *retirement*. "I'm in my ritiracy now." *Ritiracied* meant retired.

river-driver *Bartlett's* (1848) defined this old term as "A log man who conducts logs down running streams."

riz Risen. " 'I say, isn't bread 'riz' enough when it runs over the pans?" (Louisa May Alcott, *Little Women*, 1868)

riz bread Bread made with yeast, raised bread. "I'd have some riz biscuit." (Mary Wilkens Freeman, *A New England Nun and Other Stories*, 1891)

roader A good horse, a roadster. "He's some smart roader."

robin snow A light snow that comes in midspring when robins are already in evidence.

rock See quote. "Every Maine boy calls a stone of throwing size a 'rock.' " (*Expressions of the Maine Coast*, 1880)

Rock, the An old nickname for *Plymouth Rock*.

rock maple Another name for the sugar maple (*Acer saccharum*), which is widely tapped for maple sugar.

rock crab A species of crab (*Cancer irroratus*), commonly caught and eaten in Maine.

rock round the corner To stone someone for an offense or supposed offense; today such stonings are rarer than the expression.

rockweed The typical name for seaweed in Maine and other areas.

roll-way, roll-a-way An outside cellar entrance with sloping doors.

roost A term for *toilet* used in lumbering camps.

rootle A Massachusetts and Maine word for the rooting of a pig. "Pigs don't root, they rootle."

Rogues Island A humorous nickname for RHODE ISLAND in the days shortly after its founding. It was also called "the Sink of New England."

rose See RISSE.

rose bread Any bread made with yeast; a bread that rises.

Rosebud Senator A nickname for U.S. Senator Henry Anthony (1815–1884) of Rhode Island because of "the healthful glow that mantled his cheek, or as a tribute to the fact that he constantly wore a bud or other flower," according to the *Congressional Record,* January 21, 1885.

rotary A synonym for *traffic circle*.

rotten apple cider Homemade cider made from whatever apples are available, apples in any usable condition. Considered a good drink with body.

Rouge Hose See BOSOX.

round See HOUSE.

round clam An old southwestern New England word for QUAHAUG.

rowen An aftermath or second crop grown in a hayfield.

rowty Argumentative. "He's a rowty old man."

Roxbury Russet A late, long-keeping apple variety developed in Roxbury, Massachusetts early in the 19th century.

rubbage, rubbidge A pronunciation of "rubbish."

rub the time close Allow little time. "You're rubbing the time too close to catch the train." Cited as a common Portsmouth, New Hampshire expression in Frederic D. Allen, "Contributions to the New England Vocabulary," *Dialect Notes,* Vol. I (1890).

rud A pronunciation of "road."

ruddle A synonym for a house's attic. "There's a lot of family treasures up in the ruddle."

ruff A common pronuciation of "roof."

rugged weather Bad weather, though not the worst possible weather; weather when outside activities can't be enjoyed.

rummy Sometimes heard for *drunkard*. "He's an old rummy."

rum sweat A sweat worked up by drinking rum or other liquor to relieve a cold.

run a slack ship See RUN A TAUT SHIP.

run a taut ship To be a thoroughly efficient employer or supervisor. The saying dates back to the age of sailing ships and captains who ran neat perfectly maintained vessels with no slack in the rigging anywhere. The opposite expression is *run a slack ship*.

run afoul of In its seafaring use, this expression means entangled. On land in New England it means to meet accidentally. "I ran afoul of Gerald Pierce this morning." Sometimes *fall afoul of*.

running the wangan Used by Maine lumbermen for taking a loaded boat down river in swift water. See WANGAN.

russet cider An excellent cider made from high-quality apples.

rut An old expression, once common in Massachusetts, for the noise of waves breaking on the beach.

S

Sabbaday Once used as a synonym for *Sunday, the Sabbath Day.*

Saco Pronounced SAH-co or SACK-oh; a Maine town and river.

Sacred Cod (1) Cod (*Gadus callarias*) is said to be the world's most important edible fish. So important was it to the fisheries of New England that it was early called the *Sacred Cod*. (2) The pine codfish hanging opposite the speaker's rostrum in the Massachusetts House of Representatives in the State House on Beacon Hill in Boston. A wooden codfish has hung there since colonial times. One was lost in a 1747 fire, its replacement lost during the Revolution. The present cod was hung in 1784. Harvard pranksters stole the 4-foot-11-inch cod in 1933, but returned it within a few days after a great uproar.

safe as in God's pocket Cited in *The Old Farmer's Almanac* (1946) as a common New England saying.

safen Make safe. "They'll safen your brakes."

Sage of Concord A nickname for Ralph Waldo Emerson, whose home was in Concord, Massachusetts.

said it right out In plain words, bluntly. " 'I said it right out to our minister once, and he was shocked at me." (Edith Wharton, *Ethan Frome*, 1911)

sail too close to the wind To be reckless, take too many chances. Cited in William F. Macy, *The Nantucket Scrap Basket* (1916).

sakes alive! An old-fashioned euphemistic exclamation.

Salem Gibralter A candy bar first sold in the early 19th century in Salem, Massachusetts and still available recently.

salted down An old term that means money saved in a safe place; the reference is to preserved salted meat or fish. "He's got plenty salted down in the bank."

salter'n the briny ocean Extremely salty. Given as a common expression in George Allen England, "Rural Locutions of Maine and Northern New Hampshire," *Dialect Notes,* Vol. IV (1914).

salt horse Beef or pork pickled in brine was often called *salt horse* on the New England coast and elsewhere. An old rhyme went:

> "Old horse! old horse! what
>   brought you here?"
> "From Sacarap to Portland Pier
> I've carted stone for many a year;

Till, killed by blows and sore abuse,
They salted me down for sailor's
use.
The sailors they do me despise,
They turn me over and damn my
eyes;
Cut off my meat and scrape my
bones
And heave the rest to Davy Jones."

The Sacarap in the verse was a part of Westbrook, Maine, near Portland Pier. See also HARNESS CASK; LOBSCOUSE.

salt potatoes Small red-skinned potatoes, often the first of the season, are called salad potatoes on Long Island's North Fork (on the fringe of New England) because they are often used in potato salad. But along the Boston Post Road in Connecticut, less than 50 miles away across Long Island Sound, they are called *salt potatoes* (signs often advertise "Lobster and Salt Potatoes—Only $9.95) because they are cooked in salted water.

salty dog See CAPE CODDER.

same as a singed cat Said of someone very wary due to a bad experience, like a cat singed in a fire that remains suspicious of fire ever after.

same as if As though. "He acted same as if they had never fought."

samp An old name for *hasty pudding* or *cornmeal mush*.

Sam Peabody A New England name for the white-throated sparrow (*Zonotrichia albicollis*), which has been called the nightingale of the north and whose flutelike song often sounds like the words "poor old Sam Peabody, Peabody, Peabody." Also called the *Peabody* or *Peabody bird*. See PEVERLY BIRD.

san A frequent pronunciation of "sand" in the region.

sanctimonious old bastard Someone, usually an old person, who appears to be holier than thou but really has hardly any scruples at all.

sand carpets "Carpets" made of sand in early New England parlors. Housewives often drew designs and pictures in the sand, which were renewed again after company called and left. Especially valued were the blue sands from Ipswich beaches and the black sands from Mackerel Cove in Beverly, Massachusetts.

sandwich glass A pressed glass originally made at Sandwich, Massachusetts.

sannup A mischievous boy always getting into trouble; from a Maine Abnaki Indian word for *young boy*. "Get out of that tree, you little sannup."

sap coffee A New England coffee in which maple sap has been substituted for the water.

saphouse A small house or hut where maple sugar is made and stored.

sap'lasses An obsolete term for *maple syrup*.

sap orchard A sugar maple grove.

sardines A humorous name New Englanders had for *sailors* a century ago.

sarpent An old pronunciation of "serpent."

sarvant A pronunciation of "servant." "Sarvant, Ma'am (means I am your servant)." (Oliver Wendell Holmes, *The Professor at the Breakfast Table*, 1860)

sarve A pronunciation of "serve." "It sarves him right."

sass (1) Sauce. (2) Garden vegetables. (3) Impudent talk. "He was always sassing his mother."

sauceman An old name for a peddler of vegtables. "Behind comes a 'sauceman', driving a wagon full of new potatoes, green ears of corn, beets, carrots, turnips, and summer squashes." (Nathaniel Hawthorne, "The Toll-Gatherer's Day," 1837)

save out Put aside. "The old Maine fisherman said he'd 'save' out some clams for us."

saw Mainers a century ago commonly used this word to mean "scold." "Every time I turn around he's sawing me."

sawdust sorter Heard in Maine for someone whose intelligence is limited. "He's in training for a sawdust sorter."

Saw-ko The Maine pronunciation of "Saco."

saxon James Russell Lowell gives this as a pronunciation of "sexton" in *The Biglow Papers* (1866).

says I See quote under PAINT UP.

S'bay-go The Maine pronunciation of "Sebago."

S-boat A large racing boat once popular in New England. "Off 'Sconset, where the yawing S-boats splash . . ." (Robert Lowell, "The Quaker Graveyard in Nantucket," 1946)

scalawag Another name for a culpin, a freshwater fish of the genus *Cottus,* along the New England coast.

scarified pavement Sign seen in Vermont indicating pavement that has been scored to help prevent slipping.

scarlet letter, the The first mention of people being forced to wear a scarlet capital *A* that branded them adulterers is reported in the *Plymouth Colonial Records* (1639): "The Bench doth therefore censure the said Mary . . . to wear a badge upon her left sleeve." The letter *I* was used for those found guilty of incest. Any woman "suffering an Indian to have carnal knowledge of her," in John Josselyn's words (*An Account of Two Voyages to New England,* 1674), was made to wear the figure of an Indian cut out of red cloth. See also A.

scholard An old pronunciation of "scholar," a student.

schoolmarm A humorous lumberman's term for a tree that forms two trunks from its crotch, resembling someone with two legs in the air.

schooner Some etymologists say this word originated in Gloucester, where an onlooker supposedly exclaimed, "Oh, how she scoons!" when Captain Andrew Robinson launched the first vessel of this kind back in 1713 and she glided gracefully over the water. Captain Robinson, overhearing the remark, dubbed his ship a *scooner*, which came to be misspelled *schooner* over the years. The only trouble with this story is that the word *scoon* (a Scottish word meaning to skip a flat stone over the water) doesn't seem to have been used in New England.

Scituate Pronounced SIT-u-ate or SIT-u-et; towns in Massachusetts and Rhode Island.

scoff To gulp down food or drink. "He scoffed his lunch in a minute." *Scarf,* meaning the same, is more commonly heard in the United States, as in "He scarfed down his food."

scoggins A fool, an object of ridicule. "They made a scoggins out of him."

'Sconset A common pronunciation of the name of Siasconset on eastern Nantucket. See quote under S-BOAT.

scooch To crouch, hunker down. "He scooched down in the corner." Cited as a common Maine and Portsmouth, New Hampshire expression in Frederick D. Allen, "Contribu-

tions to the New England Vocabulary," *Dialect Notes,* Vol. I (1890). The word is usually pronounced *scrootch* in the rest of New England.

scottin'-long-the-shore An old name for *hashed brown potatoes,* because the dish was often made by Cape Cod fishermen while they were at work on their boats.

scoots, the; scootberry The *scoots* was 19th-century New England slang for *diarrhea* (which sent one scooting to the outhouse); because the sweetish red berries on the shrub *Striptopus roseus* almost always acted as a physic on youngsters who eagerly ate them, the plant was named the *scootberry*.

Scrap Islander A name given to Nantucketers by residents of Martha's Vineyard. Cited by William F. Macy in *The Nantucket Scrap Basket* (1916).

Scratch A name for the devil. " 'My name is Scratch. They often call me that in New England.' " (Stephen Vincent Benét, "The Devil and Daniel Webster," 1937)

scratched along Barely made ends meet, perhaps like a chicken scratching for food. "She 'kinder scratched along,' as she phrased it, and earned her living, if no more, in the various ways Yankee ingenuity can discover in a large country town." (Rose Terry Cooke, "Town Mouse and Country Mouse," 1891)

scrawl An old term for "the ragged, broken branch of a tree or bush" that I can find only in *Bartlett's* (1859).

screwed hay Hay that is baled in coils rather than rectangular bales.

scrid A little bit, a small portion. "I'll just have a scrid more of that pie."

scrimp To economize severely. Used nationally now, the word was first used in New England, where it was possibly introduced directly from England's Essex dialect.

scrimshander An old term for someone who carves SCRIMSHAW. The origin of *shander* in the word is unknown.

scrimshaw Until relatively recently sailors on long voyages, especially New England whalers, often spent their spare time carefully carving whalebone, shells or ivory into decorative and useful objects, ranging from clothespins to elaborate canes and jewelry boxes. This intricate work was called *scrimshaw*, a word whose origins are rather mysterious. *Webster's* traces *scrimshaw* to the French *escrimer*, "to fight with a sword," in the sense of "to make flourishes," while other dictionaries suggest *scrimshank*, English military slang meaning to evade duty, be a shirker. Just as many authorities believe the word comes from the proper name Scrimshaw, referring to some once-illustrious sailor-carver noted for his craftsmanship. But Scrimshaw, if he did exist, hasn't been identified. *Scrimshaw* work also

was called *skrimshander,* and today it can mean any good piece of mechanical work.

scrimshonting Another term for SCRIMSHAW. ". . . 'scrimshonting,' as it is termed by whalers, ingeniously fabricated from whales' teeth and jaw bones . . ." (William Hussey Macy, *There She Blow!* 1877)

scrod See quote.

> The story goes that the Parker, a famous old restaurant in Boston, always had the freshest fish of the day on its menu. But the manager never knew which this would be on a given day. So he invented the word *scrod* as a catch-all name for it. Thus, although scrod now officially means young cod, it is historically correct to use it for, e.g., young haddock, too. (Alan Davidson, *North Atlantic Seafood,* 1978)

More likely, the word *scrod* derives from the Middle Dutch *schrode,* "strip or shred." New England scrod may be immature cod (*Gadus callarias*) or haddock (*Melanogrammus aiglefimus*) weighing one and a half to two and a half pounds. Sometimes the term is applied to cusk (*Brosme brosme*) of about the same weight, or to pollack (*Pollachius pollachius*) weighing one and a half to four pounds. When New England fishermen use the word, they usually are referring to gutted small haddock. In an old joke, a New Englander just back from Europe and hungry for a Yankee fish dinner directs the airport cabbie to "Take me where I can get scrod." "Okay," the cabbie says, heading toward a brothel, "but I must say that's the first time I ever got the request in the past pluperfect tense."

scrods Pieces of fish cut up for boiling.

scrog A shrub or tree stunted by the wind. Used mostly in Maine and New Hampshire.

scrooch Crouch down in a small place, hunker down. "He scrooched down beside her bed." See SCOOCH.

scronch Spirit, courage, spunk. "He had a lot of scronch in him."

scummer An instrument used to skim scum or impurities when maple syrup is being made.

scunner A deep dislike, an aversion; originally a Scottish dialect word. "I took a scunner to him right off."

scup (1) Menhaden (*Brevoortia tyrannus*); from an Indian word for the fish. (2) Another name for the saltwater porgy (*Pagrus pagrus*). Also *scuppang*. (3) Short for the scuppaug (*Stentotomus veriscolor*), a marine fish of southeastern New England.

scurry funge Used in coastal areas of Maine to mean a quick straightening up of the house when someone is about to come calling. "I had to scurry funge the kitchen when I saw Hilda coming up the walk."

seabeach knotweed A rare plant now found only on beaches in Massachusetts and New York.

sea-clam See quote. "Our host told us that the sea-clam, or hen, was not easily obtained . . . The fisherman sometimes wades in water several feet deep, and thrusts a pointed stick into the sand before him. When this enters between the valves of a clam, he closes them on it, and is drawn out. It has been known to catch and hold coot and teal which were preying on it." (Henry David Thoreau, *Cape Cod*, 1865)

sea corn The eggs of the whelk, which are yellow and when piled in a heap suggested corn to early New England fishermen.

sea dogs A name frequently given to seals along the Maine coast. The Portland Sea Dogs (named after the seals) are a Maine minor-league baseball team, according to *Yankee Magazine*, April 1, 1995.

sea duck A New England name for the eider duck, because they are often found on ledges jutting into the sea.

sealer A town official in days past who inspected weights and measures.

sea room An old nautical term meaning enough room to navigate a large sailing ship; thus, by extension, a lot of room or space.

sea squall Another name for *jellyfish* in Cape Cod and along the New England coast.

seater An obsolete term used in colonial times for a settler already established on land.

sea turn A refreshing breeze off the water; a cool breeze that is a relief from the heat of summer or a warm breeze in the winter.

Sebago Pronounced seh-BAY-go; a Maine lake and village.

seem See quote. "Seem: it is habitual with the New Englander to put the verb to strange uses, as 'I can't *seem* to be suited,' 'I couldn't *seem* to know him.'" (James Russell Lowell, *The Biglow Papers,* 1867)

seen Often used for *saw.* "I seen him coming into town."

seesaw See DANDLE; TEEDLE BOARD; TILT.

selectman A member of a board of town officers chosen each year in New England towns to manage local affairs. The term has been in use for several hundred years. "Her father is first selectman in our village . . ." (Robert Lowell, "Skunk Hour," 1959)

serve A nautical term used on Nantucket meaning to fit together and then bind with cord a broken wooden object such as a broomstick or mop handle. Cited by William F. Macy, *The Nantucket Scrap Basket* (1916).

set Sometimes used for *sat,* usually by elderly rural people. "Set over there, please."

set fire, you! Pay attention. "Set fire, you, or you're not going to graduate."

setting Often used for *sitting.* "He was setting right there."

set up one's Ebenezer A probably obsolete expression meaning to make up one's mind. "He set up his Ebenezer and stood firm."

seven tribes of the sea coast See BROTHERTOWN INDIANS.

sewer of New England, the See quote. "Rhode Island . . . 'The fag end of creation' and 'the sewer of New England', Cotton Mather called the region. Never meant to be a separate polity, settled by outcasts like the bewitching, soon-to-die Anne Hutchinson . . ." (John Updike, *The Witches of Eastwick,* 1984)

shacket A word for a yellow-jacket hornet once common in the Narragansett Bay area.

shade, a A little. " 'See here—you ain't in a tight place [in financial difficulty] are you? . . . Because I *am,* a shade.' " (Edith Wharton, *Ethan Frome,* 1911)

shade it A term meaning to bring down the price when used by old-timers dickering over the sale of something. " 'Guess you don't care much whether you sell or not, Jim.' 'Might shade it a little. But Bessie's worth $60.' " (Hayden Pearson, *New England Flavor,* 1961)

shadow potatoes An interesting name Fanny Farmer's *Boston Cookbook* (1909) gives for potato chips.

shag Another name for a cormorant (*Phalacrocorax carbo*).

Shagimaw An imaginary creature of the woods with two feet like a moose and two like a bear.

sham-built Poorly built. "A mis-'able sham-built little house." (Sara Orne Jewett, "Miss Debby," 1883)

shan't Shall not. "I shan't be gone long.—You come too.' (Robert Frost, "The Pasture," *The Poetry of Robert Frost,* 1969)

sharking The old sport of fishing for sharks in Narragansett Bay.

sharp as a meat axe A simile heard in New England meaning someone or something is very sharp.

shay A carriage. "Have you heard of the wonderful one-hoss shay, / That was built in such a logical way / It ran a hundred years to a day . . ." (Oliver Wendell Holmes, "The Deacon's Masterpiece or, The Wonderful 'One-Hoss Shay,'" 1858)

Shay's Rebellion See LEFT HOLDING THE BAG.

sheers Sheer curtains. " 'Probably could see me, too, because the curtains are only sheers.' " (Stephen King, *The Dark Half,* 1989)

sheet anchor to windward Another nautical term that came ashore in New England, this expression has come to mean "to take precau-

tions." People have a sheet anchor to windward, for example, if they save money for retirement, or make sure their house has ample smoke alarms. On sailing ships, the heaviest and best anchor was the amidships sheet anchor. Putting it out to windward often saved ships from being blown onto a lee shore. Making sure one's ship had a good one was an excellent precaution.

she (he) has a leak that will send her (him) to hell Said of someone or something with a fatal flaw.

> . . . the Colonel's lady . . . appeared at meeting in a style not exactly accordant with the pastor's ideas of Christian female propriety. One morning she came sweeping into church, in a new hooped dress, which was then very fashionable. "Here she comes," said Father Moody from the pulpit. "Here she comes, top and topgallant, rigged most beautifully, and sailing most majestically; *but she has a leak that will sink her to hell.*" (Anonymous, "Father Moody," quoted in May Lamberton Becker, *Golden Tales of New England,* 1931)

sheldrake Synonymous with the American merganser duck of the family Merginia.

shell-oyster See quote.

> "Have some of these shell-oysters," said the Colonel . . . A deliberate emphasis on the word *shell* implied that the Colonel knew

what was what. To the New England inland native, beyond the reach of the east winds, the oyster unconditioned, the oyster absolute, without a qualifying adjective, is the *pickled* oyster. Mrs. Trecothick . . . knew very well that an oyster long out of his shell (pickled, that is) . . . gets homesick and loses his sprightliness . . . The word "shell-oyster" had been overheard; and there was a perceptible crowding movement towards their newly discovered habitat, a large soup tureen. (Oliver Wendell Holmes, *Elsie Venner,* 1861)

shingle In old New England *to shingle* meant to chastise a child. John Bartlett in his *Dictionary of Americanisms* (1859) explained that "A shingle applied *a posteriori* is a favorite New England mode of correcting a child."

shoal Shallow. "Letting her feet cool . . . in the shoal water." (Sara Orne Jewett, "White Heron," 1886)

shook Shaken. "You look all shook up." (Thornton Wilder, *Our Town,* 1934)

shool To loiter, saunter about idly; one who does so is a *shooler.* Cited by William F. Macy in *The Nantucket Scrap Basket* (1916).

shoot one's grandmother See quote. "A common though vulgar phrase in New England [that] means to be mistaken or to be disappointed; to

imagine oneself the discoverer of something in which he is deceived. The common phrase is 'you've shot your granny.' " (John Bartlett, *Dictionary of Americanisms,* 1859)

shop A pronunciation of "sharp" commonly heard in Boston.

shore dinner A restaurant dinner featuring clams, clam chowder and boiled lobster that originated in New England about a century ago. Not a clam bake, it is cooked and served inside a restaurant.

shore-hugger A nautical term now applied to any very cautious person.

shorts Lobsters under the legal size requirements for keeping them, the opposite of a *keeper.* "The other [lobster] was much smaller, probably a 'short,' a youngster that should be thrown back and allowed to grow for another year or two." (Peter Benchley, *White Shark,* 1994)

[A fisheries inspector] boarded a boat once, and caught a fisherman with thirty-seven shorts, all banded and plugged and ready to take home. Naturally, he asked about them. "I don't go through my catch until after I'm on my mooring," the fisherman said. "Why are they plugged then?" the inspector asked. "It keeps them from hurting each other," said the fisherman. (Bruce Ballenger, *The Lobster Almanac,* 1988)

shouldn't wonder Think. "I shouldn't wonder it's true."

show The movies. "Let's go to the show." Used in other regions as well.

show him (her) where to head in See TELL HIM (HER) WHERE TO HEAD IN.

shrub A cool fruit drink, such as *raspberry shrub,* similar to the drinks we call *coolers* today but without alcohol.

shut A pronunciation commonly heard in Boston for *shirt.*

shut down on Clamp down on, suppress, dismiss, fire. "She thought it prudent not to attempt to cut short the phrase . . . prematurely—an imputation she should incur if, without more delay she were to 'shut down,' as Verna said, on the young connoisseur." (Henry James, *The Bostonians,* 1886)

side-hill ranger A mythical animal of the lumber camps. Cited as a common term in George Allen England's "Rural Locutions of Maine and Northern New Hampshire," *Dialect Notes,* Vol. IV (1914).

side-winder See quote. "The boys of my time used to call a hit (verbal thrust) like this 'a side-winder.'" (Oliver Wendell Holmes, *The Professor at the Breakfast Table,* 1860)

sight A lot, as in "I had a sight of them." An ancient Cornish expression that is still heard in New England and was very common in 19th-century Cape Cod, according to

Shebnah Rich's *Truro-Cape Cod* (1884).

sightly Said of a good view. "The hilly view was turrible sightly."

simball See CYMBAL.

since God made sour apples For ages. "I haven't seen you since God made sour apples."

since the Concord fight A very long time, in reference to the battle of Concord during the Revolutionary War. "He hasn't been home since the Concord fight."

singing beach See quote.

> Manchester, Massachusett's peculiar attraction is that beach of ruddy sand—a warm tawny pink—which, when a carriage drives over it or people tread on it, gives forth a crisp note, something like snow under foot in dry cold weather. This odd formation of the atoms which makes them triturate together in keen musical vibration has poetically christened it the Singing Beach, a wonder of the world and a never failing source of entertainment." (Agnes Edwards, *The Romantic Shoe,* 1915)

sink of New England, the See ROGUES ISLAND.

sire A bull.

sitfast Stationary, fixed. " 'Tis good when you have crossed the sea and back, / To find the sitfast acres where you left them." (Ralph Waldo Emerson, "Hamatreya," 1847)

six weeks sleighing in April Used to describe a long winter that lasts until the end of April, often with snow on the ground at that late date.

skag Cut. "They skagged the trees with axes."

skinch Skimp on, cut short. "Don't skinch on the sugar."

skipple An old measure equaling about three-quarters of a bushel; from the Dutch *scheful*, which means the same.

skive (1) To scrape. "He skived up his shoe." (2) To skimp on. (3) To hurry, run.

skoodle An obsolete term for *squat*. "He skoodled down by the fire."

skrid Heard in Maine and New Hampshire for *a little bit*. "He et every skrid of it."

skrivvel Shrink, dry up. "The corn was all skrivveled."

skulheeg A term used in Maine for *deadfall trap*, that is, a trap for large animals in which a heavy weight is arranged to fall on and kill the prey.

skully-jo See quote. ". . . Provincetown youngsters used to carry around bits of a delicacy known as "skully-jo', which was a kind of dried fish, cured until it was very hard, and they munched on this as

other children of other places ate candy . . ." (Jeremiah Digges, *In Great Waters, The Story of the Portuguese Fishermen,* 1941)

skunk blackbird Another name for the marsh blackbird.

slacker'n dishwater Extremely dirty and untidy, slovenly. Given as a common expression in George Allen England, "Rural Locutions of Maine and Northern New Hampshire," *Dialect Notes,* Vol. IV (1914).

slack salted pollock An old-fashioned dish made of dried pollock and served with potatoes and salt pork gravy.

slat Heard in New Hampshire and Maine for *to go*. "Let's slat on over to the store."

slatch See quote. "A short gleam of fine weather, an interval in a story or heavy rain." (William F. Macy, *The Nantucket Scrap Basket,* 1916) Also means a lull between breaking waves. From an Old English word meaning the same.

slatcky sky A sky with blue showing through the clouds.

sleek as a whistle A simile once commonly heard in New England.

sleeping A tender euphemism for *buried* used mainly by old-timers. "My older boy went to war in '14. He's sleeping over in France . . . My wife died in '19. Always thought her heart never healed after Robert went." (Hayden Pearson, *New England Flavor,* 1961)

slice See quote. "It was a sort of iron shovel (by housewives termed a 'slice'), such as is used in cleaning the oven." (Nathaniel Hawthorne, "An Old Woman's Tale," 1830)

slick as a school-marm's leg Very pretty, pleasing, successful. Given as a common expression in George Allen England, "Rural Locutions of Maine and Northern New Hampshire," *Dialect Notes,* Vol. IV (1914).

slicker'n a smelt Very smoothly. "She steered her in slicker'n a smelt."

slimpsy Shoddy, cheap, poorly made. "She was wearing that slimpsy dress."

slip A term used mainly in New England for a long narrow church pew without doors, possibly because one can just slip into it.

slip gut An old-fashioned New England pudding.

slipper-down A punning name once used in Connecticut for HASTY PUDDING.

slippernoose An old term for *slipnoose.* "Ketched ye with a slippernoose, hey?" (Oliver Wendell Holmes, *Elsie Venner,* 1861)

slipper-toe A Vermont expression meaning a no-good, a no-account person. "That old slipper-toe's never worked a day in his life."

slipping An old-fashioned term for *sleighing.* "We went slippin' yesterday."

sliver To cut each side of a flounder away in one piece from the head to the tail. A Nantucket term cited by William F. Macy in *The Nantucket Scrap Basket* (1916).

slopdozzle Heard in Maine for someone very careless. "He turned out to be a real slopdozzle."

slower'n (slower than) stock-still Extremely slow. Given as a common expression in George Allen England, "Rural Locutions of Maine and Northern New Hampshire," Vol. IV (1914).

slower than a hop toad in hot tar Cited in *The Old Farmer's Almanack* (1946) as a common Yankee saying.

slumgullion A stew or soup made from whatever leftovers are at hand.

slump A fruit dumpling dessert.

slunk school, to An old term meaning to play hooky.

slut's wool Dust balls under the bed; *slut* here is an old word for a slovenly woman.

smaaht A commonly heard pronunciation of "smart."

smarm To smooth or plaster down. "His hair was smarmed down."

smart Accomplished, talented; the word also is used this way in the South.

smart as a steel trap Very smart and alert. "He'd come up again as smart as a steel trap." (Seba Smith, *The Life and Writings of Major Jack Downing,* 1833)

smart as a whip Very smart, alert, mentally quick.

smart to work Full of energy, not lazy. "The old woman always was smart to work." (Mary Wilkins Freeman, *Six Trees,* 1903)

smart up Spruce up. "It looks as natral as the hogs, / Just as you used to be, / When you get smarted up to go / And take a walk with me." (Anonymous, *Boston Globe,* May 3, 1831)

smell like a beamster To smell very badly indeed, the expression dating back to the days when tannery workers, called *beamsters,* were avoided by all because of the odors that clung to them even after a bath.

smiley Smiling. "All kind of smiley round the lips." (James Russell Lowell, *The Biglow Papers,* 1866)

smilin' Drinking. "He was out smilin' last night in Augusta."

smooth as a smelt A coastal term meaning things very smooth or pleasant. "That syrup was smooth as a smelt."

smudder Once used in Maine for a cloud of dust raised from sweeping a floor or the like. Also *smutter, smother.*

smurr up To become hazy. "It's smurrin' up to the east'ard."

smurry Hazy. See SMURR UP.

smush To mash. "She smushed everything on her plate all together."

snapper A humorous term for whatever it is in baked beans that causes gas. "The beans we serve here have the snappers removed." Incidentally, not long ago, the U.S. Department of Agriculture introduced a "gasless bean."

snedricks Snide tricks. The punning word may be nautical in origin.

snew Often used in the past for *snowed.* "It snew all day."

snicker A nationally used term meaning a snide, slightly stifled laugh. The expression originated in New England, possibly introduced there directly from England's Essex dialect.

snivver Immediately after, as in "I'll be over to your house snivver dinner." Cited by William F. Macy in *The Nantucket Scrap Basket* (1916).

snow eater A warm breeze from the sea in late February that melts the snow.

snowed up Snowed in. ". . . Tell him about the time / In Stafford's cabin, forty years ago, / When four of us were snowed up for ten days / With only one dried haddock." (Edward Arlington Robinson, "Isaac and Archibald," *Captain Craig*, 1902)

snow roller Instead of shoveling the roads in winters past, New Englanders often rolled the snow with snow rollers, packing it down for the horse-drawn sleighs. "The huge roller, looking like two big slatted barrels, went groaning and creaking down the country road, pressing down the snow." (Hayden Pearson, *New England Flavor*, 1961)

snug A synonym in Maine and New Hampshire for *stingy*.

snug by Close by. "She used to live snug by here."

soak A heavy, hard rain. "I s'pose I hadn't ought to come 'way down here in such a soak." (Mary Wilkens Freeman, *A New England Nun and Other Stories*, 1891)

soaker A swindler. "She might have heard about his temper and his reputation as a 'soaker' who put scallops in fresh water and cornmeal to make them swell [and weigh more]." (William Martin, *Cape Cod*, 1991)

Sock Saunders A mythical character of the Maine woods. "If a man . . . slips on a log, but catches himself in time, he says, 'Foxed you that time, Sock Saunders.' If he cuts his foot, he explains, 'Sock Saunders got me.' There are no stories about Sock Saunders. He's just the guy who hangs around and makes life complicated." (Louise Dickenson Rich, *We Took to the Woods*, 1942)

sody Soda pop.

so-fashion In this way or fashion. "I'll knock so-fashion and peep round the door / When I come back, so you'll know who it is." (Robert Frost, "A Hundred Collars," 1914)

soft as mush A simile heard in New England.

softer than a stewed pumpkin (punkin) An old expression used to describe a mawkish person or sentiment.

soft sawder, to To flatter someone, talk a lot of blarney. This old term is still heard occasionally, although it isn't recorded in most dictionaries. The derivation of the expression is unclear, apparently having something to do with "solder," but it is first recorded in Thomas C. Haliburton's *The Clockmaker* (1836): "If she goes to act ugly, I'll give her a dose of 'soft sawder.' "

soft water men A term New England sailors had for amateur sailors. A saying went: "Anyone who would go to sea for pleasure would go to hell for a vacation."

sofy An old pronunciation of sofa.

some Often used to mean "very," as in "He's some ugly." "She's some pretty."

some dearer Once commonly used for *more expensive*. "To the Editor of The Atlantic Monthly . . . noticin' by your kiver thet you're some dearer that wut you wuz, I enclose the deffrence . . ." (James Russell Lowell, *The Biglow Papers*, 1867)

some desperate Said of someone very ugly or otherwise undesirable. "Some desperate he is!"

some good Excellent, very good. "This chowder is some good." Also *some old good*.

something to lift the scalp Used to describe a terrible, fetid smell. See ASAFETIDA BAG.

some tired A little tired. " 'Matilda and our girls and I made 'most all the cake with our own hands, and we all feel some tired . . .' " (Oliver Wendell Holmes, *Elsie Venner*, 1861)

some ugly Mean, bad-tempered. "He was some ugly with the kids last night."

some wicked good Very good. "Some wicked good it is."

so neat she (he) squeaks Someone so neat she (he) annoys others.

son of a bitch Once a common and respectable name for boiled salt cod-fish covered with scraps of pork; heard on shipboard and in houses along the Massachusetts coast.

son of a sea cook *Son of a sea cook,* which can mean either a "good guy" or a "mean SOB," depending on the context, really has little to do with the sea. No sea cook had any hand in it. It seems that the earliest American settlers appropriated the word *s'quenk,* for *skunk,* from the Indians around the Massachusetts Bay Colony, pronouncing it *see-konk.* Thus, a *son of a see-konk* was first a stinking son of a skunk. Because *see-konk* sounded something like "sea cook," it came to be pronounced "sea cook" long after the Indian word was forgotten. The fact that sea cooks often were cantankerous old men probably reinforced the term's present ambivalent meaning.

son of a whore This commonly used epithet is not taken too seriously in northern New England, where it is heard most frequently. It does yeoman service in describing everything from a beloved friend ("How are you, you old son of a whore?") to an avowed enemy, and is applied to situations of good luck as well as bad luck, even to women as well as men. This is not to say, however, that someone might not take exception and punch you in the nose for using it.

soon or late Sooner or later, eventually. " 'Sh! not so loud: he'll hear-you,' Mary said. / 'I want him to: he'll have to soon or late." (Robert

Frost, "The Death of the Hired Hand," 1914)

sopysyvine A pronunciation of the old apple variety properly called the saps-of-wine.

sortilege A method of divination practiced in times past where a person with a problem would open a Bible randomly and study the verses on the two pages for guidance or an answer.

sot A pronunciation of "set." "All during my [Vermont] childhood and youth he was a legendary figure of 'sot' obstinacy and queerness." (Dorothy Canfield, "Old Man Warner," in *Raw Material*, 1925)

so that Used by Mainers for *as if*. "It felt so that I had broken my hand."

so thievish they [the neighbors] have to take in their stone walls nights Quoted as a contemporary saying in James Russell Lowell's *The Biglow Papers* (1867).

sounded like a bull with his pizzle caught in the garden gate Bellowed in pain at the top of his lungs. " 'You shoulda heard him . . . Sounded like a bull with his pizzle caught in the garden gate.' " (Stephen King, *Dolores Claiborne*, 1993)

souple Heard in Maine for *supple*. "He jogged a bit to get soupled up."

sour as swill A simile heard in New England.

sour milk cheese A term not much heard anymore for COTTAGE CHEESE.

sour morning A morning with bad weather. "It was what Jonathan called a sour morning for work." (Edith Wharton, *Ethan Frome*, 1911)

souse A kind of pickled pig's feet; also called *hog's head cheese, panhas* and *souse meat*.

soused clams Shucked pickled clams.

south-end An old area in Boston; early mention of it was made by Nathaniel Hawthorne in his story "Old News" (1835), in which he writes of one "Mary Salmon, who shod horses, at the south-end" ca. 1759.

sowbug A small crustacean found under logs and stones that is so called because of its piglike shape. Also called a wood louse. " 'I am a sowbug and a necrophile,' / Said Pretzel, 'and the gods are growing old . . .' " (Edward Arlington Robinson, "Captain Craig," 1902)

span, to An old term meaning to compliment each other. "The horses span well."

spandy (1) Very good or new. (2) Very, perfectly. "Her shoes are spandy new." Cited as a common Portsmouth, New Hampshire expression in Frederic D. Allen, "Contributions to the New England Vocabulary," *Dialect Notes,* Vol. I (1890).

spare room The bedroom in one's house reserved for visitors.

spark An old-fashioned term meaning to make love, court. "They've been sparking over a year now." However, this word is also used in other regions and may be of Scandinavian origin. See FELLER.

sparrowgrass A folk etymology of "asparagus." Heard in New England and other regions.

spat This word, still commonly used throughout the United States for a little fight, apparently originated in New England a century ago.

specie Once used for *species.* "It's a specie of wild cat."

spell While. "Let's set for a spell."

spell baker, to An interesting though obsolete term meaning to be fairly able, up to snuff; from the fact that *baker* was the first word of two syllables in Noah Webster's "Blueback Speller." "If an old man will marry a young wife, / Why then . . . he must spell Baker!" (Henry Wadsworth Longfellow, *Poetical Works,* 1868)

spider (1) See quote. "He was one of the kind sports call a spider, / All wiry arms and legs that spread out

wavy / From a humped body nigh as big's a biscuit . . ." (Robert Frost, "The Code," 1914) (2) A lobster, because lobsters are members of the same genus. (3) A cast-iron frying pan.

spile A spigot that is used in taking sap from a tree, or a plug in a cider barrel. "From one of [the barrels] . . . a bright pine spile stuck out alluringly." (Edward Arlington Robinson, "Isaac and Archibald," *Captain Craig,* 1902)

spills A synonym for *pine needles* in Maine.

spindle An old-fashioned term for *corn tassel.*

Spindle City Lowell, Massachusetts used to be called this in its heyday, after the thousands of spindles in its cotton factories.

spitting spell A very short spell. "He hasn't stopped working for more than a spitting spell.

spity Spiteful. "They're so spity." (Mary Wilkens Freeman, *A New England Nun and Other Stories,* 1891)

spleeny (1) A word Mainers use for someone too sensitive about pain. "Don't be so spleeny about it—it's just a scraped knee." (2) Sissified. (3) A little ill. (4) Touchy or morose.

Splendid Splinter, the The nickname of slugger Ted Williams, the best-known baseball player to play for the Boston Red Sox since Babe Ruth. Often shortened to the *Splinter.*

splinter-broom A broom made of yellow birch, close-shaved, that used to be common in New England.

spoon victuals Food for an invalid. Cited as a common term in George Allen England, "Rural Locutions of Maine and Northern New Hampshire," *Dialect Notes,* Vol. IV (1914).

spoopsie A word with some currency a century ago for a silly person.

sport Another mildly derogatory term for a nonresident vacationer in Maine, this term used mostly inland. See SUMMERCATER.

spouting A trough to carry off rain.

sprawl (1) Life, vigor, animation. "She has no sprawl." Cited as a common Portsmouth, New Hampshire expression in Frederic D. Allen, "Contributions to New England Vocabulary," Vol. I (1890) (2) energy, courage. "He's got more sprawl than most folks."

Springfield Any of many firearms made at the U.S. armory at Springfield, Massachusetts.

sprout lands An area where small young trees are growing after sprouting in a forest that has recently been cut for lumber. "And sproutlands flourish where the axe has gone." (Robert Frost, "The Generations of Men," 1914)

spruce See quote. "The kitchen was a poor place, not 'spruce' and shining as his mother had kept it in his boyhood . . ." (Edith Wharton, *Ethan Frome,* 1911)

spruce beer An old northern New England drink made from a decoction of the fresh twigs of black and red spruce trees.

spruce gum Spruce gum is still collected in Maine and New England, sometimes as a small business, but in nothing like the 150-ton-a-year quantities collected in the early 1900s. This natural chewing gum (see my *The Great American Chewing Gum Book,* 1976) is collected in winter and comes from punctures made on the trunks of both black and red spruces the previous spring.

> I knocked down a couple of good big chunks and took them back to the house. It was a good idea to trim the pieces of gum before I put them away in a shoebox . . . I got rid of the bits of bark that clung, and trimmed off the rough edges and any soft spots. Then from time to time I'd cut off a chunk and chew it into a pleasant purplish-magenta ball. If it was first-quality gum it was chewable a considerable number of times. (Hayden S. Pearson, *New England Flavor,* 1961)

"What this man brought in a cotton sack / Was gum, the gum of the mountain spruce. / He showed me lumps of the scented stuff / Like uncut jewels, dull and rough. / It comes to market golden brown; / But turns to pink between the teeth." (Robert Frost, "The Gum-Gatherer," 1916)

sprung An obsolete term for *drunk, tipsy.* "He reckoned they were a little bit sprung." (Harriet Beecher Stowe, *Deed, A Tale of the Dismal Swamp,* 1856)

spry Although this word meaning lively, active, originated as a provincialism in England, it was first used with any frequency in the New England dialect. It is part of the Americn vocabulary today. " 'Why I'm kinder sorter middlin', Mr. Slick, what you call considerable nimble and spry.' " (Thomas C. Haliburton, *The Clockmaker,* 1837)

spry as a cat Very lively and nimble. "I was fat as a doe, but spry as a cat."

spudge An old, perhaps obsolete, term for *to stick with a knife*.

spunk (1) Spirit, vivacity; a word that originated in New England. "You have convinced me of your spunk." (David Humphreys, *The Yankey in England,* 1814) (2) To kindle. "He'd spunked up a fire and hung on the kittle." (Rose Terry Cooke, "Uncle Josh," 1857)

squale *Bartlett's* (1848) defines this as "to throw a stick or stone so that it skims across the ground or water"; the expression is probably obsolete by now, *skim* generally being used.

squam A yellow oilskin hat worn by fishermen; after the fishing village Anniquam, Massachusetts.

squamish A pronunciation of "squeamish."

squantum This term was defined by John Bartlett in his *Dictionary of Americanisms* (1848):

The name of a species of fun known to the Nantucket folks, which is thus described by the *New York Mirror*: A party of ladies and gentlemen go to one of the famous water-places of resort, where they fish, dig clams, talk, laugh, sing, dance, play, bathe, sail, eat, and have a general "good time." The food generally consists of chowder, baked clams, and fun. No one is admitted to the sacred circle who will take offence at a joke, and every one is expected to do his or her part towards creating a general laugh. Any man who speaks of business affairs (excepting matrimony) is immediately reproved, and on a second offence publicly chastised. Care is thrown to the wind, politics discarded, war ignored, pride humbled, stations levelled, wealth scorned, virtue exalted, and—this is *"squantum."*

Squantum is an Indian word whose meaning is uncertain. An annual celebration held near Boston as early as 1812 and called the feast of Squantum may have inspired this Nantucket term for *clambake* or *picnic*. In any case, *squantum* was still in general use at the turn of the century in Nantucket and other areas of New England places for a good time, merrymaking, a picnic party, a high old time.

square day The whole day.

There are more kinds of weather to the "square day" in this northeastern corner of the United States than in any other part of the country. An early geographer described a sample day on the Kennebec

River. It had thunder, rain, hail, frost and snow. Perhaps if he had covered two days, he would have included fog. And he left out the sun. New England has almost 60 per cent of the total amount of sunshine possible. (Robert P. Tristram Coffin, *New England,* 1951)

See IF YOU DON'T LIKE THE NEW ENGLAND WEATHER, JUST WAIT A MINUTE.

squarenut hickory See MOCKERNUT.

squash Our word *squash* comes from the vegetable's Narragansett Indian name, *asquatasquash,* "eaten raw," which was shortened to *squash* by New Englanders.

squat Squeeze, crush. "He squat his finger in the door."

squeezay An old term believed to have been used only in Portsmouth, New Hampshire and meaning fretful.

staddles Stakes arranged in a circle in a marsh so that salt hay can be stored in cocks within them.

stands in hand Behooves. "It stands you in hand to be careful." Cited as a widely used expression in New England in Frederic D. Allen, "Contributions to New England Vocabulary," *Dialect Notes,* Vol. I 1890).

stands out like a blackberry in a pan of milk Conspicuous. Given as a Vermont expression in Charles Edward Crane's *Let Me Show You Vermont* (1937).

stars and stripes An old Boston term for *pork and beans eaten cold on Sundays.*

start Shock, surprise. "What a start you gave me!"

startle a body out of her (his) wits Scare someone greatly. " 'Startle a body out of her wits,' Miss Rainey muttered." (Susan Dodd, "Rue," 1984)

starved fit to eat the Lord's supper A colorful rural phrase meaning very hungry that was common in Maine and New Hampshire a long lifetime ago.

staver An old-fashioned term for an excellent person. "He's a real staver."

stave up To break up. "She staved up the whole place."

steam doctor A doctor who followed the medical system advocated by Massachusetts Dr. Samuel Thomson (1769–1843), who stressed the use of herbal remedies and steam baths in treating illnesses.

steboy! An exclamation used in setting a dog on an animal.

stemmy Said of males sexually aroused. "She sure made me stemmy."

stent An allotted amount, a stint. "He did his stent of work."

stewed as a fresh boiled owl Very drunk. The origin of the expression is anybody's guess. Maybe someone desperate did shoot and stew an owl whole for food and noticed its stewed resemblance to someone deep in his cups.

stiddy company See FELLER.

stiff as a church Used to describe a person ill at ease, unrelaxed; the expression was suggested by someone sitting in church in starched stiff collar and uncomfortable clothes.

stifle Vegetables sliced and fried in a SPIDER.

still as mouse work Very quiet, stealthy. "I came up on 'em still ez mouse work." Cited as a common New England expression in George Allen England, "Rural Locutions of Maine and Northern New Hampshire," *Dialect Notes,* Vol. IV (1914).

Still Corners A small town in New Hampshire. "Still Corners" (so called not because / The place is silent all day long, nor yet / Because it boasts a whisky still—because / It set out once to be a city and still / Is only Corners, crossroads in a wood.)" (Robert Frost, "New Hampshire," 1923)

sting or sting ray A name used in New England for the fish generally called a skate. It is also called the *raie* in New England.

stinkin' Benjamin Purple trillium (of the genus *Trillium*), which has a fetid odor when picked for a bouquet.

stiver An old-fashioned word meaning to get going, get moving. "Now stiver along to school, child, or you'll be late."

stivy Used in Maine for *crowded, crammed, stuffy*. "It was stivy in there." Also *stived up*.

stone drag A vehicle without wheels that is used to collect stones from fields.

stone fence Originally the New England term for what is now generally called a stone wall.

stone's got a pretty heavy mortgage on that land See quote. "A man speaking to me once of a very rocky clearing said, "Stone's got a pretty heavy mortgage on that land.' " (James Russell Lowell, *The Biglow Papers,* 1867)

stone sloop Not a ship built of stone but a ship that carried granite from New England quarries to cities along the East Coast in days past.

stone wall Used for *stone fence*. "They hev to take in their stone walls nights." (James Russell Lowell, *The Biglow Papers,* 1866)

stook An old term for a shock of corn, that is, a number of sheaves of grain stacked upright in a field for drying.

stoop one's head Stoop. "He had to stoop his head to hear her." (Edith Wharton, *Ethan Frome*, 1911)

store choppers Heard in Maine for *false teeth*.

straight ahead Words of assent, usually in reply to a question. "How about we go fishing?" "Straight ahead. Looks like a good day for it."

straight as a boar's leg An old-fashioned term for *very straight*.

straight as a gun barrel A simile once common in the region.

straight as a hair An old expression meaning perfectly straight.

straight as a yard of pump water Given as a Vermont expression in Charles Edward Crane's *Let Me Show You Vermont* (1937).

stram To stride with self-importance. "He went stramming along the street."

stram about Flounder, kick about. "He strammed about in bed."

stramming around Said of children running back and forth creating a disturbance. "Strop stramming around and sit still!"

strams An old term used in Nantucket for *children*.

straw sailor A farmer who also works at lobstering.

streaked bass Another name once used for *striped bass* (*Morone saxatilis*).

stream In Maine a creek is always a *stream,* unless it's small enough to be a *brook*.

strike-out Recorded in Maine for a new love affair; from *to strike out* meaning to start, not the strike-out of baseball.

strimmered See quote. "I looked up to the sky, such a pretty blue, and the little soft woolly clouds strimmered all over it, and I wondered if there was any dialectic [dialect] word that answered to strimmer. Seems's if there couldn't be one that pictur'd out the real thing so good. For them clouds was strimmered and nothin' else." (Annie Trumbull Slosson, "A Local Colorist," 1912)

stromp An old term recorded in New Hampshire for "a woman with a mannish or bold manner"; said to originally have been a variation of "strumpet."

struck with the Spanish mildew Said of someone who is pretending or imagining he or she is ill.

studdle Stir up. "She studdled her tea."

stuffy An old New England term meaning sullen, sulky, obstinate, bad-tempered.

stun A pronunciation of "stone" heard primarily in Maine.

stunded Stunned. " 'Been stunded', Abel said." (Oliver Wendell Holmes, *Elsie Venner*, 1861)

sub-spucky Another name for an Italian hero sandwich in Boston.

succotash The first succotash was made by American Indians, who cooked corn and beans together in bear grease. New England colonists used the word in the early 18th century, if not before then, and it apparently derives from the Narragansett Indian *misickquatash*, "an ear of corn," or *manusqussedah*, "beans."

such A pronunciation commonly heard in Boston for *search*.

sucking the nether teat Not doing very well. "I'd better make some money this year; I've been sucking the nether teat all year." The origin of the expression is unclear.

sugar bush A name Vermont and New Hampshire farmers give to their holdings of sugar maple trees that yield maple sugar.

Sugar Loaf The name of various hills and mountains in New England. The term derives from the cone-shaped loaves of sugar people used in olden times. A ski resort in Maine also shares the name.

sugar-lot A lot of rock maple or sugar maple trees from which maple sugar and syrup are made.

sugar maple *Acer saccharum*, the source of sap from which maple sugar and syrup is made; the state tree of Vermont.

Suicide Six A nickname for Route Six on Cape Cod. "Nervous damn stretch—two lanes runnin' straight and flat through pine woods for thirteen miles, speed limit fifty and damn-you-straight-to-hell if you were an old man who didn't go over forty. Somebody always itchin' to pass. Tourists comin' the other way. No wonder they called it Suicide Six." (William Martin, *Cape Cod*, 1991)

sulphur and molasses A concoction used as a spring tonic in days past.

sumac The tree (of the genus *Rhus*) is often pronounced *shoo-mak* in New England.

summer boarder An old Maine name for *summer resident*. Cited in E.K. Maxfield, "Maine Dialect," *American Speech* (November 1926).

summercater Possibly a combination of *summer* and (va) *cat* (ion) plus *er*, *summercater* is used in coastal Maine meaning people who come to the state to vacation for the summer. The term often is used in a mildly derogatory way. "That summercater's been given' us a lot of trouble." See SPORT.

summer complaint Another word used by Mainers for *summer visitor*. Also called a *dogfish* and a *rusticator*, among a number of choice terms.

sunapu Char (trout of the genus *Salvelinus*) of brilliant color found in

Sunapee Lake, New Hampshire and other lakes in New Hampshire and Maine. As one icthyologist put it, "As the October pairing time approaches, the Sunapu fish becomes illuminated with the flushes of maturing passion."

sunck A name once used for the female chief of certain New England Indian tribes. "Awaking one night . . . and finding his sunck (queen) lying near another Indian, he . . . took his knife, and cut three strokes on each of her cheeks." (*Massachusetts Historical Collection,* lx, 1804)

supawn An Indian name for HASTY PUDDING.

supper The last meal of the day, after breakfast and the noon dinner; commonly used elsewhere.

surl To be surly, mean. "He surled around the house."

surprisedly Sometimes used for *surprisingly.* "It was surprisedly cold out."

suspicion To suspect. "We suspicioned he stole it."

sut An old pronunciation in Connecticut for *soot.*

sutton A pronunciation commonly heard in Boston for *certain.*

Suz See DEAR ME SUZ.

suz a day See DEAR ME SUZ.

swad An old term for *lump, mass,* or *bump.*

swaddle out To wash clothes poorly. "She swaddled out his sheets."

swag! An old exclamation recorded as far back as 1815.

swagun Used in Maine lumber camps for *soup* or *porridge.* "We had bean swagun for dinner." Also *swagin.*

swale A marshy depression in level land; originally an English dialect word.

swallow the anchor Originally a nautical term meaning to retire from the sea but now used for retirement in general.

swamp Yankee See quote. ". . . the Speaker, after all, was a swamp Yankee from [southwestern] Massachusetts, and he was a Yankee from Vermont . . ." (George V. Higgins, *Victories,* 1990)

swan, I Also *I swang.* See I SWAN.

swan boats Famous pedal boats in the shape of swans used for rides on the pond in Boston's Public Garden.

swang, I See I SWAN.

swankie A refreshing drink made of water and molasses, with ginger and sometimes vinegar added.

swatson To chat or chew the fat; the word is probably from the German *schwatzen* meaning the same, but possibly originated in the Connecticut area.

sweeten See KEEPING VEGETABLES.

swept hold A nautical expression for an empty stomach. "I've got a swept hold, haven't eaten in two days."

switchel Recorded as early as 1779 for a drink made of sweetened water and ginger with a little vinegar and hard cider in it, sometimes with a bit of hard stuff added. It was popular on land and sea, but the word was originally Yankee sailor slang, origin unknown.

swivel-eyed Once a common nautical expression for a cross-eyed person. Sailors considered cross-eyed people bad luck, especially, for some reason, a cross-eyed Finn.

symptom book A book carried by the masters of old-time New England sailing vessels. It described the symptoms of illnesses that might befall their men and gave treatments.

syrup Often pronounced *sur-up,* as in "I'll have more maple surup."

T

t The syndrome of the vanishing *t* and *d* in New England speech is discussed in the Introduction.

t'ain't Isn't. "T'ain't a joke, is it?"

take a scoocher To ski down a slope in a squatting position. Cited as a common Portsmouth, New Hampshire expression in Frederic D. Allen, "Contributions to the New England Vocabulary," *Dialect Notes,* Vol. I (1890).

take a seat of work out on him To thoroughly criticize someone, piling complaint after complaint on the person. The "seat of work" comes from the pile of leather shoemakers used to pile around their seats, this representing the amount of work they intended to do at a sitting.

take a walk up ladder lane and down hawser street A humorous old nautical term for *to be executed by hanging,* a *hawser* being a thick nautical rope.

take to do An old-fashioned term meaning to reprove, or take to task. "I took him to do for saying that."

take up the hatchet Go to war; an Indian expression first recorded in New England in 1694.

talking big Bragging. "He was aware that he was 'talking big' . . ." (Edith Wharton, *Ethan Frome,* 1911)

tall as a beanpole A simile once frequently heard in New England.

tamarack *Larix laricina,* a common New England tree used to make railroad ties and telephone poles; also called the *American larch.*

tantoaster An old term for a severe storm.

tap the admiral To take a drink of any liquor; this expression may date back to 19th-century England when Admiral Nelson was embalmed in rum temporarily after he was killed at sea.

tarnal Eternal. " 'This tarnal son of yours got me this mawnin' to fix him a stick fer firin' apples . . .' " (Henry A. Shute, *Plupy,* 1910)

tarnation! The interjection *tarnation!* a euphemism for damnation! or damn! has been used in New England since colonial times and is familiar to millions of Americans from its use in books, movies, radio and television. The best guess is that it derives from the English tarnal!

which itself derives from the mild interjection eternal!

tarred and feathered At Salem, Massachusetts on September 7, 1768, an informer named Robert Wood "was stripped, tarred and feathered and placed on a hogshead under the Tree of Liberty on the Common." This is the first record of the term *tarred and feathered* in America. Tarring and feathering was a cruel punishment in which hot pine tar was applied from head to toe on a person and goose feathers were stuck to the tar. The offender was then ignited and ridden out of town on a rail (tied to a splintery rail), beaten with sticks and stoned all the while. A person's skin often came off when he or she removed the tar. It was a common practice to tar and feather Tories who refused to join the Liberty Boys, but the practice was known long before the Revolution, dating back at least to the days of Richard the Lion-Hearted (Richard I). Though no one has been tarred and feathered or ridden out of town on a rail in recent years, the expression remains to describe anyone subjected to indignity and infamy.

tautog An Indian name for the blackfish (*Tautoga onitis*), the term once widely used in Rhode Island.

team A Maine term for a single horse and buggy.

teared Torn. "It was all teared."

ted To spread out mown grass or hay for drying. Used mainly in New England now, the verb *ted* is first recorded in 15th-century England. The *tedder,* invented in America over a century ago, is a machine that teds hay. "He tedded the hay last week."

teedle board A name for a children's seesaw in northeast Massachusetts.

teeter totter Once common in western New England for *seesaw,* today this word is used largely by older speakers.

teethache An obsolete term for *toothache.* "He had a teethache."

tell him (her) where to head in Nautical in origin, this expression means to put a person in his (her) place, to reprimand him (her), to show him (her) who's boss. "She sure told him where to head in." Also *Show him (her) where to head in.*

tell the truth and shame the devil An old New England proverb. " 'I'm sorry if that hurts your feelings, but I've got to—tell the truth and shame the devil.' " (Thornton Wilder, *Our Town,* 1938)

tempest Heard in Masschusetts for *rain storm.*

tend Attend, work as a salesperson. "I used to tend in a store till I got worse." (Mary Wilkins Freeman, *A New England Nun and Other Stories,* 1891)

tend out on Heard mostly in Maine for *attend, attend to, watch out for.* "Tend out on him, he's pretty slippery."

tenement An apartment building; used in New England with no implications of poverty.

tennis Sometimes used for *sneakers* or *tennis shoes.* "Put on your tennis."

thack An old-fashioned Maine pronunciation of "that."

Thames A river in Connecticut, pronounced there not like the Thames (Tems) in England but as written—with the "th" and a broad "a."

thank-ye-ma'am An American courtship term that dates back to 19th-century New England. Roads at the time had diagonal earthen ridges running across them that channeled off rainwater from the high to the low side and prevented washouts. Rural Casanovas driving their carriages along these rude roads made sure that they hit these ridges hard so that their female companions would bounce up in the air and bump into them. With the head of his sweetheart so close, the gentleman could steal a kiss, and usually expressed his gratitude with a *Thank-ye-ma'am,* that expression becoming synonymous with a quick kiss or any hole in the road that caused riders to bump up and down. It wasn't long before some salacious wit took this innocent phrase between the sheets, or to the side of the road somewhere, and elaborated on it, for in 1895 we find recorded the related expression *wham bam (thank-ye-ma'am)* for *quick coitus.* As a matter of fact, the first recorded use of both expressions occurs in that year. Another explanation of the expression can be found in the following quotation:

> The thank-you-ma-am (a bump or hole in the road) only to be found in the more primitive roads in American rural districts is thus described in a newspaper: "To protect the road from wash-outs in the spring it is the custom to construct water bars, familiarly known as thank-you-ma'ams, across the road on grades." The peculiar name is said to have been suggested by the fact that, when a vehicle passes over such an obstruction, the passengers bob their heads as though making a curteous bow. (Herbert Hoswill, *A Dictionary of Modern American Usage,* 1935)

thank you kindly An old-fashioned way to say *please.* "I'll thank you kindly to leave."

that butters no parsnips That isn't worth much, means nothing at all; an old expression dating back to the 19th century but still occasionlly heard.

thatchy Said in New Hampshire of a certain taste in milk. "The milk tastes 'thatchy' because the cows eat 'thatch.' A long, coarse grass, growing in the salt marshes, is known as 'thatch' on the New Hampshire and Massachusetts seacoast. The thatch New Hampshire cows eat seems to be different from this. It is described as a sort of weed, growing in low places." (Frederic D. Allen, "Contributions to the New

England Vocabulary," *Dialect Notes,* Vol. I, 1890)

that's a fact See quote. " '. . . I won't have you gobbling like wolves. It'll stunt your growth—that's a fact.' " (Thornton Wilder, *Our Town,* 1938)

that's a great spoon An old, probably obsolete Nantucketism meaning good, promising.

thay A pronunciation of "there." "Thay's a meeting down at the church."

theah A pronunciation of "there" in Boston and elsewhere.

the child is born! An expression Mainers sometimes use to mean "a job is done."

the hell I pitch in See DOWN BUCKET!

they call a house a house, but a house with a shed is a village An old saying about Cape Cod quoted in *Massachusetts: A Guide to Its Plows and People,* 1904.

they-uh A pronunciation of "there" on Cape Cod; Cape Codders add another syllable to the Bostonian's *theah.*

thick as fiddlers in hell Very numerous, plentiful. Given as a common expression in George Allen England, "Rural Locutions of Maine and Northern New Hampshire," *Dialect Notes,* Vol. IV (1914). "It was some crowd, thick as fiddlers in hell."

thick of snow The kind of snowfall composed of big moist flakes that forms a white curtain in front of one, allowing no visibility at all. "We couldn't see land in the thick o' snow."

thimbleberry An old-fashioned term for *black raspberries* referring to their size and shape. Also called *black caps.*

thin as vanity Very thin, said of both people and things. Cited as a common expression in George Allen England, "Rural Locutions of Maine and Northern New Hampshire," *Dialect Notes,* Vol. IV (1914).

thither An old-fashioned word for *over there.* "Only one from a farm not far away / strolled thither . . ." (Robert Frost, "The Generations of Men," 1914)

three sheets in the wind Drunk. This old expression still is heard in New England. It generally is heard in the rest of the United States as *three sheets to the wind.*

three sheets in the wind and dragging anchor Someone very drunk, unable to control his or her movements. See DRAGGING ANCHOR.

three sheets to the wind and the fourth shaking Very drunk.

throughway Used for *expressway* in western New England. "He took the throughway."

throw a tub at a whale See quote. "To offer a sop to keep anyone quiet, said to be the survival of a very ancient custom when approaching a sperm whale suspected of being ugly . . . to throw a cask overboard so it would drift toward the whale to distract its attention while the boat was approaching." (William F. Macy, *The Nantucket Scrap Basket*, 1916)

throw a tub to the whale To give up and let someone have his or her own way. The expression is nautical in origin, referring to whale hunters throwing their rope tubs into the water, thus letting a harpooned whale loose, after all the rope had paid out and the whale threatened to pull a boat down with it as it sounded.

throw off To say. " 'Well, Matt, any visitors?' he threw off." (Edith Wharton, *Ethan Frome,* 1911)

throw up Jonah To be very nauseated. In reference to the biblical story of Jonah in the whale. "I threw up Jonah." Given as a common expression in George Allen England, "Rural Locutions of Maine and Northern New Hampshire," *Dialect Notes,* Vol. IV (1914).

tickled as a cat with two cocks Very happy indeed; the euphemistic version of the expression substitutes *heads* for *cocks.*

tickle grass A name used for the barbed native grass *Trichodium laxiflower.*

tie a rag to your tongue An old-fashioned expression meaning hold your tongue, be quiet.

tied hand and foot Unable to act, incapacitated. " 'I'm tied hand and foot, Matt. There isn't a thing I can do.' " (Edith Wharton, *Ethan Frome,* 1911)

tier A child's apron that was tied on rather than buttoned and used as a play garment.

tie up Used in Maine for *cow stable,* a place where cows are kept secure.

tighter than a bull's mouth in fly time Very tight. A bull keeps his mouth tightly closed during the black fly season to prevent the flies from stinging the inside.

tighter than a teddy bear Heard in Maine for someone drunk.

tight-stowed Arranged tightly, using up all available room. "Then I had told Howland that he must reserve for me a span of good horses and a sleigh that I could pack sixteen small children into, tight-stowed." (Edward Everett Hale, "Christmas Waits in Boston," 1867)

Tilbury Town The setting of many poems by poet Edgar Lee Masters (1868–1950), modeled on his native Gardiner, Maine, where he was raised from the age of one, through he was born in Head Tide, Maine.

till See INSTEAD.

tilt A name for a children's seesaw in southwest New England. Also *tilting board*.

tinker A small mackerel (*Scomber scombrus*), a common New England food fish.

tippet A cape. "Or rather—He passed us— / The Dews drew quivering and chill— / For only Gossamer, my Gown—My Tippet—only Tulle". (Emily Dickinson, "Because I could not stop for death . . ." published 1890)

tip-toe Nancy A young woman who puts on airs. Cited as a common term in George Allen England, "Rural Locutions of Maine and Northern New Hampshire," *Dialect Notes,* Vol. IV (1914).

tithing man See CHURCH STICK.

titman This word has no vulgar connotation among farmers in New England, who often refer to the runt in a litter of pigs as a *titman* or *tit*. *Tit* here derives from an old Germanic word meaning small, whereas *tit* as slang for a woman's breast comes from the Old English *titt*. A century ago *titman* meant a small or stunted person, as when Thoreau called his generation "a race of *titmen.*"

tivis To wander about aimlessly. Cited in William F. Macy, *The Nantucket Scrap Basket* (1916).

to See quote. "The corrupt use of *to* in the Yankee 'he lives to Salem,' 'to home', and others, must be a very old one . . ." (James Russell Lowell, *The Biglow Papers,* 1867)

tobacco boat See CHEBACCO.

toe injection A boot in the backside to cure someone of malingering or other ills.

toe the chalk An old expression synonymous with *toe the line*. "That 'ere's most frequently the kin o' talk of critters can't be kicked to toe the chalk." (James Russell Lowell, *The Biglow Papers,* 1862)

to hell I pitch it A common exclamation of protest in Marblehead, Massachusetts, where it is not taken as a profane or offensive term.

to home At home. "There ain't a soul but me to home." (Mary Wilkens Freeman, *A New England Nun and Other Stories,* 1861)

toil and moil Work practically without relief. " 'I shall have to toil and moil all my days, with only little bits of fun now and then . . .' " (Louisa May Alcott, *Little Women,* 1868)

tol'able A common pronunciation of "tolerable." " 'I hope you are enjoying good health.' 'Tol'able,' replied the store keeper, absently." (Bliss Perry, *"By the Committee,"* 1899)

tomally The soft green liver of cooked lobster, which many lobster lovers consider a delicacy.

tonic A bottled carbonated soft drink (soda or soda pop) in Boston and environs. Also used in Maine.

took (1) Taken. "I'd have got my ears took off." (Sara Orne Jewett, "Lost Lover," 1878) (2) Hit, struck. "He took that deer with a long shot."

took a fit Did something impulsively. "He took a fit and run up the road."

took sick Come down with an illness. " 'But I ain't never took sick,' snapped Melinda, looking like a sturdy oak-tree utterly incapable of ailments." (Rose Terry Cooke, "Town Mouse and Country Mouse," 1891)

tooser An antique word for a clay marble used in the game of marbles.

toosted Lifted. "We toosted him up in the tree." Possibly derives from *boost*.

tooth carpenter A humorous term Mainers once used for *dentist*.

top cow A bull in eastern New England; also *toro*.

top dressing Manure.

top gallant A colorful but probably obsolete term for *corn tassel*.

topping Proud. "You needn't look so topping." (Mary Wilkens Freeman, *A New England Nun and Other Stories*, 1891)

torch up Recorded in Maine and New Hampshire for *to incite, urge, inspire*.

to-rights Right away, immediately. An old poem about a slaughtered pig went: "If you eat the liver / you'll live forever / If you eat the lights [lungs], / you'll die to rights."

tortience A perhaps obsolete word for the youngest child, the baby, the pet of a family. "That there's my tortience." Origin unknown but it may derive from the Nauset Indian Taushunts meaning the same. Also *toshence, toshiens, tossance, tossiance, tossions*.

tote A Maine synonym for the verb *to carry* that is used in other regions as well.

tote road A lumber camp road used mainly for hauling supplies.

tote sled A sled used for hauling supplies.

tote-team A team of horses used for hauling.

t'other The other. "He stood a spell on one foot first, / Then stood a spell on t'other." (James Russell Lowell, *The Biglow Papers*, 1866)

touch a hundred Live to 100 years old. " 'Wust kind [of accident],' my informant assented. 'More'n enough to kill most men. But the Fromes are tough. Ethan'll likely touch a hundred.' " (Edith Wharton, *Ethan Frome*, 1911)

touchin' up Used by Maine fishermen for *stealing*. "Someone's been touchin' up my nets," that is, stealing fish from them.

touch of the holy bone, a Said to be an Irish aphorism heard among workers on the Boston docks to describe sexual intercourse.

tough as a boiled eel A simile heard in New England.

tougher than a bagful of hammers Very tough.

tourtiere A French-Canadian word for *pork pie*.

touse A fight, as in *to make a touse*, to take on someone in a fight. Given as a common expression in George Allen England, "Rural Locutions of Maine and Northern New Hampshire," *Dialect Notes*, Vol. IV (1914).

town farm A term used in the 19th century for *poorhouse*.

town fathers The SELECTMEN or elected officials of a town.

town pound A pasture once set aside for stray animals such as sheep, cows or pigs that the town field driver collected so that they would not ruin the cultivated fields.

trade Once a common term in Rhode Island for a medical prescription.

trading An old, perhaps obsolete, term for *shopping*.

train To travel with someone or a group, to be familiar with. "She trains with a fast set."

trainer An obsolete term for *soldier*.

traipsin' about Traveling around without a purpose. " '. . . it might make him discontented with Grover's Corners to go traipsin' about Europe . . .' " (Thornton Wilder, *Our Town*, 1938)

trap war A fight among lobstermen over where traps or pots are put, usually occurring when one lobsterman encroaches on another's traditional territory. "Trap wars are legendary, especially in Maine, where lobstering territories are often legacies from father to son. A half-hitch knot on a buoy spindle is a warning. A severed pot warp is a threat . . . On very rare occasions, territorial disputes flash into genuine war, as groups of lobstermen retaliate against other groups." (Bruce Ballenger, *The Lobster Almanac*, 1988)

trash Something considered worthless; one great New England poet uses the word this way: "My green hill yonder, where the sun goes down / Without a scratch, was once inhabited / By trees that injured him [the sun]—and evil trash / That made a cage, and held him while he bled." (Edward Arlington Robinson, "Archibald's Example," *The Three Taverns*, 1920)

traveler's-joy *Clematis vitallba*, a New England flower. ". . . the steam . . . tightening her rough hair into little brown rings like the tendrils on the traveller's joy.'' (Edith Wharton, *Ethan Frome,* 1911)

traverse Another word for *sled*.

tread on Step on. "Don't tread on the flowers."

tree-bender A term heard for a heavy rain in Massachusetts. See IT'S RAINING PITCHFORKS AND BARN SHOVELS.

tree squeak An imaginary creature of the Maine woods, so named because it is said to squeak like tree limbs in the wind.

triangular trade In the triangular trade, ships carried New England rum to the African Gold Coast on the first passage, traded the rum for slaves and transported the shackled slaves to the West Indies on the middle passage, where the slaves were sold for molasses and sugar, which were brought back to New England to make more rum on the final passage. The middle passage was, of course, the worst and most inhumane of the three legs of the journey.

trifflers An old New England name for *puddings*; probably derives from the dessert called a *trifle*.

trimming Cutting back on expenses. "Here followed some staggering [Newport] examples of penuriousness and 'trimming.' '' (Thornton Wilder, *Theophilus North,* 1973)

Trimontane peninsula Refers to Boston. "The dusk has settled heavily upon the woods, the waves, and the Trimontane peninsula.'' (Nathaniel Hawthorne, "Mrs. Hutchinson,'' 1830) See TRIMOUNT CITY.

Trimount City An old nickname for Boston, Massachusetts, also called *Trimountain City,* for the three mountains or hills it was built upon. See TRIMONTANE PENINSULA.

trot around all day in a bushel To be busy but getting nowhere. "He's trotted around all day in a bushel.''

troubles Minor medical problems. See COMPLICATIONS.

trout chowder A fishing camp dish made with trout and milk that is said to put New England clam chowder to shame.

trudge See U.

true as preachin'! A simile heard in New England.

tuckered Very tired. "I'm tuckered, I'll tell you.''

tumble A synonym for a haycock, a small pile of hay.

tump An Indian word used in Maine meaning to drag a deer home through the woods after it has been killed.

tunk To tap something lightly. "He tunked it with the wrench.''

tunket Hell. "He's madder'n tunket." Given as a common expression in George Allen England, "Rural Locutions of Maine and Northern New Hampshire," *Dialect Notes*, Vol. IV (1914).

tunnel Sometimes used to mean "funnel."

turned around some Lost, a less embarrassing way to say one was lost in the woods. "I would have been home soon but I was turned around some."

turn the paunch A term used a century ago meaning to disgorge, vomit.

'twarn't A pronunciation of "it weren't," especially in Maine. "If 'twarn't for you they'd have lost."

twenny A pronunciation of 20 heard in Boston. " 'He was *big*, in fact. Probly twenny-five years old, maybe twenny-six . . .' " (George V. Higgins, *Outlaws*, 1987)

twenty tailors around a buttonhole Too many cooks spoiling the broth. Cited as a Vermont expression in Charles Edward Crane's *Let Me Show You Vermont* (1937).

twice as cold as zero This old expression is still heard in northern New England on bitterly cold days.

twink! A mild oath heard mostly among women on Isleboro, an island off the coast of Maine.

twitch A distance of about 200 yards. "A good twitch is the distance a horse (called a twitch horse) can drag a full-length pulp log without resting. Distances are frequently measured in twitches or fractions thereof by woodsmen." (Louise Dickenson Rich, *We Took to the Woods*, 1942)

twizzle See quote. "Every now and then the men would come across a snare in their nets that they called a twizzle, and often a good deal of time and patience were required to pick and shake it out. 'All sorts of fish make twizzles,' Dan said. 'Sometimes a little alewife will make one of the meanest sort.' " (Clifton Johnson, *Highways and Byways of New England*, 1916)

two-holer See BACKHOUSE.

two lamps burning and no ship at sea Used to describe a foolishly extravagant person. Someone with ships at sea in the days of sail was rich and could afford to burn two expensive oil lamps. Anyone else who burned two lamps was likely a fool. Cited in William F. Macy, *The Nantucket Scrapbook* (1916). Also *two lamps burning and no ships out*.

'twould break a snake's back to follow that furrer (furrow) Said of a poorly plowed field. Quoted in John Wallace, *Village Down East* (1943).

U

u See quote. "*E* sometimes takes the place of *u* [in Yankee dialect], as in *jedge, tredge, bresh* . . . The Yankee always shortens the *u* in the ending *ture*, making *ventur, natur, pictur,* and so on." (James Russell Lowell, *The Biglow Papers*, 1867)

ugly In New England alone *ugly* is applied to cows, horses and other large farm animals that are hard to handle. "That's one ugly horse you've got there."

uncle Often used in the past as a respectful form of address for an unrelated old man as well as one's own uncle.

Uncle Sam See AFORE.

uncomfortable as a short-tailed horse in fly time An expression meaning very uncomfortable that was common in New England and other regions a century ago; a variation was *uncomfortable as a stump-tail bull in fly time.*

under the window See quote. "Nantucketers always sit *under* the window, never at the window. There is perhaps no phrase which is more noted in our speech than this . . . The reason is obviously, that Nantucket windows usually are rather high from the floor [and] we sit under them." (William F. Macy, *The Nantucket Scrap Basket,* 1916)

unfinished attic Heard in Massachusetts for *someone stupid, empty-headed.* "He's got an unfinished attic."

unthawed Used to mean "thawed out," "warmer." "He stood by the fire till he was unthawed."

up-along Sometimes used for *up* or *along.* "You going up-along to the store?"

up and died Died suddenly. An old poem goes: "Anna was a lovely bride / But Anna, damn'er, up and died." See ANADAMA BREAD.

up a stump An old euphemism for pregnancy outside of marriage. "She's up a stump and he's left the country."

up attic Up in the attic. "Then we asked was there anything / Up attic that we'd ever want again." (Robert Frost, "The Witch of Coos," 1922) See also DOWN CELLAR.

up for air See DRAWN BUCKET.

up on one's beanwater To feel good, strong, raring to go. "I'm right up

234

on my beanwater this morning."
Perhaps because beanwater, the
water beans were soaked in for hours
before baking, smelled so strong
one's head snapped up after one bent
to take a whiff of it. Given as a
common expression in George Allen
England, "Rural Locutions of Maine
and Northern New Hampshire," *Dialect Notes,* Vol. IV (1914).

up on one's shoe taps Fit and fine, as
in "He's up on his shoe taps."
Given as a common expression in
George Allen England, "Rural Locutions of Maine and Northern New
Hampshire," *Dialect Notes,* Vol. IV
(1914).

upstair Used in northern Maine for
upstairs. "I'll be upstair in a
minute."

upstropolis An unusual word for
"confused"; heard on Isleboro, off
the Maine coast.

up to the westward See DOWN EAST.

use it up, wear it out, make it do A
New England proverb illustrating native thriftiness.

V

vaggers! An obsolete exclamation.

vamp it up Strengthen, beef up, patch up. This old-fashioned expression arose among shoemakers repairing the *vamp*, or upper portion of shoes.

veal To kill a calf (for veal), used in New Hampshire and Maine. "We're going to veal the heifer."

velvet Heard in Maine for the soda fountain frappé made of milk and ice cream. See MILKSHAKE.

venture See U.

verandah Porch. "The window opened on a narrow verandah with a trellised arch." (Edith Wharton, *Summer*, 1917) Used in other regions as well.

Vermont (1) The state's name comes from the French *monts verts*, "green mountains." The Green Mountain State was admitted to the Union in 1791 as our 14th state. It was once called *New Connecticut*. (2) A horse raised in Vermont.

Vermont charity According to Hugh Rawlins in *Wicked Words* (1989), this refers to "cheapness . . . what hoboes call sympathy which is accompanied by nothing else."

Vermont gray An old, obsolete term for the common winter outer clothing long worn by rural New Englanders.

Vermontese A Vermonter or a group of Vermonters.

Vermont kindling Newspapers tightly rolled into a log for use when one is out of wood or hasn't got the money to buy wood.

Vermont psalm, the Psalm 121 from the Bible, a psalm often used to start funeral services in Vermont: "I lift my eyes unto the hills." This was noted in a *New York Times* news story on May 2, 1994 from Woodstock, Vermont: "Psalm 121 . . . They call it the Vermont Psalm here."

very poor man's dinner A Maine dish made of thinly sliced potatoes and onions fried in the grease of salt pork. A similar dish made in Massachusetts is called "Necessity Mess."

view See quote. "According to my v'oo. (The unspellable pronunciation of this word is the touchstone of New England Brahminism)." (Oliver Wendell Holmes, *Elsie Venner*, 1861)

vowel twisting See HOUSE.

voyage Sometimes used to describe a clamming or berrying expedition.

vum A New England word that means vow, or swear, as in the ex-pression of surprise, "Well, I vum!" The old term derives from the verb *vum,* dating back to the 18th century.

W

wadgetty Fidgety, nervous. Cited in William F. Macy, *The Nantucket Scrap Basket,* 1916.

wageworker A wage-earner, one who works for wages.

wagon A baby carriage. "The whole town assembled, down to the babies in their wagons." (James E. Cabot, *A Memoir of Ralph Waldo Emerson,* 1887)

wake snakes Noted in James Russell Lowell's *The Biglow Papers* (1866) as meaning "to get into trouble."

wait on Wait for. "Wait on me a minute, will you?"

wal Well. "*Wal.* Spoken with great deliberation . . . I have used *wal* in the *Biglow Papers* because if enough nasality be added, it represents most nearly the average sound of the interjection." (James Russell Lowell, *The Biglow Papers,* 1866)

Walden Pond A pond near Concord where Henry David Thoreau lived from July 1845 to September 1847, an experience that resulted in his classic book *Walden, or Life in the Woods* (1854).

walk it to him! Words urging a fighter on during a fight, meaning roughly "Give it to him good!"

wallop Heard in New Hampshire for *belch.* "I walloped up my food."

wamble-cropped An obsolete expression meaning sick at the stomach, or, figuratively, crestfallen.

wamble-jawed Recorded in Maine for *loose-jawed or loose-tongued,* given to gossiping, unable to keep a secret.

wampum *Wampumpeak* was a name American Indians in New England gave to shell money. Like most Indian names—including the longer forebears of *squash, hickory* and *raccoon*—the colonists found *wampumpeak* too long and shortened it to *wampum,* which is how it remains today. All Indians didn't have the same name for shell money. Virginia Indians called wampum *roanoke*; the Mohave Indians called it *pook*; in northern California it was called *aliqua-chick*; and in the Northwest it was *hiaqua.* But only *wampum* remains well known today.

wangan A term used by Maine lumbermen for a boat carrying supplies or tools, though the word has other meanings as well.

[Wangan] refers to the store where the cook sells candy, tobacco, snuff, and clothing . . . The cook may say, 'I lost my wangan when the work boat swamped,' and that means his dishes are at the bottom of the lake. Or he may complain, 'The wangan's runnin' low,' meaning this time that he's short of food. Or a man may take his wangan and fly—leave the job with his little bundle of personel belongings. You can only tell by the context what the word means. (Louise Rich, *We Took to the Woods,* 1948)

See also RUNNING THE WANGAN.

wanigan A boat or chest filled with lumber camp supplies. The word derives from the Ojibwa *waanikaan,* "storage pit," and is used in Alaska as well as northern New England. Also called a WANGAN.

wan't A common New England contraction of "was not."

warm from the cow A term referring to milk drunk as soon as a cow was milked, a rarity now in these days of pasturization.

War of Inequity A historical term used in New England for the War of 1812.

warm it to him Sock him, hit him. Cited as a common expression in George Allen England, "Rural Locutions of Maine and Northern New Hampshire," *Dialect Notes,* Vol. IV (1914).

warn't Weren't. "We warn't going together."

Warwick Pronounced WAH-rick; a town in Rhode Island.

wash-ashores A current term meaning summer residents or tourists on Martha's Vineyard, Massachusetts. "Seems like there's more wash-ashores on the island this year."

wash out the dishes Heard in New Hampshire and Maine for "wash up the dishes" or "wash the dishes."

watcher An obsolete term for someone who sits up, or "watches," a corpse in a time when wakes were held at home.

Watch Night An old name for New Year's Eve, when people watch the old year go out and the new year come in. In small towns services were often held on Watch Night, after which a traditional oyster stew was served.

water bar A gravel ridge that extends across hill roads at a downward angle to carry rainwater to a ditch at the other side.

water bewitched, meal begritched An old Cape Cod term for *very weak thin porridge. Bewitched* in the expression is a nautical word meaning very weak, and *begritched* means begrudged.

Waterbury A popular, inexpensive watch made by the Waterbury Clock Company of Waterbury, Connecticut.

water witch A water douser, one who divines underground water with a divining rod.

waw A pronunciation commonly heard in Boston for *war*.

wear out To beat someone thoroughly. "I'll wear out a stick on your backside!"

weather breeder The New England name for an unusually clear, cloudless day when there is extraordinary visibility. Folklore holds that such days are always followed by severe storms. "Once on the kind of day called 'weather breeder,' / When the heat slowly hazes and the sun / By its own power seems to be undone . . ." (Robert Frost, "An Encounter," 1916)

weather varieties See quote. "The varieties of weather known to Nantucketers often surprise the inland visitor, who recognizes only two kinds, good and bad. We have *fair, good, fine, foul, dirty, nasty, bad, thick, rough, heavy,* and several other sorts, including *owlish* and 'mirogenous', whatever that may mean." (William F. Macy, *Nantucket Scrap Basket,* 1916)

wedding-elms A New England custom calls for newlyweds to plant a pair of elm trees known as *wedding-elms* by the front door.

wedgy A name given in Rhode Island to large sandwiches made of loaves of Italian bread and most commonly known as *heroes* in the rest of the United States. See GRINDER.

wee-wawing Shaking, bouncing, as in "The wagon was wee-wawing all over the road." Given as a common expression in George Allen England, "Rural Locutions of Maine and Northern New Hampshire," *Dialect Notes,* Vol. IV (1914).

we have two seasons: winter and the Fourth of July An old New England saying quoted in Louise Dickinson Rich, *Happy the Land,* 1946.

well James Russell Lowell, in *The Biglow Papers* (1867), gave five different New England ways of pronouncing *well* at the time:

> "A friend of mine . . . told me that he once heard five "wells," like pioneers, precede the answer to an inquiry about the piece of land. The first was the ordinary *wul,* in deference to custom; the second, the long, perpending *ooahl,* with a falling inflection of the voice; the third, the same, but with the voice rising, as if in despair of a conclusion, into a plaintively nasal whine; the fourth, *wulh,* ending in aspirate of a sigh; and then, fifth, came a short, sharp *wal,* showing that a conclusion had been reached."

well, I'll be Shorthand for *well, I'll be damned* often heard in New England.

well, I vum! See VUM.

well, knock me off the Christmas tree! An old expression indicating great surprise. "Well, knock me off the Christmas tree if she hasn't gone and done it!''

well to live To be so drunk that one had no cares. "He's been well to live all night."

we must take it as it comes from the cook A saying, nautical in origin, meaning we must accept things as they are. Cited in William F. Macy, *The Nantucket Scrap Basket*, 1916.

went A euphemism for *died*. See SLEEPING.

weren't Sometimes used as a singular verb. "He weren't home."

wet Humidity. See MILDEN.

wet as sap Sweating profusely; a Mainism.

Whaleman's Chapel The Seaman's Bethel, a famous church in New Bedford, Massachusetts, with many memorials to New England whalemen. "In this same New Bedford there stands a Whaleman's Chapel, and few are the moody fishermen, shortly bound for the Indian Ocean or Pacific, who fail to make a Sunday visit to the spot. I am sure that I did not." (Herman Melville, *Moby Dick*, 1851)

whale the daylights out of Give a beating to. "She whaled the daylight out of him."

whaler (1) A whaling man. "Dan and Shorty . . . brought up from the depths of their chests . . . fancy articles or "scrimshonting,' as it is termed by whalers . . ." (William Hussey Macy, *There She Blows*, 1877) (2) Something very big. "That's a real whaler."

whaling A beating. "She gave him a good whaling."

whap over Knock over. "He whapped it over."

wharves Bartlett points out in his *Dictionary of Americanisms* (1848) that this plural of *wharf* originated in Massachusetts in about 1735; the English always said *wharfs*.

whatcheer See quote.

The shibboleth of the people of the State of Rhode Island. When Roger Williams, the founder of the ancient colony, pushed his way from Salem, Massachusetts, in the year 1636, through the wilderness, he embarked in a canoe with five others, on Sekonk river, and landed near the present site of the city of Providence. As the party approached the shore, they were saluted by a company of Indians with the friendly interrogation of "What cheer?" a common English phrase which they had learned from the colonists, equivalent to the modern How do you do? and meant by the natives as Welcome! The cove where the party landed is called *"Whatcheer Cove,"* which term is also applied to the lands adjacent; besides which there is in Providence a *"Whatcheer* Bank," a *"Whatcheer* Church," *"Whatcheer* hotels," a *"Whatcheer* Insurance Company," and, last of all a

"Whatcheer Lager Beer Saloon!"
(John Bartlett, *Dictionary of Americanisms,* 1848)

what-da-ya-think? A common greeting when two people meet in Maine. The reply is often: "I think, damn, that's what I think."

what in tarnation! An old-fashioned euphemistic exclamation.

what in tunket! A euphemism for *what in hell!* "What in tunket do you mean?"

what's the state of your mind and the stem of your constitution? A joking man-to-man inquiry about the state of one's health. See STEMMY.

what's the word? Another Maine greeting.

what time be it? Heard in Maine and other areas for *what time is it?*

wheat and Indian A historical term recorded as far back as 1643 for "a mixture of white flour and the meal of Indian corn," in *Bartlett's* (1848) words.

wheel An early name for a bicycle. ". . . his brother helped me select a 'wheel,' as we generally called them in those days." (Thornton Wilder, *Theophilus North,* 1973)

wheelbarrow fashion See quote. "They were . . . ordered to kiss each other 'wheelbarrow fashion'—You would then see a young man and a girl meet on the floor, close their right and left hands, on both sides; and with a whirl . . . turn through their arms, bring the back part of their shoulders in contact—each with the head resting upon the other's right shoulder, their mouths meeting." (*Yankee,* April 1828)

when it rains porridge hold up your dish Take advantage of a situation. Probably an old New England proverb. " 'When it rains porridge hold up your dish,' said Mrs. Flagg, but Miss Pickett made no response . . ." (Sarah Orne Jewett, "The Guests of Mrs. Timms," 1895)

when you don't know what to do, do nothing An old Yankee maxim.

where are you preaching? Said in Maine to somebody all dressed up, formally dressed.

where you going? Where are you going? "Are" often is omitted after "where."

whickering owl A small screech owl (*Otis asio*).

whick-whack Heard in Nantucket for *run here and there.* "They were whick-whacking back and forth."

Whip City An old nickname for Westfield, Massachusetts, which in 1900 had 40 whip factories that turned out 90% of the world's supply of horse whips.

whippet (1) A small person. (2) A female animal. Heard mostly in Maine.

whistling up the wind Talking wishfully. The expression has its origins in the superstitious practice of sailors in the days of sail whistling for a wind during a calm.

white-faced New England What P.T. Barnum called "the meanest kind of New England rum."

white flannel hash See RED FLANNEL HASH.

White Graveyard of the Atlantic, the A name given to the shifting shoals of Race Point, Nauset and Monomoy on Cape Cod, where so many ships were wrecked over three centuries. Noted in Elizabeth Reynard's *The Narrow Land,* 1934. See MOONCUSSERS.

white hen's chickens Very pleasant, desirable people. "She thinks he's one of the white hen's chickens." Cited as a common expression in George Allen England, "Rural Locutions of Maine and Northern New Hampshire," *Dialect Notes,* Vol. IV (1914).

White Mountain freezer The first hand-crank ice-cream machine sold in America; made from New England pine and cast iron by New Hampshire's White Mountains Freezer Company beginning in 1853.

White Mountains Famous mountains in New Hampshire. ". . . we had been loitering towards the heart of the White Mountains—those old crystal hills, whose mysterious brillancy had gleamed upon our distant wanderings before we thought of visiting them." (Nathaniel Hawthorne, "Sketches from Memory," 1835)

white oak *Quercus alba,* the state tree of Connecticut.

whittle Used in Nantucket to mean "to fuss," "to be uneasy"; also "to tease or pester." Cited in William F. Macy, *The Nantucket Scrap Basket,* 1916.

who beat? Who won? " 'Who beat?' interjected a voice that should never have been allowed to disturb the silence . . ." (James Brendon Connolly, "From Reykjavik to Gloucester," 1920)

whole boodle, the An old slang term meaning the whole lot, everything. "I would like to have the whole boodle of them." (Oliver Wendell Holmes, *The Autocrat of the Breakfast Table,* 1858)

whole caboodle An old expression heard in New England and elsewhere for *everything, all of it, the whole thing.* "He has a whole caboodle of baseball cards."

whole tote, the Everything. "I'll take the whole tote."

whore's egg A colorful name fishermen give to the sea urchin (*Arbacia punctulata*), which is unattractive to all but other sea urchins.

Wianno Pronounced we-ON-o; a village on Cape Cod, Massachusetts.

wicked good Very good. "The fishing was wicked good."

widow maker (1) A sailing ship's bowsprit or job boom, so called because sailors who lost their hold on it while working on the headsails in rough seas often lost their lives. (2) The sea. (3) A tree in a precarious position that looks as if it will fall and kill a man.

widow's walk An elevated observatory on a dwelling, usually with a railing and affording a good view of the ocean. These watchtowers, often seen on the roofs of old houses in New England, date back to colonial times and were so named because many woman walked in vain on them, waiting for incoming ships that never returned. Taking the form of a cupola, railed-in deck or balcony, they also have been called, less poetically, the CAPTAIN'S WALK, *the lookout, the observatory* and *the walk.*

wife of It was once common in New England to call wives by the first and last names of their husbands to distinguish them from relations with the same name; for example, Mrs. Peter Walker. A lengthier way to make the same distinction uses *wife of*: "This is Mrs. Mary Walker, wife of Peter Walker."

wigs on the green An all-out fight, a donnybrook. The expression dates back to times when men wore powdered wigs and suggests two or more such men fighting on the village green, their wigs having fallen on the ground.

wilcox To spend an uneasy, sleepless night. "I wilcoxed all night long." The term is said to have originated with a Nantucket family named Wilcox that had to sleep five in a bed one night when they had a lot of company. Cited by William F. Macy, *The Nantucket Scrap Basket,* 1916.

wildcat trail A steep, fast skiing trail with sharp curves for expert skiers. See POLE CAT TRAIL.

wild geese Sparks flying up and out of a chimney.

wind blew straight up and down, the A Yankee description of a gale cited in *The Old Farmer's Almanack* (1946).

wind is out, the Used to describe wind blowing in from the sea. "The wind is out."

window stool Used in Maine for *windowsill.*

wind-pudding See quote. "It is all of piece with wind-pudding, which is a (joking) word for a dinner consisting of tightening the belt." (Robert P. Tristram Coffin, *Kennebec, Cradle of Americas,* 1937)

winkum An old word for cider brandy once heard in Connecticut.

winter never rots in the sky This old saying assures us that though spring may be here at last, there's always the chance of winterlike weather around the corner.

wishing book A rural name a century ago for the Montgomery Ward and the Sears catalogs, both no longer published. Also WISH BOOK.

witchgrass A weed (*Panicum capillare*) that is called *quack grass* in other regions.

witching wand A divining rod, a branch or stick thought to help a dowser locate water. "The water for which we may have to look / In summertime with a witching wand . . ." (Robert Frost, "Two Tramps in Mud Time," 1936)

with all sail set A nautical term used on land to mean "hurriedly," "with great determination." "He was on his way home with all sail set."

Witherlick A mythical animal of the lumber camps. Cited as a common term in George Allen England, "Rural Locutions of Maine and Northern New Hampshire," *Dialect Notes,* Vol. IV (1914).

with-its The vegetables and other dishes served with the main course of a dinner. "We had leg of lamb and with-its."

without Unless. "He done it, without I'm mistaken."

withy Strong and wiry. Given as a common expression in George Allen England, "Rural Locutions of Maine and Northern New Hampshire," *Dialect Notes,* Vol. IV (1914).

wizzled Wrinkled, wizened. "The grapes were all wizzled up on the vine."

wolf fish *Anarchichas lupus,* an excellent eating fish caught in New England waters. Also called *ocean catfish.*

wonder A word once used in Nantucket for *doughnut.*

> Here in my adopted city of Providence I have produced occasional merriment by calling a doughnut . . . a "wonder." The name is a "quaint" belonging exclusively to the place (Nantucket) where it is used . . . Wonders were simply doughnuts made in a certain prescribed regulation form—cut out round, jagged across and separated in the center two or three times, but not cut through to the edge; made in that way the fat, while they were frying, passed between these jagged cuts, with the result of crisp, deliciously browned crosspieces, so that the "wonder" easily broke into such separate sections, or bars, and was peculiarly appetizing." (J.E.C. Farnham, *Brief Historical Data and Memories of My Boyhood Days in Nantucket,* 1923)

wonder cakes Doughnuts in the shape of twisted fingers that are dipped in sugar syrup.

wonderful (1) Exceptionally, wonderfully. " 'The morning star always gets wonderful bright the minute before it has to go—doesn't it?"

(Thornton Wilder, *Our Town,* 1938)
(2) Very. "He's wonderful hand-some."

woodchuck (1) A New England name for the groundhog (*Marmota monax*), *woodchuck* probably derives from a New England Algonquian Indian word meaning the same. "A boy always had woodchuck holes to explore after the leaves were down in the fall . . ." (Hayden Pearson, *New England Flavor,* 1961) (2) A derogatory slang term currently heard in New England for a poor white person, according to the *New York Times Magazine,* March 27, 1994.

wooden nutmegs See YANKEE PEDDLER.

woodpile cousin A very close friend.

woods A term New Englanders chiefly use for the forest.

wood's queer See quote. "[Getting out of touch with conventional society] is known in Mrs. Rich's country as going 'wood's-queer.' " (Clifton Fadiman, *The New Yorker,* November 21, 1942)

wood wax A yellow flower that grows plentifully on poor land and has a bitter taste. "This deceitful verdure was occasioned by a plentiful crop of 'wood-wax,' which wears the same dark and glossy green throughout the summer, except at one short period, when it puts forth a profusion of yellow blossoms. At that season to a distant spectator, the hill appears absolutely overlaid with

gold . . ." (Nathaniel Hawthorne, "Alice Doane's Appeal," 1835) Also called *green grass.*

woolyneag A name once used in New England for the fisher (*Martis pennanti*), the largest member of the mink family; from an Abnaki Indian word meaning handsome squirrel.

wopse Wrap up quickly, entangle. "She's all wopsed up in the blanket."

Worcester Pronounced WUSS-ter; a city in Massachusetts.

world's a sorry schoolroom sometimes, the A Maine saying " 'I still believed . . . that love would eventually rise to the top like cream in a bottle of milk. I learned better over the next ten years. The world's a sorry schoolroom sometimes, ain't it?' " (Stephen King, *Dolores Claiborne,* 1993)

worse than a Massachusetts driver Used in Maine to describe the worst, most reckless type of driver; there is no record of *Maine driver* being used for the same in Massachusetts.

wosh The usual pronunciation of "wash" in the region.

wotta A Cape Cod pronunciation of "water."

wouldn't give him (her) hell room The very lowest estimate of a person, that is, one wouldn't provide room for him (her) even in hell. (Though this suggests that there must be some worse place where he (she) would have to find room).

wouldn't know him (her) from a side of sole leather An old expression meaning I don't know him (her) at all, never saw him (her) before. A "side" was shoemaker talk for half of a cow's hide.

wouldn't touch it with a ten-foot pole This expression may have been suggested by the ten-foot poles that New England boatmen used to pole their boats along in shallow waters. Possibly the words were first something like *I wouldn't touch that with the ten-foot pole of a riverman,* this shortened to the present phrase with the passing of pole boats from the American scene. The image first appears in the Nantucketism *can't touch him with a ten-foot,* meaning he is distant, proud, reserved. In the sense of not wanting to get involved in a project or having a strong distaste for something, the words aren't recorded until the late 19th century. The expression is now used throughout the United States.

wouldn't touch with a barge pole A variation heard in Boston on *wouldn't touch with a ten-foot pole.* " 'Screw this package, buddy, I wouldn't touch this one with a goddamned barge pole.' " (George V. Higgins, *Outlaws,* 1987)

wouldn't wear it to a dog fight Said of apparel very unfashionable: "I wouldn't wear that shirt to a dog fight."

wreck The Maine pronunciation of *rack.*

wreck of the Hesperus A huge submerged rock off the coast of Gloucester, Massachusetts caused so many shipwrecks in the 18th century that it was called Norman's Woe. Wrote Henry Wadsworth Longfellow in his diary for December 17, 1837: "News of shipwrecks horrible on the coast. 20 bodies washed ashore near Gloucester, one lashed to a piece of wreck. There is a reef called Norman's Woe where many of these took place; among others the schooner *Hesperus* . . . I must write a ballad upon this." The ballad proved to be "The Wreck of the Hesperus," which became so well known that "wreck of the *Hesperus*" also became an expression for any, battered or disheveled thing, as in "You look like the wreck of the Hesperus."

wringing wet Soaking wet.

wrote up Written up, reported. " 'He chose his own epytaph . . .' 'Why, it's just some notes of music—what is it?' 'Oh, I wouldn't know. It was wrote up in the Boston papers at the time.' " (Thornton Wilder, *Our Town,* 1938)

wudge Recorded in New Bedford for a little bunch. Also *wudget.*

wunt A common pronunciation of "won't."

wust A pronunciation of "worst." See TOUCH A HUNDRED.

X

x See EX.

Y

Yale Yale University, ranking after Harvard and William and Mary as the third oldest institution of higher education in the United States, is named for English merchant Elihu Yale (1649–1721). Founded in 1701 as the Collegiate School of Saybrook, Connecticut, the school was named Yale College at its 1718 commencement, held in the first college building at New Haven. Yale might have been called Mather University, for Cotton Mather suggested naming it so in return for his financial support, but Elihu Yale won out when he donated a cargo of gifts, books and various goods that were sold for about 562 pounds.

Yale banger An obsolete term for a club like a cane or stick, a blundgeon once used by students at Yale University. "This challenge is accepted by the Sophmores and in the evening a 'banger rush' takes place." (L.H. Bagg, *Four Years at Yale,* 1871)

Yale blue A reddish blue that takes it name from the colors of Yale University. It is the royal blue of the Egyptian Ramses dynasty, also called Ramses.

Yalensian A Yale student or graduate. Also *Yalie.*

Yale lock The Yale lock has no connection with Yale University. New England inventor Linnus Yale (1821–1868) invented numerous locks, including the trademarked key type with a revolving barrel that bears his name. Linnus founded a company to manufacture locks at Stamford, Connecticut the same year that he died.

yank *Yank,* meaning to pull abruptly or vigorously, is of uncertain origin. A U.S. invention, probably originating in New England early in the 19th century and much used since then, it has nothing to do with the word YANKEE, for a New Englander. It may be akin to the English dialect word *yerk,* a variant of *jerk,* but there is no proof of this.

Yankee (1) The source of this word has long been disputed and its origin is still uncertain, despite all the research devoted to it. Candidates, among many, have included a slave named Yankee offered for sale in 1725, a Dutch sea captain named Yanky, the Yankos Indians and the Dutch name *Janke* ("Johnny"), which the Dutch applied to the *English*. The most popular explanation, also unproved, is that Yankee comes from *Jan Kees,* a contemptuous Flemish and German nickname for the Dutch that the English first applied to the Dutch in the New World.

In any case, *Yankee* seems to have been first applied to New Englanders by British soldiers serving under General James Wolfe in the French and Indian War prior to 1758. A letter written by Wolfe himself in that year uses the word as a contemptuous nickname for New Englanders.

> My posts are now so fortified that I can afford you two companies of Yankees, and the more as they are better for ranging and scouting than either work or vigilance . . . [they] are in general the dirtiest most contemptible cowardly dogs that you can conceive. There is no depending on them in action. They fall down dead in their own dirt and desert by battalions, officers and all. Such rascals as those are rather an encumberance than any real strength to an army.

Wolf's low opinion of the New Englanders and further contemptuous use of *Yankee* is seen in a 1775 chronicle, which also is notable as an early description of the practice of "mooning." "They [British soldiers] abused the watch-men on duty, and the young children of Boston by the wayside, making mouths at them, calling them Yankeys, showing their posteriors, and clapping their hands thereon."

It wasn't until the Battle of Lexington, the first battle of the Revolution in 1775, that New Englanders began applying the nickname *Yankee* to themselves, making it respectable. Soon after, the process of dignification began and the story about the Yankos Indians was invented. In this tale a mythical tribe of Massachusetts Indians are said to have been defeated by a band of valorous New Englanders. The defeated Yankos so admired the bravery of their victorious adversaries that they gave them their name, *Yankos,* which meant Invincibles, and was soon corrupted to "Yankees"!

Yankee has been an admirable or contemptuous nickname for New Englanders ever since, depending by whom and in what context it is used, as the many entries herein clearly show. At any rate, *Yankee* described a New Englander by the middle 18th century and was used by the British to designate any American during the Revolution, the most notable example found in the derisive song "Yankee Doodle." Nowadays the British still use the word for an American, Southerners use it for Northerners and Northerners use it for New Englanders, who, despite its early history, are proud of the designation. "What will we come to / With all this pride of ancestry, we Yankees? / I think we're all mad . . .' " (Robert Frost, "The Generations of Men," 1914) (2) To cheat or outsmart. "He Yankeed them at every turn." (3) The large job topsail on some racing yachts that originated in New England. (4) Yankee dialect. "I kin write long-tailed, ef I please— / But when I'm jokin', no, I thankee; / Then, 'fore I know it, my idees / Run helter-skelter into Yankee." (James Russell Lowell, *The Biglow Papers,* 1867) See YANKEE DIALECT.

Yankee beverage SWITCHEL, vinegar and water sweetened with molasses and drunk in hot weather.

Yankee bullets Bullets made by housewives from household pewter during the Revolution.

Yankee bump See THANK-YE-MA'AM.

Yankee cheese-box on a raft An apt Southern description of the U.S. armored warship the *Monitor,* which fought the famous naval battle against the Confederate *Merrimac.*

Yankee clipper A name given to the famous clipper ships that were the aristocrats of the sea from 1850 to the end of the 19th century. They were by far the fastest ships of their day, and their leading builder was Donald McKay of Boston.

Yankee Coast An old term for the New England coast.

Yankee comfort A comforter made in New England.

Yankee dialect The English dialect used by New Englanders. The term *Yankee dialect* has been used since at least 1832; before this, at least as early as 1772, New England speech was simply called *Yankee.* Wrote James Russell Lowell in *The Biglow Papers,* 1866: "Of Yankee preterites I find *risse* and *rize* fer rose in Middleton and Dryden."

Yankeedom The domain of the Yankee. Also *Downeast, Yankeeland.*

Yankee Doodle (1) Legend has it that during the French and Indian War, the shabbily dressed troops of Colonel Thomas Fitch of Norfolk, Connecticut inspired a British army surgeon with musical talents, Dr. Shuckburgh or Shackburg, to write the derisive song "Yankee Doodle."

According to local tradition, Elizabeth Fitch, on leaving the house to bid goodbye to her brother (Colonel Fitch), was dismayed by the ill-sorted costumes of the "cavalry". Exclaiming, "You must have uniforms of some kind," she ran into the chicken yard, and returning with a handful of feathers announced, "Soldiers should wear plumes," and directed each soldier to put a feather in his cap. When Shuckburgh saw Fitch's men arriving at Fort Crailor, Rensselaer, New York, he is reputed to have exclaimed, "Now stab my vitals, they're macaronis!" sarcastically applying the slang of the day for fop, or dandy, and proceeded to write the song, which instantly caught popular fancy. (Federal Writer's Project, *Connecticut,* 1938)

There is no firm proof of this theory about the origin of the song, which ironically came to be popular among patriot troops during the Revolutionary War. It is said to have hundreds of verses. Before the Civil War, the tune, identified with New England, was often hissed off the stage in the South. (2) An obsolete term for *Yankee.*

Yankee-doodle   dandeeism The plucky spirit of Yankees, New Englanders or Americans.

Yankedoodledom A humorous old term for *New England* or *America.*

Yankee drawl See the Introduction.

Yankee female, the See quote.

> The little medical lady struck him as a perfect example of the "Yankee female"—the figure which, in the unregenerate imagination of the children of the cotton-states, was produced by the New England school-system, the Puritan code, the ungenial climate, the absence of chivalry. Spare, dry, hard, without a curve, an inflection or a grace, she seemed to ask no odds in the battle of life and to be prepared to give none. (Henry James, *The Bostonians*, 1886)

Yankeefied Make like Yankees, either New Englanders or Americans in general. "Japan becomes more Yankeefied every year."

Yankee grit Great persevering courage. "Their Yankee grit saw them through the battle."

Yankee Hastings Cambridge, Massachusetts farmer Jonathan Hastings of the early 18th century used "Yankee" in the sense of good or excellent so frequently that—according to one theory, at least—the word was widely adopted as a nickname for New Englanders. Students at Harvard are supposed to have given Hastings his nickname.

Yankee ingenuity See quote under SCRATCHED ALONG.

Yankeeism A word, phrase, pronunciation, trait, whim or peculiarity characteristic of New Englanders.

Yankee jacket See FIT WITH A YANKEE JACKET, TO.

Yankeeland New England, of which the inhabitants are Yankeelanders.

Yankee leave French leave. "He took a Yankee leave, cleared out leaving all his debts unpaid."

Yankee nation An old term for *New England*.

Yankee neat A nautical term meaning shipshape that came ashore.

Yankee notions These were originally the mirrors, needles, beads, pocket knives and the like that Yankee sailing ships traded with for native goods in foreign ports. Yankee peddlers also carried them. Today *Yankee notions* sometimes refers to small items sold in gift stores.

Yankee Notion State See quote. "The Yankee Notion State, as Connecticut has often been called, earned its title in the early part of the 19th century, when there was a great impetus given to the manufacture of almost all sorts of implements for the farm and the household." (*Hartford Courant*, October 29, 1904)

Yankee peddler "The whole race of Yankee Peddlers," wrote an observer of American character in 1833, "are proverbial for dishonesty. They go forth annually in the households to lie, cog, cheat, swindle; in short to get possession of their neighbor's property in any manner it can be done with impunity." In fact, the name "damn Yankee," coined long before the Civil War, probably came from Yankee peddlers who worked the rural South. Yankee peddlers were known as far away as Europe for their trickery and sharpness, especially for their wooden nutmegs (it took an expert wood carver a full day to make just *one* in a recent experiment), when these kernels of an evergreen tree cultivated in the Spice Islands sold for less than a penny apiece. But whether carved wooden nutmegs ever existed (no one has yet turned up an authentic one), many country people did believe that Yankee peddlers sold them, along with carved wooden hams painted pink ("Basswood hams"), carved cigars, and wooden pumpkin seeds. Connecticut still is called the Nutmeg State for this reason, and the warning *don't take any wooden nutmegs* probably influenced the coining of the still-current phrase *don't take any wooden nickels.*

An old rhyme went: "There is in Yankeeland / a class of men called tin-peddlers, / A shrewd, sarcastic band / Of busy meddlers." And an old joke went: "Know how to revive a Yankee peddler when he drowns?" "Just turn out his pockets!" But though they were well-versed in the Yankee art of giving people "a steer in the wrong direction," as P.T. Barnum put it, Yankee peddlers helped settle America, carrying the materials of civilization to sparsely inhabited regions. Wherever a man swung an ax in the wilderness, an old saying went, a Yankee peddler would show up in the clearing the next day. "They stood halfway between the merchant and the gipsy, with a faint touch added of the mountebank . . . To say the Yankee peddler was a consummate liar was considered . . . an assertion of the obvious." (Odell Shepard, *Pedlar's Progress, The Life of Bronson Alcott,* 1937)

Yankee Pirate, The A nom de guerre of American sea hero John Paul Jones.

Yankee rum Rum made in New England. Also called *Yankee* and *stink-e-puss* in days past.

Yankee schoolmarm (schoolmaster) A schoolteacher in New England or from New England teaching in another state. The *Congressional Globe* of April 5, 1871 reports "A Yankee schoolmarm was stoned and murdered by her own pupils."

Yankee states, the (1) The New England states. (2) Also once applied to Ohio, where there were many settlers from New England.

Yankee trick A deception or fraud often associated with Yankees, especially Yankee peddlers.

Yankee twang See quote. "The familiar twang given to the Yankee speech of words like *now* and *cow* . . . was extended beyond the limits of permission." (*Harper's Magazine,* September 1880)

Yankos See YANKEE.

yarned Pulled, hauled. "He yarned the trailer around all day." Pronounced *yahned*.

ye An old-fashioned form of "you" probably obsolete today.

yokefellows Partners working closely together like oxen in a yoke. "She's [New Hampshire] one of the two best states in the Union. / Vermont's the other. And the two have been / Yokefellows in the sap yoke from of old . . ." (Robert Frost, "New Hampshire," 1923)

yon See quote. "The Yankee says 'hither an yon', for 'to and fro.' " (James Russell Lowell, *The Biglow Papers*, 1866)

yonder Over there. "My green hill yonder, where the sun goes down / Without a scratch . . ." (Edward Arlington Robinson, "Archibald's Example," *The Three Taverns*, 1920)

York shilling An old coin worth 12½ cents. Also a *Yorker*.

you Sometimes added for emphasis, as in "That's a fact, you!"

you better believe This popular national phrase, meaning you can be sure, is first recorded in New England about a century and a half ago in the *Yale Literary Magazine* and was used by Oliver Wendell Holmes, among other Brahmins. See BITTER AS BONESET.

you could carry me out with the tongs! An exclamation of great surprise. "Well, you could carry me out with the tongs!"

you might as well talk to a post Said of someone dumb or determined not to answer. " 'Wal, I swan,' Dart ejaculated . . . 'You might as well talk to a post.' " (Rowland Robinson, "The Paring Bee," 1900)

young-uns Often pronounced *yow-wuns* in Maine. " 'Not at all,' he said. 'Lookin' forward to having young 'uns around again.' Except "that the sound of this, exotic to their Midwestern ears as a foreign language, was yow-wuns." (Stephen King, *Pet Sematary*, 1983)

your ox won't plow An old expression meaning something doesn't work, anything from a faulty argument to a defective machine.

yow Recorded in Maine and New Hampshire for *female*. "That's a yow cat."

Z

zanzibar An old-fashioned candy originally made in Salem, Massachusetts over a century ago.

zero Said of someone considered worthless, without any importance. "He's a total zero."

zip See BLACK AS ZIP.

zone Short for the Combat Zone, a seedy area of topless bars, porno shops and the like in Boston. "Just to wear that with a pony-tail took a lot of nerve, but to wear it into the Zone and then to wear it into the Pussy Cat on a Thursday at midnight meant the son of a bitch was from another planet." (David Huddle, "Apache," 1987)

About the Author _____

ROBERT HENDRICKSON is the author of more than 25 books, including several critically acclaimed works on language and literature. For Facts On File he has written *American Literary Anecdotes*, *British Literary Anecdotes*, and *World Literary Anecdotes*, as well as *Whistlin' Dixie* and *Happy Trails*. He is also the author of *The Facts On File Encyclopedia of Word and Phrase Origins*, which he has recently revised. He lives in Peconic, New York.

Other volumes in the Facts On File Dictionary of American Regional Expressions series are *Whistlin' Dixie: A Dictionary of Southern Expressions* (0-8160-2110-4) and *Happy Trails: A Dictionary of Western Expressions* (0-8160-2112-0). Forthcoming are volumes on *Mountain* (0-8160-2113-9) and *New York* (0-8160-2114-7) expressions.